WH

Thi... of
Hoc...
It h... s
and... te
cau... e
role... d
the... e
did
Th... n,
phi... s
exp... ed
by... t
anc... ost
co...

THE STORM OVER THE DEPUTY

EDITED BY
ERIC BENTLEY

GROVE PRESS, INC. NEW YORK

Second Printing

Library of Congress Catalog Card Number: 64-8187

Manufactured in the United States of America

Contents

Foreword
by Eric Bentley 8

PART 1 HOW THE PLAY GOT PRODUCED
Introduction to *The Deputy*
by Erwin Piscator 11

PART 2 WHAT THE THEATRE CRITICS SAID
Understudy for *The Deputy*
by Albert Bermel 16
History as Drama
by Robert Brustein 21
A Theatre Review
by Harold Clurman 25
The Meaning of Silence
by Tom F. Driver 28
The Deputy Arrives
by Richard Gilman 31

PART 3 THREE EDITORIALS AND A PRESS RELEASE
Silence
from The New York Times 35
Echoes of *The Deputy*
from the New York Post 36
A Statement by Cardinal Spellman
from The New York Herald Tribune 37
Character Assassination
from America 39

PART 4 HOCHHUTH INTERVIEWED
Interview with Rolf Hochhuth
by Judy Stone 42

Interview with Rolf Hochhuth
by Patricia Marx 52

PART 5 HOCHHUTH'S ENCOUNTER WITH TWO PERSONS CONCERNED

Pius XII and the Jews
by G. B. Cardinal Montini (Pope Paul VI) 66
Reply to Cardinal Montini
by Rolf Hochhuth 69
The Pope and the Jews
by Albrecht von Kessel 71
The Playwright Answers
by Rolf Hochhuth 76

PART 6 COMMENTS OF LITERARY CRITICS AND PHILOSOPHERS

Rolf Hochhuth's *The Deputy*
by Lionel Abel 81
The Deputy: Guilt by Silence?
by Hannah Arendt 85
The Possibility of Individual Choice
by Robert Gorham Davis 94
On *The Deputy*
by Karl Jaspers 99
The Vicar of Christ
by Alfred Kazin 102
The Deputy and Its Metamorphoses
by John Simon 109
Reflections on *The Deputy*
by Susan Sontag 117
Drama or Pamphlet: Hochhuth's *The Deputy* and the Tradition of Polemical Literature
by Rolf C. Zimmermann 123

PART 7 AND OF JOURNALISTS, SOCIAL SCIENTISTS, HISTORIANS

The Harassed Pope
by Carl Amery 149
Pius XII: A Symbol
by Arthur C. Cochrane 157
The Dilemma of Pope Pius XII
by Desmond Fisher 162

The Need for Confession
by Friedrich Heer 166
Pius XII
by Robert Leiber S.J. 173
Pius XII, the Jews, and the German Catholic Church
by Guenter Lewy 195
The Real Accomplishment
by Golo Mann 217
The Real Issue
by James O'Gara 219
Pope Pius XII and the Nazis
by Leon Poliakov 222
What Some People Have Forgotten About God's "Deputy"
by I. F. Stone 234

PART 8 BIBLIOGRAPHY
by David Beams 237

Foreword

That *The Deputy* raised a storm has been obvious since the world première in Berlin, and was no doubt predicted by Erwin Piscator — and intended by Rolf Hochhuth. Only much more recently has it become clear how unusually large this storm is. *It is almost certainly the largest storm ever raised by a play in the whole history of the drama.* When this staggering fact has sunk in we may try to minimize it by observing: "But it's all because of modern communications. Never in the past could a play be performed so soon in so many places or mentioned in so many copies of so many newspapers." The observation is insufficient because, for one thing, even other modern playwrights have not attracted attention on anything like this scale. And it is not for lack of trying. Only think of Brecht. Who more than he wished to speak to the whole modern world on burning issues that concern everyone? Yet the most one can say for the audience of *Mother Courage,* even where the play has been received most enthusiastically, is that it interests a rather considerable minority group. It may well be that *The Deputy* has fewer friends than *Mother Courage*. What it certainly has is more enemies. And there is an irony in this too. For Brecht did not court popularity but gloried in the thought of being a threat, a maker of enemies. Hochhuth, by comparison, is such a nice young man — and such an idealist!

Well, Bertolt Brecht did not "attack Pius XII." Any explanation of the difference between the impact of Brecht and the impact of Hochhuth's first play is going to have to start there — wherever it ends. And that is why what would otherwise seem an inordinate amount of space in this book is given to Pius XII. I would not claim to be a neutral observer but I have taken it as my editorial task to present more than one side. A very essential part of the evidence that can be mustered in Pius's defence is to be found in the eloquent address of his helper and admirer, Father Leiber. It seemed to me also essential to print a little of the impassioned journalism which has championed Pius and attacked Hochhuth: hence the presence here of Desmond Fisher's piece and the *America* editorial and Cardinal Spellman's extraordinary press release. And of course there is the comment of the present Pope — surely this must be the first time in history that the première of a play has been noticed in the Vatican? What makes the situation even more extraordinary is that Pope Paul is also *in* the play, though not as a character on stage. The same is true of Albrecht von Kessel whose exchange with Hochhuth is also printed here.

I do not marshal here evidence inimical to the personal character of Pius XII. Such as there is has been provided in the text and appendix of *The Deputy*. What most of us needed, I thought, was knowledge of the historical circumstances. Here the contribution comes from a non-Catholic source, Guenter Lewy. Leon Poliakov has a somewhat similar tale to tell, and from a somewhat similar viewpoint. Carl Amery suggests seeing the whole subject in a different light: his is perhaps the most original and thought-provoking piece in the whole book.

All this concern with Pius and his Church is not to say I would have *The Deputy* considered as history rather than drama. The drama is always about something, and it is good that its audiences receive, from time to time at least, a sharp reminder of this fact. The editor of *The Reporter* was recently very shocked because his drama critic followed up an analysis of James Baldwin's *Blues for Mister Charlie* with some remarks of his own on the Negro problem. How shocking to find either that the drama deals with life or that a drama critic is himself alive! To which one must add that a particular kind of drama — to which Baldwin's play, like Hochhuth's belongs — has as its very purpose to react back upon life. Baldwin intended to drive the attention of *The Reporter*'s critic in a certain direction — and succeeded. After Guenther Lewy's necessarily lengthy analysis of the historical problem, the longest piece in this book, justifiably, I believe, is Rolf C. Zimmermann's essay on the kind of play Hochhuth is attempting, its history, and its special relation to its audience.

Of the critical sections of the book (2 and 6), while I may have done a little balancing of one opinion against another, and made some slight attempt to represent different schools of thought, I should like to believe that I have picked some of the best criticism that was written, irrespective of opinion and school. What school of thought a critic of art belongs to is not the most important thing about him unless he is a very feeble critic.

If the selection of theatre critics seems eccentric, it is not really so. Given that, for reasons of space, I limited the field to American theatre critics, I picked the critics of the weeklies, almost en bloc. Are there not good reasons for preferring their work — in general and also in their reviews of *The Deputy* — to that of the daily critics? The work of critics in monthlies and quarterlies, on the other hand, comes out so much later that all sense of the immediate occasion is lost. It tends to be omnibus reviewing (a detestable genre), and too exclusively literary.

As for the literary criticism, in a case like this it shades off imperceptibly into philosophic commentary, and so I feel justified in lumping together Karl Jaspers' piece with Alfred Kazin's, and Hannah Arendt's with Lionel Abel's.

Of the many newspaper, radio, and television features, the most serviceable for my purposes were the unusually full interviews of, respectively, Judy Stone and Patricia Marx.

Finally, I thought it only right that the book should lead off with a statement by Erwin Piscator because —second only to Hochhuth — he provided the occasion for all subsequent statements about *The Deputy*.

Only thirty commentators are represented out of some thousands. Obviously then this book would be a mere beginning for the thorough-going student of "the storm over *The Deputy*." Where he might go from here is indicated in David Beams' remarkable bibliography. And that bibliography may serve to give even the most casual reader an impression how very widely *The Deputy* has been discussed in print.

ERIC BENTLEY
Spring 1964

1 | How the Play Got Produced

ERWIN PISCATOR

Introduction to The Deputy

Hochhuth's play *The Deputy* is one of the few substantive contributions toward mastering the past. Relentlessly it calls things by their names; it shows that no tale written with the blood of innocent millions can ever be out of date; it apportions to the guilty their measure of guilt; it reminds all the participants that they could have made their decision, and that in fact they did make it even when they did not.

The Deputy makes liars of all those who assert that a historical drama as a drama of decision is no longer possible because decisions as such are no longer possible for man, given the featureless anonymity of social-political arrangements and pressures in an absurd construction of human existence that sees everything predetermined. Thus to blot out historic action is a theory that recommends itself to all those who today would like to escape the truth of history, the truth of their own historic acts.

This play is a historical drama in Schiller's sense. It sees man as acting; and in his actions as a representative, or "deputy," of an *Idea*: *free* in its fulfilment, free in his insight into the necessity of *categorically* ethical, essentially human behavior. This freedom which we all possess, which we all possessed under the Nazi regime as well, must be our point of

---

Mr. Piscator, director of the Freie Volksbühne in Berlin, and author of *Das Politische Theater,* produced the world première of *The Deputy* there. This reprint of the introduction to the German edition of the play published by Rowohlt, Hamburg, 1963, was translated by Clara Mayer.

departure if we wish to master our past. To disclaim this freedom would be to disclaim the guilt each took upon himself who did not make use of his freedom to decide *against* inhumanity.

II

Already a literary genre of plays may be discerned that deals with our most recent past. The best one can say of the majority of these plays as, for the most part, they gather dust in the agencies, is that on the whole they are meant well. In many of them the authors have liberated themselves from their own life experiences. They should be recognized as a kind of confession. But it is evident that life alone writes no plays, at least no good ones. Only in rare instances is the view of individual destiny comprehensive enough to be symbolic, exemplary in the original meaning of that word, "deputized" for the generality, as it were. In addition, there are the purely technical inadequacies.

Hochhuth relates nothing he has lived through; his is the stuff of drama that played behind closed doors and that he could make his own only through long years of persevering historical research. Even in the crowded history of the Nazi period, Hochhuth's material is extraordinary. He confronts society as a theater audience with one of the most radical of historic conflicts, not just of the Hitler regime but of the West altogether. The stage business is expressed through content that had been shrouded in carefully guarded silence more zealously than any that had preceded.

When in the spring of 1962 I was chosen as the artistic director of the Freie Volksbühne in Berlin, I had determined by means of this very instrumentality of the People's Theatre and a People's Theatre repertory to check this general forgetfulness, this general desire to forget in matters of our most recent history. In the midst of my deliberations as to how to shape such a repertory (Gerhart Hauptmann's *Atrides Tetralogy*—a mythologically keyed evocation of the Hitler barbarities—was what I had chosen as the point of departure) in the midst of my deliberations a telephone call reached me from Mr. Ledig-Rowohlt: he had received a play from his friend, Karl Ludwig Leonhardt, acting as intermediary, the first work of a young German author, which was really more than "just" a play. Everyone in his publishing house who had read it had been profoundly shaken. No one had any idea how the play could be staged since it went beyond any and all dimensions. But—if I had time and the wish to read it, it would not be kept from me.

The play was sent to me, not in manuscript as usual, but in galley proofs, set not by Rowohlt publishers but by a publisher who had to acknowledge, after typesetting, that he lacked the courage for publication. Rowohlt, on the other hand, to whom the play was then offered, had the courage, had the boldness—as he always does; he was determined to publish the book.

Extraordinary circumstances, confounding, exciting. An extraordinary, confounding, exciting, great and necessary play—I already felt it after reading the first pages. The theme, of course—the fate of the Jews under Fascism—was in itself not new. We knew—for example—the *Diary of Anne Frank*, had felt its great effect on our emotions, an effect that still made itself felt in the American dramatization of the book. We had just seen *Andorra* on the stage, an important, "timely" play, even though the critics, not wrongly perhaps, pointed out that the play had become entangled in the construction of its plot and failed to emerge from the "novelistic" despite the addition of a few "epic" spotlights.

But surmounting "the novelistic," the unheard-of, the unique, the "exceptional case" is Hochhuth's great achievement. His play aims not at the "interesting," at making the point, at constructing the plot—mark of the novelistic, the storyable, perilously close to this unusual, "exceptional" content—rather it aims at objectivizing, exploring the total human attitude not in story but in history. Hochhuth unfolds and artistically formulates the material he has worked over scientifically, he orders and articulates his material with the means—I say it consciously, deliberately—of a distinguished dramatist.

If ever a play appropriately becomes the central point of a repertory program that seeks to concern itself with political-historical groups and sequences of events, then this is it! This play makes it worthwhile to produce theater; with this play the theater again gets a mission, a value, becomes necessary.

III

The epic in drama, epic drama itself, does not trace its existence to Brecht; Shakespeare's history plays are basically one single epic drama. Schiller calls his *Robbers* a "dramatic novel," and where, for example, he puts Wallenstein's camp on the stage, he does it as an epic writer (a historian!) who does not want to suppress even the somewhat peripheral, which, often enough, is central, nuclear. To do this requires legitimate disregard of the so-called norm of dramatic length. It is, after all, a matter of complete indifference how long a play is if it is a good, a necessary play. Not how long an audience can listen is decisive, but how much an author has to say to his audience. By this gauge, which is the only one applicable, the span of *The Deputy* is fully justified. An epic play, epic-scientific, epic-documentary; a play for epic, "political" theater, for which I have fought more than thirty years: a "total" play for a "total" theater.

What is meant by this?

Expressionism had already recognized that the reality of our century could no longer be conveyed in "private" situations and conflicts; it strove toward extending its objects into "types," in some sort allegorical (*the* man, *the* woman, etc.) by which it arrived at only partial truths and remained inexact, lyrical, in the examination of historical-political events. Expressionism was on intimate terms with all men without knowing them, which in time caused it to acquire fantastic, unreal features. I have been reproached for "expressionism" repeatedly—senselessly, because I begin where expressionism left off. The experiences of the First World War taught me with what reality, what realities I had to reckon: political, economic, social repression; political, economic, social struggle. Theater for me was the place where these realities were to be put under the microscope. At that time—in the twenties—there were few authors, Toller, Brecht, Mehring and some others, who strove to draw these new realities into their plays. Their efforts were not always adequate. I had to add what the plays themselves did not contain.

By extending and changing the dramaturgic forms, by using new technical and scenic devices, I tried to make visible in the theater the vastness and the complication, the totality of our basic life problems (always materials of conflict, "occasions for war" if you like). Means such as projection, film, commentary, treadmill, I called epic even before Brecht had formulated *his* concept of the "epic." They penetrated a production with scientific, documentary material, analyzed, elucidated.

Hochhuth's play, *The Deputy,* is already fixed in its literary form as fully epic. The most essential instructions for scenery and direction, the characteristics of persons, etc., are blended into the dialogue as inseparable from the play itself. (Likewise the documentary supplement.) The verse form gives structure and support to the manifold facts. Hochhuth himself told me he could only master his overwhelming material by using free verse to give it form; thus the danger was avoided "of a documentary naturalism without a style in the manner of news-of-the-week. . . ." The documentary and the artistic have merged indissolubly.

Of course, it is difficult to make a stage version of this "total" play, to cut a play out of the play, not because it is too large for the theater, too burdened with matter, but because the theater, the vision of our society and its attitude toward the theater is too limited for this play, at least at this moment. "Too long to be good," ran the heading of the recent drama review of a production which lasted three and a half hours! As for Hochhuth's play, I would rather say, "Too good to be long." Nevertheless—although a production continued on two or three evenings would be the only really adequate one—cuts will *have* to be introduced to make the audience, which indeed does not want the whole play, acquainted with the essential parts. (Perhaps I may subsequently "deliver" the omitted scenes in special productions, matinees, etc.). In any event, I have agreed with the Rowohlt publishing house that the book will reach the public at the same time as the initial Berlin production, as necessary underpinning and supplement.

I hope that attack and defense of the play will reach *all*, as they have the few who have read it to date; I hope that the value of such a work lies not only in the artistic, the formal, the aesthetic, but first and last in its words and with its reach into life; I hope this play will be a force *for change*. My "atrocious," anti-Schopenhauer optimism—despite natural wear through resignation—is still strong enough to believe in a change in human history through *understanding*—a peaceful change, not a violent material change which acknowledges evolution henceforward as evolution exclusively toward catastrophe. But from objective recognition a passionate avowal of values can develop, for which Hochhuth attempts a new formulation in this play. This new author, Rolf Hochhuth, seems to me not only a good playwright and poet: he is a man confessing! The discovery of such a confessor is healing and consoling in a world of silence, silence that is empty, without content, useless.

Berlin, November 6, 1962

2 | What the Theatre Critics Said

ALBERT BERMEL

Understudy for The Deputy

As a play *The Deputy* has been praised for its historical accuracy, its angry insistence, and little else. Advance reviews out of Berlin, Paris and London, and recent criticism in New York describe Rolf Hochhuth's drama as a social document rather than theater; as a diatribe against Pius XII, if not against the Church itself, cast arbitrarily into the shape of a five-act play and supporting an overload of factual material; as a slab latter-day Schilleriana; as a setback to the 20th-century schools of symbolic, psychological and absurdist playmaking; and as a sprawling, immature first effort.

Finally, we can see for ourselves. *The Deputy* comes to us in two English versions. Grove Press has issued an American edition of the entire play and a compendious essay to go with it, translated by Richard and Clara Winston. And Herman Shumlin has co-produced and directed a condensation, adapted by Jerome Rothenberg and placed on show at the Brooks Atkinson Theatre. The Shumlin production represents about one-third of the total playing time, and it has been suggested that bringing the script into line with Broadway dictates has strengthened its impact by deleting the undramatic frippery.

As it happens, the exact opposite is true. The production, a

Albert Bermel, the author of two plays which have been produced at the Royal Court in London, as well as translator of a number of plays from the French, is the drama critic for *The New Leader,* in which this piece appeared March 16, 1964.

heap of disconnected fragments, is a reduction in every sense of what Hochhuth has written. But before saying what the production is not, I should try to outline what the full play is. To start with, it is an example of classical theater, and that comes as a shock and a relief after the avalanche of romanticism that has been tipped on to American and European stages in recent years: the self-defensive pleas of the playwright as hero, the tiger-biting-his-own-tail searches for identity, the case histories, the fluting social tracts, the poky and impoverished one-acts in double bills.

The Deputy is concerned with its subject matter, not with its author. It has richness of literary and political reference, but it rises to a fervor of which most dramatists today seem incapable. It is a cry from the mind as well as the heart, for it is not, in fact, dominated by its content. On the contrary, Hochhuth has imposed a severe discipline on himself, and the dramatic progression controls the flow of information at all points. In other words, this is a play by design and craftsmanship, not by accident. Its ambition is deeper, its scope wider, its ferocity more sustained than those of any other play written since the war, with the possible exception of Sartre's *Lucifer and the Good Lord*. In contrast with, say, Ben-Zion Tomer's *Children of the Shadows* (which arrived in New York at about the same time, courtesy of Habimah), *The Deputy* is not choked up by guilt but propelled by indignation.

Observing Mme. de Staël's precept that intellect does not attain its full force unless it attacks power, Hochhuth has mounted an all-out assault on indifference and inaction in high places. His theme—that Pius XII should have condemned the persecution of European Jewry—is reiterated in every scene, not simply as repetition but from different vantage points that give a freshly illuminating emphasis each time.

Near the opening, for instance, the Papal Nuncio in Berlin wishes that the Pope would authorize him "to take a stand/the way my brother Nuncio in Slovakia/did two weeks ago when he spoke up/against the wholesale killing of Jews from Bratislava. . . . . He made a strong protest." In the next scene, one German tells another that the Concordat drawn up between the Vatican and Hitler was "a stroke of luck." Farther on, a high-ranking layman in the service of the Holy See asks his son whether the Pope could bear to see even a single man hungry and in pain: "His heart is with the victims." The son, a priest, retorts bitterly: "But his voice? Where is his voice?" And later still, when a Cardinal argues that a statement from the Pope will be construed by Hitler as a threat that is bound to aggravate the situation—and this is the crux of the play—

the young priest replies that 100,000 Jewish families in Europe face certain murder: the situation "could not possibly be worse."

As is indicated, the play is written in free verse which transposes from conversational realism to intricate dialectic, to polished aphorisms, to rhetorical storming. I have not read the original text and am told that, like Brecht's (or, come to that, Goethe's) German, it is not easily brought into an English of comparable quality. In the Winstons' translation the play does not by any means shape up as a triumph of style. It is resolutely flat in language. Hochhuth knows that naturalistic dialogue is out of fashion, but he deliberately shuns metaphors; for him they "screen the infernal cynicism of what really took place." Two other European plays, raised on topics similar to that of *The Deputy* but treated in unrelenting symbols, happen to bear witness to Hochhuth's claim. Max Frisch's *The Firebugs* and Brecht's *Arturo Ui* have to dip into hysteria to counteract the sloppiness of their metaphors.

The drama, then, is not overtly poetry. Is it tragedy? Any attempt to define tragedy is liable to touch off a critical brawl. Nevertheless, it is worth noting Lope de Vega's comment that "tragedy has as its argument history," and remembering that Hochhuth can footnote almost every line of his work to the events themselves, which constitute an unsurpassed disaster. But that is not enough. Putting aside academic considerations, I think that Hochhuth has achieved an authentic, artistic tragedy by the sheer disposition of his facts and eloquence and the crushing logic of his story. By negative definition, if this play is not a tragedy neither is Goethe's *Egmont,* which also tells of a hero's self-sacrifice.

The characters in the play may be graduated by moral arithmetic from near good to outright evil. At one end of the scale is Kurt Gerstein, drawn from a real-life figure of the same name, a pacifist who has insinuated himself into the SS and the concentration-camp program in the belief that "dictatorships can be abolished only from within." Gerstein is trying to bring to the outside world an accounting of the exterminations at Auschwitz: "Seven hundred and fifty persons/in each of four chambers — /each room with a volume of sixty cubic yards — /three thousand human beings . . . The gassing operation takes twenty-five minutes. Now they want to speed it up. . . . Like marble columns the naked corpses stand . . . with hooks they're pulled apart. Jews have to do that job/Ukrainians lash them on with whips."

Gerstein makes contact with Riccardo Fontana, an Italian priest from an aristocratic, undemanding background. It is

Riccardo who, haunted by Gerstein's descriptions, tries to persuade the Pope to "raise a hue and cry/to stir the world to pity,/to outrage and to action." Gerstein and Fontana are the twin subjects of the tragedy; like classically tragic figures they are thinking and talking, toward the end of the play, in ethical absolutes.

Moving down the scale one encounters a succession of secondary characters — clerics and laymen, Jewish prisoners and Jewish-Catholic converts—until at the nether extreme are the German officials, including Salzer, a police captain, Adolf Eichmann, August Hirt ("an anatomist and collector of skulls at the University of Strassburg") and, at the nadir, a man known only as The Doctor; or rather, not a man but the devil, "only playing the part of a human being." Once again one may hark back to Goethe. Hochhuth has taken this "cool and cheery . . . handsome and likable" incarnation from his researches into the person who was in charge of "medical" operations at Auschwitz, but he seems equally to have delved into the Mephistopheles of *Faust*. The Doctor's relishing of his victims' spiritual and bodily torments leads to some of the most passionately defined and gruesome moments in the play.

It is the center of Hochhuth's scale, however, that has provoked the public outcries against him. There he situates Pius XII and a certain unnamed Cardinal, and this act looks like a profanation to people who cannot imagine them placed any lower than the top. Some plaintiffs swear that Hochhuth has turned Pacelli into a malefactor and fool. He has done nothing of the sort.

True, he admits some rancor into his portrait; he objects to the Pontiff's remoteness and the doctrine of Papal Infallibility alike; and he has not been able to resist undercutting the Cardinal by making him slightly comical and the Pope by making him slightly prissy. In addition, he has restricted Pius to one appearance, holding him back until act four in an endeavor to forge awe out of expectation. In this he succeeds. In his picture of Pius he does not, and this failure is the outstanding weakness of Hochhuth's play.

A dramatist has the right to make of his characters what he can, but Hochhuth owes his audiences a "bigger" Pius, if only as a worthy adversary for Riccardo. Even so, in the speeches Hochhuth gives the Pontiff he strives to be just to the historical character's intelligence and persuasiveness, as a careful study of those speeches reveals; and the Cardinal, like the Pope, is a sophisticated man who uses the language of *Realpolitik* as adeptly as that of religion. "Germany must remain viable," says Pius, "not only to hold the frontiers against the East,/but also to hold the balance of power./The balance of the Continent is more important/than its unity which hardly corresponds/to Europe's national traditions."

If I have dwelt on the play rather than on the New York production, it is because I hope that Hochhuth's work will survive for what it is, rather than what has emerged from it. The Shumlin-Rothenberg version is, to use a heavy word, a disgrace. Three entire scenes have been lopped off, and the remaining ones have been cut down to Broadway measurements.

The complexity of the plotting and sub-plotting, a subtle reticulation of happenings and people, has given way to a harsh, simple-minded story line. Important episodes, such as the Pope's washing his ink-stained hands, the seizing and deporting of prisoners, the bowling party attended by a group of upper-echelon Germans, and the very climax of the plot have vanished. Some of the central characters have gone altogether; the others—Gerstein, Riccardo, the Pope, the Cardinal, the Doctor—have been so levelled off by gross editing that they are now mere silhouettes. If it be argued that spectators in other cities also saw a foreshortened adaptation, I can only reply: so much the worse for them.

With the excision of so much drama, the production becomes a static exposition running into discussion. And strangely worded discussion at that. For example, the Nuncio in Berlin says to Riccardo, "Father, stay out of this." A monk mutters, "People are crazy is what I say." And Riccardo talks about "a poor priest like you or I."

The staging offers no help to the ineptitudes of the script. Its one exemplary feature is the costuming by Edith Lutyens Bel Geddes. As for the decor, tubular hangings, looped cords and oversized doorbell chimes designed by Rouben Ter-Arutunian hang and wave distractedly above the realistic props. The lighting faltered more than once on the night I attended. The actors tripped and hesitated.

Since the characters have been snipped down by the adapter, the director has presumably tried to compensate for their diminution by having them roar like wind tunnels. Emlyn Williams presents a startling physical likeness to Pius XII, but is restrained by the cutting of the text from showing his capacity as an actor. Jeremy Brett uncovers some of the heroism and goodness of Riccardo, although not the fanaticism; watching him, you are never aware of the steel spine of the role. As Gerstein, Philip Burns plays his two scenes with frantic sincerity, as if to make up for his absence from the three other scenes in which Gerstein appears in the full play. And Fred Stewart, a rouged and rotund Cardinal, is forced by his narrowed role into skilled embroidery. The other acting ranges downward from inadequate, the director for the most part keeping the cast on their feet when they should be on their toes.

The question is: Why do the play at all in this crippled form? The answer is another question: Why indeed? I suspect that the pressure to get it on the boards this season, come what may, for the sake of its implications as historical evidence, simply pushed it into the wrong hands. And that has cost *The Deputy* dear as a work of art. If it is to be an overpowering experience and not a titillating knock at big names; if it is to register anything like its full meaning; if the performance is to be the play and not a feeble understudy for it, a large work like this must be given complete, or as nearly complete as possible. It may have to run on two successive nights, or it may have to begin early or end late. On those rare occasions when a drama as bold as *The Deputy* reaches us, Broadway conventions ought to bend to it, if not break. As things stand, Hochhuth is justified in asking with Dryden, *Who would excel, when few can make a test/Betwixt indiff'rent writing and the rest?*

ROBERT BRUSTEIN

History as Drama

Rolf Hochhuth's *The Deputy* reads like a German doctoral dissertation in verse: two or three epigraphs precede each of the five acts, the acts themselves are divided into discrete sections and titled as if they were chapters, discursive passages

---

Associate Professor of English at Columbia University, Mr. Brustein is drama critic for *The New Republic* and author of *Theatre of Revolt*. This article is reprinted from *The New Republic* of March 14, 1964.

and author's asides are generously mixed in with the dialogue, and sixty pages of prose, called "Historical Sidelights," are appended at the end, accompanied by footnotes. The presence of so much scholarly paraphernalia in a published dramatic work suggests, for one thing, that the author has prepared himself for trouble ahead. And since *The Deputy* deals with an extremely inflammatory subject—the failure of Pope Pius XII to condemn unequivocally Hitler's extermination of the Jews—he has acted wisely: the work is born unto trouble, as the sparks fly upward. There is no need to rehearse here the controversy that *The Deputy* has provoked in Europe and America; the slanders, the innuendo, the protests, the riots. Suffice it to say that the customary conditions following the publication of an unpleasant truth have prevailed, and humanity has managed to disgrace itself again.

Hochhuth's painstaking research, on the other hand, does raise difficulties of a quite different kind, for although *The Deputy* is a remarkable work in many ways, it is an *animal amphibium*—a compound of fiction and fact which can be classified neither as good history nor as good literature. While Hochhuth's historical facts are unassailable, for example, some interesting questions have recently been raised about his interpretation of these facts, particularly his assumption that the silence of the Vatican—though partially determined by Church policy, which held the Bolsheviks to be the greater danger than the Nazis—would have been broken had another Pope (say, Pius XI) been in power. Guenter Lewy[1], in *Commentary,* has suggested that, on the contrary, Vatican policy was the logical culmination of Catholic anti-Semitism, while Hannah Arendt [2], in *The New York Herald Tribune,* has emphasized that it was Pacelli's predecessor who first praised Hitler and signed the Concordat with Nazi Germany. The temporizing of Pacelli over the fate of the Jews, even as they were being rounded up under his window, then, was not an isolated instance of passivity in the face of evil, but rather reflected the general moral and spiritual collapse of European Christianity, Protestant and Catholic alike.

Hochhuth's tendency to make the individual accountable for the failures of the institution is a heritage of his German idealism, an influence which can also be seen in the shape and substance of his play. *The Deputy* is written in the ponderous heroic style of Schiller, full of vaunting speeches, generous sacrifices, and externalized emotions—angry confrontations dominate each scene, the verse pitches and rolls,

[1] See p. 195.
[2] See p. 85.

and indignation keeps the tone at a high boil. As for the characters, they are larger than scale, and, therefore, not always very convincing. When the author permits himself artistic license, he can create an interesting and complex individual—the Doctor, for example, whose fatigued cynicism, experimental cruelty, and intellectual arrogance make him a figure of absolute evil, a creation worthy of Sartre or Camus. But more often, Hochhuth's characters are members of a cardboard nobility: Gerstein, for example, the compassionate German who joined the SS, risking his own life to help the victims of Hitler, or Father Riccardo Fontana, the anguished Jesuit priest, who pinned the Jewish star to his cassock when the Pope refused to protest, and accompanied the Jews to Auschwitz.

Although Father Fontana is fictional, Kurt Gerstein is based on an actual figure whose heroism Hochhuth wished to celebrate in his play. But this is one of the difficulties: historical fact does not always make for very profound art, unless it is supported by a good deal of invention. This is even more obvious in Hochhuth's characterization of Pacelli who appears, a cold, forbidding diplomat, in a climactic obligatory scene, endorsing checks from the Society of Jesus, discussing the various financial holdings of the Church, condemning the Allied bombing of San Lorenzo, and composing a highly ineffectual Article against suffering and misfortune which never once mentions the Jews by name. By adhering so faithfully to contemporary accounts of the Pope, Hochhuth has protected himself, as he must, against charges of tampering with history, but he has left us with a superficial and shadowy character, whose motives remain unplumbed. Unlike Hannah Arendt, who was able to create an extraordinarily complex portrait of Eichmann because the materials were so abundant and her insight so acute, Hochhuth is limited by a scarcity of information about his subject, and by his own apparent lack of interest in the inner workings of character. Cataloguing his personages almost exclusively according to their attitudes towards the Pope's silence, Hochhuth preserves the moral integrity of his work, but at the cost of its aesthetic weight and complexity.

The New York production of his play, however, preserves no integrity at all, and I have confined my discussion to the printed text because the Broadway performance is beneath discussion. The adaptor, first of all, has confused the need to cut this six-hour work with the license to butcher it, for he has hacked away at the most interesting feature—its intellectual heart—exposing the weakest part of the anatomy

—its melodramatic bones. Aside from excising four whole scenes, two of them essential to the theme, decimating characters (the Doctor and Gerstein are mere shadows now), and cutting out just about every literary, historical, political, and religious reference in the text, the adaptor has also methodically proceeded to soften the horror of the work and weaken the accusation of the author, sometimes by rewriting whole portions of dialogue. What the adaptor has left undone in the way of carnage, the director and actors have completed. Were it not so sloppy and unfinished, Herman Shumlin's direction might remind one of certain Hollywood Nazi movies of the forties, because it features exactly the same clichés: the jagged line of prisoners, rags carefully arranged, moving stagily behind barbed wire, threatened by guards; the immaculate Nazis, cracking whips against their boots and curling their lips contemptuously at their victims; the idealistic martyr-heroes, striking lofty postures, pumping up emotion, and spilling righteous rhetoric. Except for Emlyn Williams, whose characterization of Pacelli is suitably frozen and fastidious, none of the actors gives more than a stock performance, and they are using so many different styles that everyone seems to be performing in a separate play. Broadway may have had the initial courage to produce *The Deputy*, but it has not finally been able to transcend its ingrained cowardice and artistic inadequacy.

Still, the play is available in published form—a document of power and persuasiveness, whatever its aesthetic and interpretive shortcomings. If Hochhuth has not entirely proven himself yet as either an historian or a dramatist, he has certainly proven himself as a man of discriminating moral intelligence and outstanding courage, which makes him rare and valuable enough in the modern world. Appearing at this time, *The Deputy* may, as one American religious group complained, endanger the cause of "harmonious interfaith relations," but if such a cause is contingent on the suppression of truth, then we are better off without it. As Hannah Arendt has observed, after suffering her own ordeal at the hands of groups with special interests, the truth *always* seems to come at the wrong psychological moment, but in the words of the Catholic historian whom she quotes at the conclusion of her article, "Only the truth will make us free. The truth which is always awful." I am not so certain that the truth will make us free, but a courageous confrontation of the terrible is still the most exhilarating thing I know, and the greatest source of metaphysical joy.

HAROLD CLURMAN

A Theatre Review

Though there may be doubts as to the merit of Rolf Hochhuth's *The Deputy* as a play (Brooks Atkinson Theatre), there can be no question as to the absorbing interest of its material. The blunt fact is that I found myself so intent on the subject that I very nearly ceased to concern myself with the performance as an evening in the theatre.

Before saying anything further about *The Deputy*—which has been produced in Berlin, London, Paris, Vienna, Stockholm, Athens—I should like to comment on the implications of that opening remark.

It is nonsense to maintain that we see and judge plays entirely in the light of their "creative" values. If we have no personal relation to a play's human content, we are not likely to understand it all or care anything about it. Imagine a person incapable of passion at a performance of *Romeo and Juliet* or *Tristan und Isolde*. True, there would still be the language of the one and the music of the other, but even these would lose their affective force for such an auditor. He might well ask, "What's all the excitement about?"

Allardyce Nicoll, the English theatre historian, made a point some years ago at an international drama conference, citing a passage from my book *The Fervent Years* which describes the opening night in 1935 of Odets' *Waiting for Lefty* as follows: "When the audience at the end of the play responded to the militant question from the stage—'Well, what's the answer?'—with a spontaneous roar of 'Strike! Strike!' it was something more than a tribute to the play's effectiveness. . . . Our youth had found its voice. The audience was delirious. It stormed the stage. . . ." Professor Nicoll held that such a response to a play was a form of mass hysteria and thus not a proper attitude for a theatre audience. It lacked the necessary objectivity for artistic appreciation.

A leading stage director and author of well-known books such as *The Fervent Years,* Harold Clurman is drama critic of *The Nation.* This review is reprinted from *The Nation* of March 16, 1964,

Perhaps so. We always hope for and seek perfect unity between form and content in a work of art, but I suspect that complete "Apollonian" detachment from the sources of an artist's inspiration—the living matter which generates his work—is even more foreign to relevant judgment in the arts than is complete identification with those sources. I very much doubt that the Athenians who attended the plays of Aeschylus, Sophocles, Euripides and Aristophanes viewed them with the contemplative calm presumed by doctors of aesthetics to be the correct frame of mind for cultivated enjoyment. All of which makes me sympathize with the critic who, when asked about his favorable review of Dore Schary's *Sunrise at Campobello,* "You really liked the play?," answered "I liked Roosevelt."

An evaluation of *The Deputy* at this moment is difficult, to begin with, because while it was written as a Schiller-like epic drama—the published text would take more than six hours to perform—each of its versions has had a different translator, and been staged and cut by a different director. Even more taxing to strict criticism, an ambiguity in the dramatist's motivation has led to a confusion in the audiences' reception of the play everywhere.

Apparently Hochhuth set out to write a dramatic "poem" on the existentialist question: Why should a young Jesuit priest, martyring himself on behalf of the Jewish victims of Nazi savagery, cling to his belief in God when all the evidence of his actual experience contradicts any rational justification for such faith? But this theme was lost sight of in the development of the work because the author was carried away by the more burning question of why the Christian world—embodied in its most organized Church—failed to protest the blackest crime in history: the systematic slaughter of six million Jews between 1941 and 1944. The outraged moralist and historian in the author superceded the religious artist.

The climatic scene of the play becomes, therefore, the one in which Pope Pius XII (Pacelli) refuses to denounce the Nazi action against the Jews or to abrogate the Concordat between Hitler and the Church. It makes the play appear to be primarily an attack on the Pontiff and, by extension, on the Catholic hierarchy.

This is a distortion of the play's significance and value. It should not be construed as anti-Catholic. Even the Pope's role in the dramatic context should not be considered central. The play's real protagonist is Father Fontana, whose tragic outcry and assumption of Jewish martyrdom lie at the heart of Hochhuth's message. What the play tells us is that we all share in the guilt of those years, for none of us acted with sufficient vigor, none of us protested bitterly, clamorously, specifically enough. The governments of Britain and France, to go no further, are as open to the play's accusation on this score as was the Church's chief deputy.

If the audience misses this point, its failure is largely due to a weakness in Hochhuth's dramatic thinking, his inability to bring the play's larger issue and the detail of its scenes into focus. Father Fontana is less vividly and convincingly drawn than are his more compliant fellow clerics. Yet, despite these grave defects of dramatic statement, it would be false to deny the play's hold on our attention or its power to stir.

Herman Shumlin's production is unfortunately not nearly as gripping as it should be. It lacks impetus and bite. Jeremy Brett is a good choice for the role of Fontana, though his part seems underwritten in this version. But most of the cast on the second night, except for Fred Stewart as an unctuous cardinal, struck me as insecure, either from insufficient rehearsal or lack of aptitude.

Emlyn Williams, on the other hand, possesses all the skill and authority needed to play the Pope, but his (or the director's) choice of interpretation was misguided. It damages the play to make the character soft or to suggest, even in the slightest degree, a suave insincerity. The part is not written that way. From a political standpoint, the Pope's arguments are "sensible" enough. His behavior toward the Italian Jews was irreproachable and his general attitude in the circumstances was less reprehensible than, let us say, that of Chamberlain in respect to the situation in 1938. The part could and should be read with dignified strength, masterly self-possession and with the firm conviction that the Pope is "right."

TOM F. DRIVER

The Meaning of Silence

The American production of *The Deputy,* Rolf Hochhuth's famous play about the Papacy and the Nazis, has been launched with the force of a rocket. Even before blast-off it drew fire from several anti-missile strongholds, and later it attracted the shots of more, including the Archdiocese of New York. Now that the missile is in trajectory, the only question is what target it will hit.

The Deputy will not succeed in blasting the reputation of Pope Pius XII, if that is what was intended. Nor is it likely, under the circumstances, to touch that more important mark, the public conscience. Where it will have an effect, however, is on the box office of the Brooks Atkinson Theatre.

The phenomenon of this production, hastily mounted by producer-director Herman Shumlin and following in the wake of controversy touched off by the play in Europe, does not evoke much admiration. It does not, in my opinion, fairly represent the play that Hochhuth wrote. Meanwhile half the public shouts angry defenses of Pope and Church, while the other half luxuriates in a "confession" of corporate "sin," safe in the knowledge that no one can be punished for *that.* A sort of merchandising of guilt is going on. Some people are buying and others are trying to sell. The theatre owner makes a profit either way.

Some of the blame for this debacle belongs to Hochhuth, who wrote a script so long that those producing it on stage have had to cut it substantially. But a larger share of the blame must be addressed to the producer. As written, the play, while by no means a great drama, is interesting and subtle. In this production, it has become simply an anti-Catholic tract of almost no subtlety.

Dr. Driver wrote this piece for *The Reporter* when he was drama critic of that magazine. Dr. Driver parted company with *The Reporter* in June 1964 in a quarrel over his review of *Blues for Mister Charlie.* He teaches at Union Theological Seminary.

The published text of *The Deputy* (Grove Press) is larger in scope. It shows not only the response of various Catholics and the Vatican to Hitler's *Endlösung;* it shows also the face of that evil as it appeared in the behavior of Eichmanns, Krupps, SS men, and other people. We see Jews being rounded up for the death camps. We see them reaching their destination. We see the anguish in them and the anguish of another sort in their persecutors. All the while the question grows: Who speaks for man? Why doesn't someone whom the whole world can hear name this evil for what it is?

The play is designed so that in its fourth act this question can be carried to the Vicar of Christ. But Hochhuth's Pope cannot answer it clearly. He is the head of an institution, and he has a duty to see that the institution survives. All his calculations, including his underestimation of the evils being done to the Jews and his fear that Bolshevism is a greater menace than Nazism, are based on that duty. His morality is not that of an individual but of a corporate body with branches in many nations, and for that reason it is equivocal.

The protagonist of the play is Father Riccardo Fontana, a young Jesuit. His Jesuit training must have been somewhat lacking, for he is unable to understand one of the first principles of ethical theory—namely, that the morality of a group cannot equal that of an individual. He speaks more like a young St. Francis, who once suggested, as Riccardo does, that perhaps the Pope should be martyred.

If Pius XII, in Hochhuth's play, finds the language of "responsible restraint" coming too quickly to his lips, Riccardo is a hothead. When Riccardo at last realizes that the Pope will not speak unambiguously, he pins a Star of David to his soutane in the very presence of the Holy Father. Later he rides one of the Jew-trains to Auschwitz, where he dies a Jew's death. His is the freedom, the courage, and the martyrdom of a heroic individual, and it puts the morality of the hierarch to shame.

At Auschwitz, nevertheless, the question of silence is carried beyond the Pope. The fifth act is concerned with the silence of God. Auschwitz is a machine run by diabolic minds. Its purpose is to prove that Man the Destroyer can challenge God the Creator with impunity. Forced to work at the gas chambers, Riccardo says he felt as if he were "burning God." He is taunted by the doctor in charge of the killings (based on the actual Josef Mengele):

Riccardo: Why . . . why? Why do you do it?
Doctor: Because I wanted an answer! And so I've ventured

what no man has ever ventured since the beginning of the world.

I took the vow to challenge the Old Gent, to provoke him so limitlessly that He would have to give an answer . . . .

Well, hear the answer: not a peep came from Heaven, not a peep for fifteen months, not once since I've been giving tourists tickets to Paradise . . . .

The truth is, Auschwitz refuses creator, creation, and the creature. Life as an idea is dead.

These lines are not spoken in the acted version, for very nearly all of the act in which they occur has been cut. Where Hochhuth's play is basically a questioning work, Herman Shumlin's jaundiced adaptation turns it into a diatribe. (The playbill says Jerome Rothenberg did the adaptation, but Shumlin has publicly assumed credit for it.) The aim of the adaptation is to accuse the Pope of cowardice. The picture it draws perpetuates two gross illusions about history: first, that the famous men of history may be divided into sheep and goats because their moral choices are simple; second, that the Roman Catholic Church has enormous power which it uses more often on behalf of the goats than the sheep. In this way, history is turned into melodrama. If I read Hochhuth's play correctly, however, one of its main points is that although history sometimes looks like cheap melodrama, its reality is something more complex.

It has been suggested that the German people may be pleased with this play because in impugning the Pope for his silence it exonerates them for theirs. On the contrary, I think the intention of the play was to show that the buck cannot be passed. In the play it is handed all the way up to God, who in His silence refuses to accept it. If, instead of seeing that point, the audiences of *The Deputy* prefer to hurl accusations at one another, there is nothing to stop them. But let them not imagine they are in that way helping mankind to avoid a repetition of the evils they deplore.

The production of *The Deputy* in New York suffers not only from a butchered script but also from bad casting and, I am sorry to say, slovenly direction. Moreover, the stage designs are impractical. The evening displays no unity but merely a series of effects thrown together for the occasion. Only the performance of Emlyn Williams as Pius XII is worth remembering, and that not because it is character creation but skilled caricature. The interest of this production does not reside in what we see on stage, which is flat, but from facts and ideas extrinsic to the theatrical event. It need not have been so.

RICHARD GILMAN

The Deputy *Arrives*

The arrival on Broadway of *The Deputy* has turned out to be an anti-climax, an intellectual one at least, since everything had been expended long before, all argument, partisan response, exhortation and cool theory. Yet physically the first performances were in every sense climactic. Outside the theater the hate-groups picketed, stirring eddies of disgust but also that peculiar nostalgia we feel for periods during which hatred has clear objects and know-nothingism a face in the streets. And inside there was an atmosphere of expectation beyond anything in recent years, an edgy solemnity that curiously outran the knowledge most of us presumably had. It was as though no matter how much we had read or heard about the play, or whether we had read the text, we could not really believe in its existence until it became actual, subjecting us to its argument in the flesh. The difference might have been that between a lecture on concentration camps and a visit to the site of Buchenwald.

The expectation was never fulfilled, the demonstration was discovered to be almost wholly the lecture it was supposed to supplant. But what is so unprecedented, the reality which makes so much of the public discussion irrelevant, is the way in which Rolf Hochhuth's work manages to survive its own deficiencies and even its incorporeality, persisting in the memory as an instigation, a catalyst and an obduracy. The play as adapted and performed is very much less than the printed text, that text is in turn less than the truth of history, yet something remains that cannot be appeased, neutralized or overthrown.

We have been doing our best to accomplish one or all of these things, and not least by the insistence that despite perversions and reductiveness the play sets going a moral energy outside the framework of history and independent of its

---

Now drama editor of *Newsweek,* Richard Gilman was formerly drama critic of the Catholic magazine *The Commonweal.* This review is reprinted from *The Commonweal,* of March 20, 1964.

details. This is the high, or soul-supporting interpretation. On lower levels *The Deputy* is regarded as a strict historical assertion which can only be established or disproved, or alternatively, as a no less strictly intended work of art obliging us to canonize it or deflate its pretensions. But what is so significant about Hochhuth's work is that it cuts through categories, being neither art nor history nor pure moral gesture nor autonomous call to arms. If it is anything at all it is an act of frustration in the face of categories and complexity, an attempt to give definition and location to an overwhelmingly diffuse and imprecise moral anguish.

In this sense there is a strong resemblance between *The Deputy* and the trial of Adolf Eichmann. Eichmann became the local, identifiable, graspable source of the horror, the foul consciousness which could explain all unconsciousness, the bounded agency which could account for unbounded crime. It is half the universe from Eichmann to Pope Pius XII, but we will be doing ourselves and the play a great disservice if we allow our natural indignation at the linking of the two names to prevent us from seeing what is being constructed here. As Eichmann was, for the people who tried him, the active principle, upon whom was heaped all the rage and frustration that stemmed from the fact that there was no other agent at hand and, even more, from the intolerable pressure of historical complexity, so Pope Pius, in Hochhuth's sortie against the past, is the negative principle personified, the fixed point of silence who is made to account for and bear the responsibility of silence everywhere.

Dramatically, this seizure of the late Pope for the purposes of finding a location for and giving intelligibility to the fact of silence serves Hochhuth as both a thematic center and an organizing principle. There is no tension springing from Pius' possible courses of action within the play; we know he will not denounce Hitler for the extermination of the Jews. But there is a tension which rises from the return to history, the illusion of having the agonizing events unfolding again, and another which issues from the figure of the Jesuit priest, Riccardo Fontana, who adopts an opposite course, sacrificial and circumstance-defying. He is Hochhuth's imaginative alternative to the Pope, his corrective to moral history; by his action in physically aligning himself with the victims Fontana offers the possibility of redeeming the past at the same time as he most radically indicts its failure as exemplified by Pius' inaction.

Two things go wrong, however, in Hochhuth's drama, if not in his moral vision or at least his moral impulse. The first is contained in the enormous blunder of ascribing to the Pope's personality and human deficiencies more of the responsibility for the Church's failure to speak than rests upon the institutional nature of the Church herself. As Michael Harrington and Guenter Lewy have pointed out, by failing to take into account the nature of German Catholicism, with its pervasive anti-Semitism and, beyond that, the nature of the organized Church itself, perpetually risking shame by its considerations of physical survival, Hochhuth has reduced the issues to an intolerable degree.

It is true that he inserts some explanations from the realm of policy—the Vatican's desire for an independent, mediating role, its fear of Russia—but his portrait of Pius as a narrow, tight-lipped, terrifyingly abstract and unfeeling man is so unrelenting and is made so central to his thesis that the effect is to abase history to the level of personality. But what is essential to keep in mind here is that exaggerated and unfair as this portrait undoubtedly is, the real crime is not against Pius but against moral complexity, just as the real failure of imagination rests not in an ignorance of what Pius was but in an ignorance of what we all are in our relations to fact, evil, necessity and transcendence.

This imaginative deficiency is perhaps even more sharply revealed in the figure of the Jesuit, Fontana, who might have been the locus for a true examination of conscience, an arena for moral debate and illumination. But Hochhuth is unable to make more of him than a narrow agency of opposition and indictment, an emblem of revulsion from moral failure and an unchanging container for the corrective act. Dramatically, there is no growth on the part of this character; once he has learned the facts about the extermination of the Jews he simply swings into predictable motion, approaching every so often a pseudo-Dostoevskian confrontation with the anguish of faith besieged by social horror but sinking continually back into mere functionalism, a rod of indignation with which to beat Pius and a weight to throw into the scales.

All this having been said (there has been no space to describe the play's technical and structural weaknesses—its wobbly stance between a Brechtian epic mode and a portentous lyricism, nor to comment on the way in which Jerome Rothenberg's adaptation serves to reduce to the vanishing point such complexity as the text possesses) there remains the truth that *The Deputy* cannot be measured by its own dimensions. It survives in part by its very inadequacy, which is to say that its attempt to locate guilt instructs us in the supreme difficulty of the task, once the obvious man with the gun has been dealt with, and its vulnerable resurrection of history teaches us how vulnerable are our own efforts to make history transcend itself.

Pius failed to speak, and in the ultimate moral region beyond fact and physical necessity the silence is to be condemned and mourned. But we would be getting off easy if we persisted in seeing *The Deputy* as merely a reminder of his or anyone's failure, as a prick to conscience or the grounds for a reformation of spirit. Things of this sort have a way of floating like balloons above the carnage; we comfort ourselves by their presence in the empyrean. The real value of Hochhuth's play is precisely that it can force us back into history, into the intricacies of the relationship between spirit and aggrieved body, between personal responsibility and institutional indifference. If it does this inadvertently, through a passion ill-matched with its instruments, it does it in any case. *The Deputy* can be described as an accident which rides the weight of necessity, an error which can lead to truth, a failure which makes most of our successes strangely unsatisfying.

3 | Three Editorials and a Press Release

FROM "THE NEW YORK TIMES"

Silence

The Deputy, by Rolf Hochhuth, is a play, a book, a news story—and a factual and philosophical statement, one of the most controversial theatrical works of recent years. To say merely that a serious play or book—regardless of how hard it cuts and what passions it arouses—should be allowed before the public would be begging the question. Of course it should. People can see it or read it, avoid it or picket it at their pleasure. But thoughtful people will discuss the theme as part of our recent and possibly our future history.

It is now nearly two decades after the *Walpurgisnacht* of Nazi Germany ended. The ripples of the holocaust still reach the far corners of the earth. In courtrooms of West Germany today, war criminals are still being tried for bestial acts at Auschwitz and elsewhere. It can never be forgotten that six million Jews and millions of other innocents in the path of war were deliberately killed by Hitler's Third Reich and its active supporters on many levels in Germany.

Could the innocents—or at least some of them—have been saved? In *The Deputy,* the playwright contends that Pope Pius XII, then the Sovereign Pontiff of the Roman Catholic Church, might have prevented deportations and mass murder by speaking out against the Nazi extermination camps. The

---

This editorial appeared in *The New York Times* on February 28, 1964, and is reprinted by permission.

facts may be in dispute; the history imperfect; the indictment too severe. But the philosophical issue is ever alive. In a word, it is: silence.

Specifically applied to the years of Hitlerism—which, after all, were slowly building in the 1920's and 1930's—there were many governments, and many political, religious and other leaders who failed to speak up, let alone act. First Hitler swallowed the lambs; then the jackals; then he tried to lie down with the lions.

Those who appeased the dictator, those who wished to be innocent bystanders, those who closed their frontiers to the refugees, and those who merely remained silent contributed in different degrees to the downfall of man and his conscience in the twentieth century.

FROM THE "NEW YORK POST"

Echoes of The Deputy

The Deputy, the controversial play by Rolf Hochhuth, a young German Protestant, raises momentous issues which cannot be evaded simply because they are painful and delicate. The nature of Cardinal Spellman's attack on the production obscures rather than clarifies the issues.

To avoid the subject would make our generation guilty of the same kind of silence of which Hochhuth accuses Pope Pius XII. The question is not whether Hochhuth's portrayal of Pope Pius is historically just or overdrawn; there is evidence to suggest it is open to challenge on many points. The question is whether the conduct of nearly all institutions and leaders, during the years when one of the most monstrous crimes in human history was committed, is an appropriate theme for debate and dramatization.

Such searching reappraisal should be troublesome for all of us. At the time of the Eichmann trial, when Hannah Arendt charged that European Jewish leaders cooperated in the destruction of their own communities, the resulting outcry in many Jewish circles showed that a sensitive nerve had been touched. We believe Mrs. Arendt overstated her case; but we never questioned her right to present it.

Khrushchev's outrage at the poet Yevtushenko for suggesting that Russian anti-Semitism was an accomplice of the Nazi extermination squads at Babi Yar was the anger of a man who wanted to avoid confronting the problems of conscience posed by the poet.

There has never been a full assessment in the West of the blame of the Allied leaders who, when asked to do things that might have saved many Jewish lives, asserted the higher urgencies of war diplomacy and strategy.

As the managing editor of the Catholic weekly, *The Commonweal,* James O'Gara recently wrote, "It is altogether too easy to lay the blame on Pius XII, and this can easily be just one more act of evasion where there has been too much evasion already."

It is not Cardinal Spellman's passionate defense of Pope Pius XII that concerns us. Surely it is his right to speak his mind. What is disturbing is his statement of the case in terms designed to discourage free discussion of the dilemmas and responsibilities created by the violence and inhumanity of our age.

FROM "THE NEW YORK HERALD TRIBUNE"

A Statement by Francis Cardinal Spellman

In the fall of 1958, the whole world grieved when Pius XII died. He was mourned not by Catholics alone but by people of all faiths, especially by Jewish people to whom he had been a loyal friend in the tragic hours of Nazi persecution.

Today a play is being shown in our city which attempts to reverse this judgment and in effect holds Pius XII guilty of the Nazi crimes. Only six years after his death our Holy Father is being tried and condemned on the stage. This is an outrageous desecration of the honor of a great and good man, and an affront to those who know his record as a humanitarian, who love him and revere his memory.

It was my privilege for many years to know him intimately and to work at his side, and I testify that he was utterly incapable of any base motive of personal cowardice. Compassionate and courageous, he dedicated and sacrificed his life for God and for all his fellow men.

Because such a slanderous and divisive drama is calculated to stir strong emotions and bitter feelings, I plead for moderation and charity in meeting the crisis which it provokes. I pray that the people of New York will not allow it to drive a wedge between Catholics and Jews, with whom we have suffered together, for whom we have the greatest respect and the friendliest feelings — and for whom also we have deep and heartfelt sympathy in the terrible and tragic sorrows which they have known.

The statement reproduced here was released by the Bureau of Information of the Archdiocese of New York. *The New York Herald Tribune* of March 3, 1964, in reporting the statement, quoted some remarks made by Cardinal Spellman when asked whether the statement might be construed "as an order to Roman Catholics to stay away from performances of *The Deputy*." The Cardinal's reply follows: "The statement says all I wish to say. I have refrained until now from commenting on this play, which was first presented in Europe a year ago, because it was not until recently it was made available here. I have not seen nor read it, but like most people, I feel I know its tack — so much has been written and said about it."

In the same issue of *The New York Herald Tribune,* Richard Cardinal Cushing was quoted as having made the following remarks: "I don't think it would do any harm for any intelligent person to see the play, but I think prior to seeing it, they ought to know the real facts and not imaginary conditions that are described. They should really be familiar with what Pope Pius XII, while he was the Nuncio in Germany, and while he was the Supreme Pontiff, really did to help the Jewish people . . ."

FROM "AMERICA"

Character Assassination

A drama written by a young German named Rolf Hochhuth came to New York on February 26, preceded and accompanied by an unusual amount of press and radio-TV coverage—not to speak of an unusual outpouring of emotion. And small wonder. Entitled *The Deputy,* the play deals with the fate of Hitler's Jewish victims slaughtered by the millions in the gas chambers of Auschwitz and elsewhere. The hero is a priest; the villain is a Pope, Pius XII. The Pontiff is portrayed as having been criminally responsible for the death of the Jews, indeed as the chief culprit, after the Nazis, for the holocaust. For a word from him, allegedly, could have stayed Hitler's hand.

This is a grave indictment of a historical person, and its validity obviously depends not on a dramatic production but on a serious and competent study of the vast forces at work during the 1939-1945 conflagration. We do not take seriously the claim that author Hochhuth has based his play on such a study. But this does not prevent him from stating his estimate of Pius XII: "Perhaps never before in history," he tells us in his so-called historical notes (*The Deputy,* p. 304, American edition. Grove Press. 1964.), "have so many human beings paid with their lives for the passivity of a single statesman." The Pope is a criminal—a judgment with which the American producer-director, Herman Shumlin, is in accord.

Making allowances for incidental changes in the actual Broadway script, the basic Hochhuth-Shumlin thesis is an atrocious calumny against the memory of a good and courageous world leader occupying the venerable Chair of Peter during one of the great crises of humanity. Pius XII needed no lectures from small men far away on how to comport himself with dignity and conscientiousness before monumental catastrophes. Popes have always had to cope with these throughout

---

This editorial is reprinted from *America,* (The National Catholic Weekly Review), March 7, 1964.

the long history of the papacy. Another Pope might have acted differently—though just how differently will always remain a matter of conjecture. But the thrust of the Hochhuth charge is not at the correctness of decisions made in good faith, on the basis of knowledge available at the time, but at the motivation that inspired those decisions. These motives, in *The Deputy,* are the basest—greed, fanaticism, power politics, even anti-Semitism. To reverse the estimate made by Hochhuth: perhaps never before in history have so many vicious, tendentious and mean imputations of motives been based on such flimsy, distorted and falsified historical arguments. *The Deputy* is character assassination.

In the present state of public feeling on the Broadway production, it may be well simply to recall what responsible Jewish spokesmen themselves said about Pius XII during his lifetime and when he died, in 1958. Those statements ring with a note entirely different from what we now hear emanating from Broadway. These testimonies were freely and sincerely rendered.

We recalled, in an editorial last August 24, the statement of Mrs. Golda Meir, Israeli foreign minister, who declared: "In the decade of Nazi terror, when our people was subject to terrible martyrdom, the voice of the Pope was raised in compassion for the victims." We recalled the gracious gesture of Leonard Bernstein, who, before beginning a concert of the N.Y. Philharmonic, called for a moment of silence "for the passing of a very great man, Pope Pius XII." But in May, 1955, the Israel Philharmonic had already presented a concert in the Vatican, in the presence of the Pope, as a gesture of thanks for his services to the Jews during the war.

The voices of rabbis were not hushed in 1958 or even earlier. Rabbi Julius Mark of Temple Emanu-El in New York, which counts among its members some of the most distinguished families in American Jewry, declared, in the name of all, that "possessed of a brilliant mind, a compassionate heart and a dedicated spirit, His Holiness gave of himself generously and self-sacrificingly to the sacred task of world peace founded on justice." In October, 1945, the World Jewish Congress made a token financial gift to the Vatican in recognition of the work of the Holy See in rescuing Jews from Fascist and Nazi persecutions. On December 1, 1944, at its war emergency conference in Atlantic City, the WJC sent a telegram of thanks to the Holy See for the protection it gave "under difficult conditions to the persecuted Jews in German-dominated Hungary."

Since the plight of the Jews of Rome, "under the windows of the Vatican," figures prominently in *The Deputy,* it is instructive to learn what the persons directly concerned thought about the Pope's handling of the situation. Dr. Israel Goldstein of the WJC said, in his own 1958 tribute: "In Rome, last year, the Jewish community told me of their deep appreciation of the policy which had been set by the Pontiff for the Vatican during the period of the Nazi-Fascist regime, to give shelter and protection to the Jews, wherever possible."

Hochhuth and his backers argue that Pope John XXIII would have acted differently had he been in the shoes of Pius XII. And they cite with admiration Roncalli's own rescue record as Apostolic Delegate in Istanbul. But the same Pope John XXIII never failed to insist that what he did then, he did with the approval and even on the orders of his chief.

Attempts are also made, as in *The Deputy,* to give the credit for any Jewish rescue work to individuals, as though, in the case of the hero-priest, they were actually working against the will of the Church. Adequate commentary is provided on this maneuver by L. Poliakov. This French Jewish scholar is not particularly philo-Catholic and is cited by Hochhuth as a witness for himself. But in the November, 1950 issue of *Commentary,* organ of the American Jewish Committee, Poliakov cut the ground neatly from under such palpable attempts to downgrade the papal role: "And this direct aid, accorded to the persecuted Jews by the Pope in his position as Pope of Rome, was only the symbolic expression of an activity that spread throughout Europe, encouraging and stimulating the efforts of Catholic churches in almost every country. There is no doubt that secret instructions went out from the Vatican urging the national churches to intervene in favor of the Jews by every possible means."

As we have asked before in these pages: What has happened since 1958 to erase with one sweep these informed and unsolicited tributes to the memory of Pope Pius XII? Why do they count for nothing when *The Deputy* comes to town? By what dialectic, or through what human fickleness, has a great benefactor of humanity, and of the Jews particularly, now become a criminal? Frankly, we have no answer.

4 | Hochhuth Interviewed

JUDY STONE

Interview with Rolf Hochhuth

For a man who has provoked a storm of conscience and controversy in the Christian community and shattered the inviolability of the Vatican, Rolf Hochhuth is surprisingly shy and diffident, but he has the courage to examine the most terrible moral problem of our time: "How does man exercise his responsibility?" The 32-year-old German Protestant and former member of a Hitler youth group was not looking for easy answers or a scapegoat when he wrote his searingly anti-Nazi play *Der Stellvertreter*.

The question that haunts him, and all guilt-ridden young Germans is: "How could our people have killed six million Jews?"

He talked about the German reaction in an interview during the Christmas holidays while visiting his parents in Eschwege, the small town in which he grew up. Hochhuth is a slender man with a look of pain on his face, the physical residue of a partial paralysis compounded by some inner struggle. A slight imbalance of the eyes compels attention and the level sincerity in them commands respect. His grave and lovely wife Marianne, whose own mother was decapitated by the Nazis, acted as translator.

"If I had killed someone," Hochhuth said slowly, "I can

Miss Stone is editor of the daily drama, music, and art section of the *San Francisco Chronicle*. Her interview is reprinted from *Ramparts*, Spring 1964.

never get rid of it, no matter what I do. So I must live with this feeling of guilt and gradually I get used to it. It's the problem of each individual: how he can live with guilt. Whether he gets indolent or superficial. I wrote this book; that's how I lived with it." He paused for a long time and murmured, "But if you measure it [writing a book] against the murder of only one child, it is, of course, nothing."

The uproar in Berlin when the play opened in February 1963 under the direction of the famous Erwin Piscator has since spread to Switzerland, Paris, England, Denmark, Vienna and the United States where it opened in New York in February, produced by Herman Shumlin. For the play, Hochhuth won the "Young Generation Playwright Award" of the 1963 "Berliner Kunstpreis"; shared the Gerhard Hauptmann Prize of 1962; he has been praised as a social conscience, a mantle he wears awkwardly and reluctantly, and he has been damned variously as a Nazi, a Communist and an anti-Semite.

To those who asked him to refute the charges, Hochhuth replied with quiet dignity, "I will not answer. I want them to judge my play independently of my person. Whoever reads my play and still maintains the opinion that I am an anti-Semite, or Nazi, or Communist, this one cannot be answered."

In all the controversy about the Pope, Hochhuth said, his major point has often been overlooked. Perhaps because the truncated, over-simplified three-hour stage versions have lacked the moving complexity of the eight-hour original drama.

"To me," Hochhuth explained, "Pius is a symbol, not only for all leaders, but for all men—Christians, Atheists, Jews. For all men who are passive when their brother is deported to death. Pius was at the top of the hierarchy and, therefore, he had the greatest duty to speak. But every man—the Protestants, the Jews, Churchill, Eden, Cordell Hull, all had the duty to speak."

It is absurd, he said, that people should accuse him of trying to diminish the guilt of the Germans because he has accused the Pope of silence: "The arsonist does not become less guilty because a fireman resigns in front of a great fire."

"I hope that this play will give a lecture for the future," he said, "because I think the terror against the Jews in our time is only one example of the terror which reigns on earth at all times, in all epochs, in every century. In every nation there are feelings that wait for a Hitler to awaken. In other centuries there was the Inquisition. Nearly all times have known horrible examples that certain groups of men were persecuted in dreadful ways: The Christians in Rome, the heretics persecuted by the Christians. Therefore, I fear that this will never cease. Today there is race persecution between white and black; the persecution of the Communists by McCarthy and others and the persecution of others by the Communists. There was McCarthy on one hand in America and Ulbricht on the other in East Germany and Kadar in Hungary.

"I believe that this play may be a lesson for the future if only people will accept it. A friend asked me, 'Why do you take such pains to write about the final solution? In 20 years' time no one will talk about it.'

"I have studied enough of history to know that he was probably right; actually the victims have always been forgotten very quickly. But in spite of that, I am convinced—not only in spite of it, but because of it, that the play can teach a lesson which is timeless."

To oppose injustice, Hochhuth said, "one needn't be a moral man. It is enough to do nothing which damages others." (To a critic who asked, "Is this indeed enough?" Hochhuth replied, "It may not be much if you measure saints by it, but for people it is enough.")

How could a young German grow up under the Hitler regime and retain a moral sense?

Hochhuth was born in 1931 in the little town of Eschwege in Northern Hesse, near the river Werra, now just a few miles from the East-West border, a border that torments the playwright. "You must see the border," he urged repeatedly. When finally we did, it was an odd sight: after their heavy noon-day dinners, the West Germans come on Sunday outings, with powerful field glasses, to look at the border. What are they looking for? What do they see?

Hochhuth sees for the Germans a tragic fate, inextricably linked to that of the Jews, and in the border, an almost mystical analogy to the Jewish Diaspora.

Asked if he thought that Germany could ever again be a threat to the world's peace, he replied, "Only in an indirect way. A country of 70,000,000 which is cut into two pieces against nature can never come to peace. The Germans should be forbidden atomic weapons for all time, but they should be given their unity. The occupying powers can stay; they don't disturb us, but the border between the Germans should be removed. One should always think of it and see it. It's idiotic, this border.

"This border in Germany may be the beginning of a Diaspora like that of the Jewish people. I think that German history will become as sad and tragic as the Jewish history. I feel that the tragedy of the Jewish history has not come to an end by the foundation of the state of Israel. This small country with a small population in the midst of the Arab world is menaced so terribly. I fear for it . . . And when one thinks of the anti-Semitism in Russia leading to persecution again . . . The Germans and the Jews seem to have the quality of always getting themselves disliked and persecuted."

Hochhuth has refused to let his play be performed in Eastern Europe or in any country where the Church is suppressed by the State, but he wonders if his decision is correct. "When I read now in a leading Jewish newspaper in West Germany that the Jews are actually persecuted in Russia, I ask myself if it wouldn't be important to publish my play in Russia for evidently the Church is less suppressed at the moment than Jewry. A Hungarian anti-Communist in Paris who left Hungary during the revolution, wrote that it was great folly not to allow my play to be published in the East. He said the play calls people against all forms of terror and for that reason the people in the Eastern bloc would understand."

But Hochhuth who has had offers from Poland, Prague and Belgrade, said, "I am convinced they would abbreviate it in a radical way and I couldn't do anything about it. I'm afraid the Communists would use it for propaganda against the Church."

He himself had little formal religious training in Eschwege where his father ran a shoe factory which had been founded by Rolf's great grandfather. The elder Hochhuth had been an officer in World War I and an officer for three months in the second World War before being retired because of his age. One brother served in the army in Hungary and two cousins died in the war.

In 1941, at the age of ten, like all other boys, Hochhuth became a member of the Deutsches Jungvolk, a Hitler youth organization. When still a boy, he met his future wife, Marianne Heinemann, editor of a recent book of German poetry. Her personal tragedy is nowhere reflected in the serene warmth of her blue eyes, but unspoken pride shines in them when she speaks of her mother. She has achieved a matter-of-fact tone when she tells of the day two Nazis in civilian clothes came to their home in Berlin to take her 35-year-old mother away "for questioning." The 10-year-old Marianne watched as the men found the hidden, forbidden books by authors whose works had lit the unforgettable bonfires of 1933. Marianne's grandmother, a poor peasant girl who had worked and studied to become one of the first women Social Democrats and served on the Frankfurt town council until removed by the Nazis, trembled and sank into a chair. Her mother, tense and pale, tried to summon reassuring words for the child. Nine months later, Marianne was told her mother had died of a heart condition, but years later, she learned of her decapitation in prison. Her father, a former teacher, died serving in the Wehrmacht in Romania and 11-year-old Marianne was sent to Eschwege to live with relatives. She and Rolf met in school toward the end of the war.

Hochhuth, trying to recreate the mood of those black, wartime days, said, "To the end of the war, the little boy Rolf wished that Germany would win. My parents did not wish it and they would never have thought it possible that Germany could win after the invasion of Russia, but of course, they could not tell their feelings or they would have been killed. They heard the English and American broadcasts even though there was a death penalty for anyone caught listening. My mother entered a restaurant one day and told someone that the Americans were in Brussels. Since the German radio did not announce it until the following day, it was clear she had heard it on the enemy radio. She was denounced to a Nazi organization, but the leader was an old teacher of hers, a good man, and he told my uncle, who later became burgermeister for the Americans, to warn her not to do it again. That time they tore up the report.

"We feared the Russians," he said, "and because of the bombing of the Allies, we hated the Allies. From a propaganda point of view, it was not a good idea for the Allies to bomb civilian centers. As boys of the Hitler youth, we had to pick up pamphlets and leaflets dropped by the Allies. On these leaflets, it was written, 'We are not fighting the German people but the Nazis.' But we boys mocked those words because we saw dead women and children and we were impressed and hated those who had done it. The Americans who attacked Eschwege tried to find the military targets only and it was only bad luck they bombed the streets near the airport. But the English destroyed Kassel. We saw the town burning from here and my 14-year-old brother had to go there at night to help. The English didn't care where they bombed, but now I understand the English point of view."

Although Eschwege had many Jews living there, by 1941 the last ones were driven out to nearby Kassel and from there to Riga where they worked in the mines and were later killed. Rolf remembers with grief the act of charity extended by his mother to the Jewish wife of their cousin, a well-known doctor in Wiesbaden.

"A Jew married to a non-Jew was considered half-Jewish so they were not deported in 1941, but they had to wear the yellow star. My parents invited her here in 1943 and we boys were ashamed and wondered what people would think. She was very sweet to us and grateful. She stayed for a few weeks although people wondered and talked in a small town. When she returned to Wiesbaden, she had an 'invitation' to go to the Gestapo and she poisoned herself. Her husband was asked to help revive her, but he would not because he had promised to respect her wishes about her own fate."

Meanwhile, the townspeople heard from soldiers returning from Russia of rumors that the SS had engaged in mass shootings, but the rumors were all very quiet, very hush-hush.

"We thought it could not be true," Hochhuth said. "It was so ugly and brutal. But in a war, people's feelings become insensitive. The Jews had disappeared from our lives but we knew from books and school lessons that Jews were described as *untermenschen* and that all other people were second class. We also knew that the Russian prisoners of war in Germany and the German prisoners of war in Russia were treated badly and died of starvation, but this didn't affect one; each one had his own problems; we trembled for members of our own families."

After the Americans occupied Eschwege, they nominated as mayor Rolf's uncle, a well-known businessman who had not been a Nazi. He appointed the 13-year-old Rolf to be his messenger between Town Hall and the military government.

"The first week of the occupation was not very agreeable for the occupied. My parents and others had to leave their homes, but we were relieved because the war was over. My brother who had been taken prisoner of war by the Americans was released. And then the cruel things of the concentration camps became known. The photographs were shown in the papers and it shamed and sickened us. We didn't dare to believe . . ."

In the turmoil, he said, "The American army would have won the hearts of the German youth at once if they had treated the German soldiers better. Of course, they made great speeches that the Germans must not for the next 1000 years have guns, but you must take into consideration that the boys liked soldiers and ships and suddenly they heard it would be forbidden for the next 1000 years. On the one hand, they understood how guilty they were and the disaster we had brought to Europe, but these were the feelings that struggled inside us. And we were terribly frightened of the Russians. We heard about the most dreadful crimes the Red Army had committed in the Eastern Zone and this was no more Nazi propaganda, but facts.

"I say all this knowing that we Germans have started with

all these cruelties and that 'who sows the wind will reap the storm.' "

The young people today, he said, consume great quantities of non-fiction pocket books about the Third Reich and they ask, "How could it have been possible?"

"The people who were adults at that time and who silently feel guilty do not want to get near these problems. They have made great sacrifices through the war to Hitler. It is not very rare to find German families who have lost two sons and there is almost no family who has not lost one. I do not want to weigh the victims of the battlefields against the gassed people. I am not trying to make an accounting. Auschwitz was the top in inhumanity. But I will try to make you understand a little more. The old people are tired of torture. They want to be left in peace from politics. And also of the politics of today. One can be glad they come out for elections. But for the young people as truly as I am sitting here, there is no anti-Semitism. They don't know Jews. (One man said, 'Jews are like Martians to them.') Towards the Jewish people they feel guilty. 'How could our people have killed six million of them?' "

When the war ended and the realities of daily politics became too complex and confusing to young Rolf, the introspective youth kept to his books and began writing poetry. Then he discovered Thomas Mann and *Buddenbrooks*. It was a great revelation.

"The world of Buddenbrooks was the world of my ancestors. The firm my mother came from was also founded in 1797 and the last of the family was no more a businessman, but a sensitive artist. This touched me; the decay of a family fascinated me because I saw it in all the families I knew."

While reading the book, he learned that Mann had voluntarily left Germany because of his opposition to Hitler. "Mann has influenced me most," Hochhuth said. "The early Thomas Mann, his attitude towards life, his humanity, his engagement in politics. I have learned from Thomas Mann that the poet always must be active in politics. That he is also responsible. *The Deputy is* politics."

At the age of 17, Hochhuth left school to become a bookseller because he believed that he could come closer to literature and writing than by taking German lessons and studying natural science. After a few years as a bookseller in Marburg, Kassel and Munich, he fell ill for a year with an undiagnosed sickness which left one side of his face partially paralyzed. When he recovered he still could not work and he decided to attend the University of Heidelberg and the University of Munich to study history and philosophy.

In 1955, he became a reader and editor for the largest book club in the world, the Bertelsmann Lesering, and he edited a collected edition of the famous 19th-century anti-clerical satirist and caricaturist Wilhelm Busch. The book included among hundreds of caricatures of people and animals, some drawings of Jews, a fact which led to an attack on Hochhuth as an anti-Semite.

"Busch was not an anti-Semite," Hochhuth said. "One of his stories is about an innocent Jew who is hanged for a crime committed by Christians. But Busch was anti-clerical and I have discovered that in certain historical periods, one must be anti-clerical in order to defend oneself."

However, in an edition of Busch for children—his Max and Moritz characters became a model for the Katzenjammer Kids—Hochhuth omitted the pictures of Jews "so that German children would not mock the Jews."

At the same time, he wrote an unpublished novel in the form of letters called *Occupation,* a picture of the last weeks of the Nazi regime and the first month of the occupation. But he was writing more history than fiction and in studying the documents of the Nuremberg trials, he discovered the strange and improbable figure of Kurt Gerstein, the SS officer who plays a major role in *The Deputy*.

Gerstein had been active as an Evangelical Church youth leader. He wrote and distributed anti-Nazi pamphlets of the Confessional Church until his arrest in 1936. Upon his release, he decided to enlist in the SS and led an almost suicidal double-life there to determine the truth behind all the rumors of genocide. Gerstein finally made his way into the SS "Institute of Hygiene" and was responsible for taking delivery of consignments of Zyklon B, the lethal agent used in the death camps. In August 1942, he set about trying to sabotage the destruction process and from that time on was "driven without respite" to make the facts known to Protestant and Catholic leaders, including an attempt to reach the Apostolic Nuncio in Berlin. After making a full report to the Allies in 1945, Gerstein's trail disappeared in a Paris prison and his name has been placed by the Paris Jewish community on their memorial tablet for the victims of Fascism.

Fascinated by the figure of Gerstein, Hochhuth felt that he was a Christian "of a type so modern that to understand him completely one needs to read Kierkegaard. What interested me was that Gerstein was a Protestant in the most literal translation of the word. I believe that the Christian spirit as he expresses it, is the real spirit, the form of Christian spirit for our time."

He became so excited reading the documents on Gerstein that the drama inescapably began to form in his mind, although he had never thought of writing drama before.

"Then in the autumn of 1958, Pius died," Hochhuth said. "In Germany, the newspapers and radio declared that a holy man had died. The Germans loved Pius whose three closest advisors were German and they called him the German Pope."

But Hochhuth, stirred by Hitler's murder of almost 2500 Catholic priests, felt that "the holy men were those people who had died in concentration camps and not a man who died in his bed at a high age. Those Catholic priests whom Hitler killed are the true martyrs of the Catholic Church in our time, not the man who personally never tried to protest.

"I saw that this was the tragedy, the tragedy that the Vatican out of reasons of state did not support those members of their own church who sacrificed themselves."

He dedicated his play to the memory of two of them. One was Father Maximilian Kolbe, Internee No. 16670, a Polish Franciscan priest who died in 1941 in a starvation cell at Auschwitz after asking to take the place of a prisoner who was going to be among ten men punished to death by starvation in retaliation for the escape of one prisoner. He died too slowly for the SS and they finally gave him an injection to hasten his end. The other was Provost Bernhard Lichtenberg of the Cathedral in Berlin who prayed publicly for the Jews, was arrested and who asked to be allowed to share the fate of the Jews in the East. But he was taken to Dachau and died on the way there in 1943.

Hochhuth's fictitious figure of Father Riccardo Fontana, S.J., who confronts the Pope with the fact of his official silence, is based on the deeds and aims of Provost Lichtenberg who was concerned with the Pope's reaction to his attempt to share the fate of the Jews. In the play, Fontana, disappointed with the Pope's response, pins a yellow star on his cassock and goes with the Roman Jews to Auschwitz.

"I did not discover the fact of the Pope's silence," Hochhuth said. "In 1944, Albert Camus had posed the question: 'How was it possible that Pius kept silence?' François Mauriac asked the same question, as did the Catholic philosopher Friedrich Heer in Austria."

Leaving Germany, Hochhuth went to Paris and London to study all the relevant documents, the ones published and the ones lying unread in archives. Later he spent three months in Rome, living near St. Peter's, studying the atmosphere, talking to Swiss guards, Romans and Jews who had been hidden in Italian monasteries. He posed a series of questions to one Bishop whose name he will not reveal. After avoiding Hochhuth for weeks, the Bishop finally agreed to see him, confirming the belief of the author in his thesis.

Since the publication of the play a year ago and two books dealing with the controversy, there has been no real answer from the Vatican, Hochhuth said.

"If the Vatican had in its archives documents to throw doubt, even only to throw doubt, on my play, they would have found them and published them," he believes.

Shortly before his election to the Papacy, Cardinal Montini[1] wrote a letter commenting on newspaper reports of Hochhuth's play (cut nearly in half for the theater) to the *Tablet,* the leading Catholic periodical in England. In it, he did not deny the fact of the Pope's silence, but defended the character of Pius and told of his concern for all the victims and fear of bringing on even greater tragedies.

In Basle, Switzerland, where the Hochhuths now live with their three-year-old son, Hochhuth said, "I was visited by a prominent Jesuit father. We talked one whole Sunday, but believe me, we hardly spoke about the Pope. We were mainly concerned about Act 5: 'Auschwitz or the Question Asked of God.' "

"The padre told me that another Jesuit, very old, had said in a circle of Church people, that the fact that Hochhuth had attacked Pius was not so important and should not lead the discussion away from the fact that I had said inexcusable things about God.

"Pius is a historical figure, one of 260 Popes and his attitude is not enough to characterize the institution of Popedom, either in its good or in its bad sense. But the question about God is timeless, as the atrocities are timeless," Hochhuth said.

He quoted the German poet Trakl: "Silently over the heap of skulls, God's golden eyes open."

"Now for our contemporary sensibilities," Hochhuth commented, "this might have been said somewhat too beautifully, but whether God looks on the heap of skulls or if one says with Lichtenberg (an 18th century physicist and author) 'no invention has been easier to people than the invention of heaven,' this question about God is more essential than the silence of death of the so-called confessional peace which my

[1] See page 66.

play has been accused of endangering. That is unimportant to me. Luther once said, 'There must be upheaval in Christendom.' The Christians live much too comfortably today. The Churches have never before been even remotely fed with tax money as they are today, and on top of this one should leave them in peace? Why?"

PATRICIA MARX

Interview with Rolf Hochhuth

MISS MARX: Mr. Hochhuth, *The Deputy* is your first play to be published. Had you been thinking of writing a drama before you became interested in this subject?

MR. HOCHHUTH: No, I had not started a play before *The Deputy*; and, before that, I wrote non-dramatic prose.

MISS M: Why did you decide to treat such a vast historical subject in the form of a play?

MR. H: Because I believe that this subject is, in itself, such that this is the appropriate form, when you consider, for example, that the argument of the play hardly had to be invented by me, but could be taken directly from actual events—I mean, Gerstein bursting in upon the Papal Nuncio. I believe that in a play historical events can be marshalled toward the dramatic climax, and different points of view can be made to clash more sharply, and forcefully, than in a work of fiction.

This interview with Rolf Hochhuth, recorded during his visit to the United States in February 1964, was broadcast first over WNYC, the city-operated radio station of New York. Excerpts from that interview are reprinted here by permission of *Partisan Review*, where an edited text appeared in the Summer 1964 issue, Volume XXXI, No. 3, The translation of Mr. Hochhuth's answers is by John Simon who served as interpreter of the broadcast.

Also, I felt challenged by the notion of writing a play in free verse—something that has been ignored in German literature for some forty years; to be precise, since *Der Rosenkavalier* and other works by Hofmannsthal. Whereas, in England and America, it was common practice; for instance, Christopher Fry and T.S. Eliot. And I was particularly influenced by Auden's *The Age of Anxiety*.

MISS M: Why did you use free verse rather than prose?

MR. H: That, too, hinges on the choice of the dramatic form. Free verse carries its speaker along much more readily than prose, especially when it concerns a subject which is so closely involved with contemporary events and depends so extensively on historical documents. Then, things must be transposed, heightened by language. Otherwise, it would often be likely to sound as if one were merely quoting from the documents.

MISS M: But why is your free verse so very close to prose? Couldn't it just as well have been printed in prose form?

MR. H: No, I don't think so. I wrote certain scenes of the play in prose, then transposed them into free verse; and, in so doing, I was repeatedly able to cut the length one-third, sometimes even one-half. Free verse concentrates enormously; and, clearly, it gets its actual rhythm only in the interpretation.

Not only have actors, after the first rehearsal in Berlin, told me that they found it much easier to memorize the play, because it was written in this free verse; but, also, people who had not read a play since they graduated from high school said that they could read it more fluently.

There are certain rhythmic principles involved which have not yet been sufficiently explored. Little is known about it, so far. Of course, one must be very careful not to go too far. Occasionally, I incorporated a line of blank verse to put "stays," so to speak, on a whole group of lines. But one can't do that very often. When you have six consecutive lines of blank verse, of the kind that classical dramatists used, in a play today, it already sounds forced and unnatural.

Of course, the choice of a heightened language—whether we convey it through free verse or however—was made easier for me by the milieu of the play. Anyone who talks, for example, to high church dignitaries, will find that they do not speak in an ordinary, everyday, language, but that they express themselves, as a matter of course, in a more ceremonial manner—words on cothurni, as it were. I do not think, however, that it is still possible to write a drama in classical verse form when the characters are people from our walk of life.

MISS M: Mr. Hochhuth, did you feel constrained, as an artist, to be historically accurate? Was there a conflict between you as an artist and you as an historian?

MR. H: Only inasmuch as writing a play about events that lie only two decades behind us required a much more intensive research into historical documents than one might need if one were writing, say, a play about Luther.

MISS M: It has often been said that it is impossible to deal with such huge and complex historical situations in the context of a work of art, because one must simplify and condense. Did you find this a difficulty?

MR. H: I was, of course, aware of these difficulties; and, for that very reason, I considered it necessary to add to the play a historical appendix, fifty to eighty pages (depending on the size of the print). However, I expressly wrote the play in such a way that it is all very understandable and can be played by itself; and neither historical documents nor appendix has to be used (or has been used) by any of the productions of the play, except the Paris production, which did use one of the documents—but, in my opinion, unnecessarily.

MISS M: How did the idea for the play present itself? How did it take shape?

MR. H: Well, I only got the courage for the free verse after I had delved into the structure of the play to a considerable extent, and after I had visited Hans Egon Holthusen in Munich, and resolved the problem with the help of his long-line versification—as well as that of other contemporary German lyricists. It all happened a long time ago, and it is very hard for me to reconstruct exactly how it all began. I think I took down a few notes referring to the character of Gerstein, because my idea was to write a short story about him — quite a long time ago.

Later, however, in 1956, I met a man in Austria, who had helped with the gassing in Auschwitz; he had been transferred there as political punishment. And I read accounts which referred back to this old subject. Then it first became clear to me what the form of the play must be.

Also, at that time, the book, *The Third Reich and the Jews,* which contained the Gerstein report, was published. And then, in 1958, a book appeared containing the documents concerning the Vatican's attitude toward the deportation of Jews from Rome. At that time, I was living in

Münster because my wife was a student there; and I heard accounts of a vain attempt to arrest Bishop Galen—or rather, of the Nazis' hesitation to imprison him. I cannot say more than this. It is now seven years ago. It all fitted itself together like a mosaic.

Then, the actual work on the play began—my daily work on it—starting in the spring of 1959.

MISS M: How did the Pope enter into the play?

MR. H: That came about with the consideration—with the question—how, in this so-called Christian Europe, the murder of an entire people could take place without the highest moral authority of this earth having a word to say about it.

MISS M: In the beginning, then, the Pope wasn't in the play at all?

MR. H: Well, there had appeared, as I said, some documents about the attitude of the Vatican, which already have a voice in the play. It all simply developed in such a way that the most meaningful antagonist to Riccardo could be none other than the highest moral authority—precisely because he makes a demand which only this highest moral authority can meet.

MISS M: Mr. Hochhuth, what writers influenced you the most?

MR. H: Dramatists did not influence me so much as novelists or letter-writers.

I am always being asked why I did not study Brecht. When I started writing, I was so much under the influence of Thomas Mann that everything I wrote painfully echoed this great man. As a beginner, one simply cannot resist him; indeed, there exists a very well-known German writer who today, in his sixties, is still so much under the spell of Thomas Mann that he practically has no independence; which was very much my case, too. That is why I wanted to prevent, at all costs, something like this happening to me with Brecht, and I went out of my way to ignore him.

Naturally, I read many classical plays: the ancients, and Shakespeare, and also the German ones including Hauptmann. But, as concerns my concept of life in the perspective of history, I was influenced much more by novelists and story-tellers and also, above all, by the great German historians—Mommsen, very decisively.

I read him not for his subject matter, which of course is Roman history, but simply because man's bearing, his historic stance, can most readily be deciphered through the study of history. This, for me, is, and will surely remain, the most interesting area for investigation. I shall never forget (though it does not strictly bear on this) a sentence in Mommsen that really sank in, that I shall probably always carry with me. It concerns an invasion of Sicily. Mommsen writes, with icily laconic concentration: "The men were killed; their women and children distributed among the soldiery." You see, I find that such sentences contain all of history; and, when such insights are later combined with the experiences one has had in one's own time — during the aerial bombardments or just altogether during the Third Reich—then one realizes that history is man's great fatality, and, God knows, a great field of study for the man of letters.

MISS M: Many critics feel that your work has greater historical and moral value than artistic value. I wonder what your response is to that evaluation of your play?

MR. H: That is a question of who is doing the criticizing. The historians, with few exceptions, find it interesting as literature—and the *literati* find it historically interesting. I cannot defend myself against this, and can only hope that time will sort it all out—and, in any case, I will not allow myself to be deterred from writing about what I find interesting, even if my next play should again be a historical one.

I think that literary criticism, in some measure, was thrown into mild consternation by the fact that someone had, again, written historical drama. None had been written—not for decades, I mean. Brecht's *Galileo* is, in this sense, not so much a historical play. But the simple fact that the writing of historical plays is no longer practiced does not mean that one shouldn't try one's hand at it all the same.

History is such a wide-open area, and such a devastating phenomenon, that human demeanor can, presumably, be interpreted only from those extreme, those polar situations, into which history places us.

It is scarcely conceivable why, for example, a marital drama should be more interesting than a play which deals with, let us say, the extermination of the Albigensians. With this prerequisite, however: a historic drama today, I believe, is legitimate only when the author makes use of history merely as a blueprint from which to construct the behavior of the man of our time. When he is, in other words, not just giving a picture of the times, a giant fresco of the past, but rather something indicative, with characters who behave in a way significant of our actions and feelings. The condescension with which a few—and it was only a few—men of letters tried to dismiss me as a mere historiographer, is especially funny because it is particularly in the realm of literature that I conquered new ground, at least in Germany, by writing the first verse play we have these days.

I am highly skeptical of the celebration and the fuss made about novels that have no bearing on reality and that are each time hailed as the great event for some four weeks by twenty-two people.

I must tell you that when I recently saw Ingmar Bergman's *The Silence* I left that Hamburg movie house with the question, "What is there left for the novelist today?" Think of what Bergman can do with a single shot of his camera, up a street, down a corridor, into a woman's armpit. Of all he can say with this without saying a single word. The entire film consists perhaps of three pages of typescript. What then can a novelist offer of comparable interest with mere words?

MISS M: Mr. Hochhuth, how does this relate to the drama? Is it the same thing to some degree?

MR. H: I don't think the drama faces the same problem. Film has this more pronouncedly epic, narrative character, whereas drama is tied to theses, to the conflict of ideas. These are things that a film cannot tackle in its nonverbal way, such as the confronting of arguments with counter-arguments. The drama cannot dispense with words. In film, the narrative element may well be bound up much more with the image that can be conjured up without words if one only knows how to command one's camera.

MISS M: Are you thinking of writing a film yourself?

MR. H: Never. I lack the technical orientation and know-how. But if something I have written lends itself to being adapted to the film, well and good as far as I'm concerned.

MISS M: What did you mean earlier, Mr. Hochhuth, when you referred to history as fatality?

MR. H: I'm influenced in this by various writers. Theodor Lessing, for instance, the author of *History as Rationale of the Irrational*. Theodor Lessing's very life was depressing proof of the rightness of his thesis. In 1933, he was shot to death by the Nazis as he sat in his study.

And already as a boy of thirteen I felt history in a very blunt, subconscious, sub-intellectual way, as a fatality that has sway over us and against which we can defend ourselves only very partially.

MISS M: To what degree is man responsible for his own fate or his own actions, then?

MR. H: I have just been involved in a heated debate with a German periodical which accused me of being so very primitive in my thinking as still to maintain that it is great men who make history. And I have not been aware of the fact that this is not so. But the periodical did not say who, then, does make history; and I am very much of the opinion that the history of World War II would have looked very different if Hitler and Churchill had never been born. And indeed I would subscribe to the notion that it would be the end of the drama if one were to take the position that man cannot be held responsible for his fate.

At the end of my "Sidelights on History" I quote Melchinger: "But if the individual can no longer be held responsible, either because he is no longer in a position to decide or else does not understand that he must decide, then we have an alibi for all guilt. And that would mean the end of drama. For, there can be no suspense without freedom of decision in each given case."

MISS M: How can this be reconciled with the idea of history as fatality then?

MR. H: This very contradiction is the fatality. Man is meant to act, to be responsible. He should be the master of his fate. He should be moral, and history continually brings him into conflict with powers which condemn him to defeat, which are stronger than he and which destroy him. I am thoroughly of the opinion that this is an area which should be of interest even to the gentlemen of literature. Consider merely one very fruitful example: obligatory military conscription in this twentieth century. Compulsory military service is an invention of the French Revolution as much as is the secret police and has indeed completely changed the lives of people.

Consider only what insoluble conflicts arise from the fact that as one completes one's eighteenth year, he is simply forced to put on a uniform and start shooting.

MISS M: But if you're being attacked by an enemy, isn't it necessary that you defend your country?

MR. H: Absolutely. I am not a pacifist at all because I'm of the opinion that it is irresponsible to allow oneself to be driven into traps. Imagine simply what would have happened if the Russians in 1941 had not defended themselves against the Nazis. What would have become of the Russian people? However, for the Russian soldier this did not produce a tragic situation, or hardly. He was fighting for his country. A tragic situation occurred for any particular Russian soldier who was a passionate anti-Communist and who nonetheless had to fight with the Communist army against the invaders, for the benefit of Communism just as much as for the benefit of his country. This same kind of tragic situation occurred, of course, for many Germans, who could not possibly have wished that Hitler triumph, but who no more wished that the Russians march all the way to the Rhine. Indeed there is no human conflict possible—conflict, let us say, in marriage or in love or anywhere else, which does not get its most fundamental intensification in the context of history.

MISS M: In the context of history as fatality, how would you define the Pope's guilt or responsibility in terms of not protesting against the slaughter of the Jews?

MR. H: That is a question whose answer cannot possibly be reduced to a simple formula. So very many things have contributed to the Pope's behaving as he, unfortunately, did. Looking at it purely from the outside, one can say, for instance, that fatality began with the fact that on the very eve of the Second World War Pope Pius XI, who was a very brave and very resolute man, should have died. Furthermore, again looking from the outside, it may have been only a coincidence, but then again perhaps truly fatality, that his successor should have been a Pope who in his perfectly legitimate predilection for everything German, for the German people, overlooked the fact that the Nazis were not "the Germans" but the despoilers, the perverters of Germany, as well as of everything else.

MISS M: Granting that the Nazis might have retaliated do you feel that the Pope should have protested anyway?

MR. H: Absolutely. And I say this not merely off the top of my head but out of the very reasons which Riccardo cites in his conversation with his father in the second act of my play. This is emphatically expressed in the play, always presupposing that one takes the office of the Pope seriously, and that one is really ready to measure this man by his own pretensions which are of course enormous.

MISS M: Was the Pope then under a different kind of moral obligation toward his fellow man than a man of another faith?

MR. H: Well, the Catholic Church lays claim to being the only church that bestows salvation. It should naturally devolve on it to feel responsible for all human beings, all religions, all races. This is all the more so—though many Catholic priests deny it—because Pius XII had without doubt no anti-Semitic feelings. You might be interested, if we have a little time, in hearing an anecdote which was actually the most terrifying experience I had since the publication of my play.

I received a visit one day from a very intelligent, older, and quite well-known Jesuit priest, who spent an entire Sunday with my wife and me, chatting. What this man said so enormously frightened me that twice I countered him with a quotation which stands at the very beginning of my play, and comes from Bernard Shaw, "Beware of the man whose God is in Heaven." This Jesuit father spoke to me as follows: "If humanism were right, but humanism is only a fashion, then you too would be right in your play. For man is not really the measure of all things. Antiquity is wrong when it asserts that man is the measure of all things." He went on, literally: "Man is excrement, at least in the aspect of eternity."

And that, presumably, is to this day—much more than she admits it—the view of the Church. The Jesuit went on, "Certainly it is frightful, what was done to the Jews and to the 56 million people of all faiths who were devoured by the Second World War, but then again it is not *so* frightful, because all of them are with God, not one of them was lost. They are all preserved. No soul is lost, not even that of Hitler or of Himmler. Before God this will all someday become unsubstantial and forgiven." And he went on, "The Bible has an example ready which really cuts the ground out from under *The Deputy.*" And he said, "Jesus did not lift a finger to have St. John the Baptist rescued from Herod's prison, for obviously Jesus must have felt that this man had fulfilled his mission on earth." I on the other hand, not being conversant with the historical circumstances of that particular time, asked: "Father, was Jesus in a position to do something about that in the first place?"

The Jesuit could not answer my question precisely, but he said that he believed Jesus could have acted, because already he had the people very much on his side. I said to him then, because his tremendous hardness impressed me, "Father, I am ready to believe that you would not bat an eyelash if you were informed that in ten minutes you would be beheaded." He smiled at that. He liked that. I then continued, "I also believe that you would not bat an eyelash if you were in the cell of a human being who, five minutes later, would be executed." And on this Sunday I became cognizant for the first time of what bottomless cunning lurks in the Church's insistence on celibacy. That these priests are obliged to live alone, that they do not have a single human being to whom they can get thoroughly attached. They have no child, no wife, and this gives them that unbelievable hardness, which enables them to reckon years not in the terms of a human life, but incommensurably under the aspect of eternity. They are not permitted to live. They are not permitted to have a life of their own, and therefore life itself, the life of other people, is not of the same consequence to them as life is for those to whom that is all there is.

And it is from this position—I am now completely clear about this—that the Church was able, from the beginning, to draw the strength to demand for 2,000 years such unheard-of sacrifices and victims. This brutality is true of all great promulgators of ideas. So, too, the Nazis were willing to sacrifice one half of the German people in the Second World War because they felt they were building an empire, a kingdom of a thousand years. The Bolshevists, too, reckon not in our measures of time but in terms of centuries. They do not think of the happiness of the living but of generations and generations to come—that eventually things will become better. But it is always terribly inhuman to think in this way.

MISS M: Mr. Hochhuth, your characterization of the Pope emphasizes his concern for earthly things, such as factories and the political realities of Europe vs. Russia. Were you at that time unaware of his transcendental view of life?

MR. H: Well, first of all, I must say that in no part of my play did I submit that the financial concerns of the Vatican caused the silence of the Pope. That I did not maintain anywhere. I put this scene dealing with finances before the actual drama concerning the deportation of the Jews from Rome, because I'm fully of the opinion that the Vatican does indeed have very substantial earthly interests, but I do not reproach it with that. I must, however, add that this conversation with the Jesuit did not occur until after the appearance of my play, and that today it seems to me very good that this conversation occurred as late as it did. I am now firmly convinced that this calculation in terms of eons, of gigantic chunks of time, played its part in the Pope's decision.

But even today I would hardly dare to represent the Pope with this kind of metaphysical hardness. Let us hope that he was really concerned with the political and historical arguments, the charitable arguments, which are proposed in the fourth act as his motivation, and that it was these arguments alone which brought him to this awful decision. If it were otherwise, then the decision and indeed the Church itself would have to be conceived of as altogether inimical to life. I found this attitude of the Jesuit extremely inimical to life and indeed I told him so. But this did not concern him very much, for life is, for him, not the first and last consideration, whereas to us ordinary mortals who are not firmly embedded in our faith —and who is nowadays?—to us, life is very much the first and last concern.

That Pius XII himself, of course, was influenced by this kind of ecclesiastic thinking or that he embodied it himself to a very large degree is proven in any case by a speech which I transcribed and included in my fourth act, a speech he made about the Poles when, in their need and despair, they asked him for help:

"As the flowers of the countryside wait beneath winter's mantle of snow for the warm breezes of spring, so the Jews must wait, praying and trusting that the hour of heavenly comfort will come."

I didn't change anything in this except one single word. Instead of the word *Poles* I used the word *Jews*. That is the whole story.

MISS M: Mr. Hochhuth, is a religious faith in another world inimical to the kind of humanism that you value? Is it a necessary consequence of this belief that human life is not taken seriously on this earth?

MR. H: For God's sake, no. Faith is a good thing, and I envy any human being who is firmly established in it. But he must not, or he should not, be led by his faith into any kind of neglect of the matters of this earth. Obviously our turn will come, the turn of all of us, someday; and probably everyone has, at least for a moment of every day, the feeling of resignation toward the things of this earth. A moment when he knows that to founder here below is the ultimate, that which is destined for all of us, no matter how great our earthly involvement, no matter how great our ambition. Then it is very good to have faith. Then it is probably the sole salvation to have faith. But as long as we have the courage or the brutality to bring children into this world, a world which, for example, has an atom bomb in it, for that long we must not *reckon* in terms of eternity, and, out of regard for eternity, neglect our earthly involvements.

MISS M: Mr. Hochhuth, would you care to define or describe your own religious views?

MR. H: I would rather not, because they are extremely vacillating and because it was really only while I was working on *The Deputy* that I noticed that these things lie much more deeply inside me than I realized. I have many Protestant churchmen among my ancestors, but these matters have become buried, and nothing is very clear and firm. I cannot state anything here that would help other human beings. At the utmost, I can quote a saying of Bismarck's, which has perhaps been made use of all too little, even though it should be of help to the intellectuals.

A friend once asked Bismarck how he had overcome the radical nihilism of his youth. He said, "I recalled the advance patrols of my doubts, which had ventured too far forward, with all firmness." In other words, an act of the will, and probably that is the only way it can be done. One cannot wait for grace to bestow faith upon one.

MISS M: Do you mean that it's a matter of will to quell doubts and to accept a faith?

MR. H: I think that absolutely, that it is an act of the will, because, after all, we are daily attacked by doubts and could not live if we did not chase them back into the corner.

MISS M: Is there any principle that guides you in regard to what things you will choose to believe in?

MR. H: I don't believe so, but I haven't thought enough about it. I think that the personal experiences of every individual life, which will be different from one person to another, must be the determining factor.

MISS M: Mr. Hochhuth, you were only fourteen at the end of the war. How do you feel that you would have behaved if you had been a responsible adult during the war?

MR. H: I would have behaved just as well or as badly as all other contemporaries. I am sure that I would not have been a particularly brave fellow. I think it also depends on whether one has a family or not. I find that there are many excuses, very legitimate excuses, for fathers of families, who well know that they have children and a wife who will be killed if they, the men, dare go too far. That should not be overlooked by us today.

MISS M: Mr. Hochhuth, were the actions of Riccardo, the central figure of the play, the ones that you respect the most? Was his behavior, leading to his martyrdom, the only right way to act?

MR. H: For artistic reasons I tried, of course, to make Riccardo a living human being, with all the contradictions that entailed. He was not to become a mere moral trumpeter, but a human being who makes mistakes, who goes too far, who overshoots the mark, who, for instance, considers Hitler's chances in Russia much better than they actually were, which was exactly how contemporaries felt at the time. Or if you think of that central passage in the drama, Riccardo's foolhardy decision to do away with the Pope and to make the SS take the rap for the murder, in order to mobilize the world's indignation against them. This scene, to be sure, is not intended realistically at all. It is merely a vehicle for pushing theoretical thought to its extreme limits. This is why I cannot answer your question with an unqualified yes. But the essential concern of Riccardo, the moral impetus which propels him, and his coming out strongly for the victim — this I find indeed to be essentially what one should have expected of the priests in such a situation, and what many of them, more than a thousand, actually did.

MISS M: Would you expect this from a man who is not a Catholic?

MR. H: It cannot be expected or demanded of anyone. One cannot even demand it of a priest. The determination to become a martyr is a very personal decision which not even the Pope can demand of his priests. But this is why I laid the scene of the deportation of the Jews precisely in Rome, the Pope's own diocese, where the Pope was personally, as an individual, as Eugene Pacelli, confronted with this problem and able to make a personal decision.

MISS M: If you can't demand martyrdom, where do you place limits on what you can expect of a moral human being?

MR. H: That is a very important question. You yourself said before that I established in great detail all the diplomatic possibilities of the Vatican toward the co-signatory of the Concordat, Hitler. Opportunities which would not have placed the Church in danger, but which could nonetheless have been exploited to resist Hitler. These possibilities should have been fully exploited: anything that within the realm of diplomacy could have been mustered up by way of threats against Hitler. But beyond that I would say that the Pope also had the duty to obligate the countless Catholics in the East—in Poland, in Hungary, for example, and also certainly the Catholics in Germany—to obligate them not to participate in the mass murder. It is inconceivable how many people could have been saved just in

Poland if the population had been summoned by the Church to offer Jews a hiding place.

MISS M: So, short of martyrdom or risking the lives of Catholics, you feel it was incumbent upon the Pope and the Church to do what they could for the welfare of the Jews.

MR. H: Of course.

5 | Hochhuth's Encounter with Two Persons Concerned

G. B. CARDINAL MONTINI

Pius XII and the Jews

DEAR SIR—It gave me much pleasure to read the article entitled 'Pius XII and the Jews,' which appeared in your excellent periodical on May 11th, 1963: it was a most welcome defence not only of Pope Pius XII, of venerated memory, and of the Holy See, but also of historical truth and sound logic, not to speak of common-sense.

It is not my intention here to examine the question raised by the author and the Berlin producer, Rolf Hochhuth and Erwin Piscator respectively, of the play *Der Stellvertreter* (The Representative): namely whether it was Pius XII's duty to condemn in some public and spectacular way the massacres of the Jews during the last war. Much, to be sure, might still be said on this point; for the thesis of Herr Hochhuth's play—that to quote Mr. George Steiner's review in the *Sunday Times* of May 5th, 'We are all accomplices to that which leaves us indifferent'—bears no relation whatever to the personality or the work of Pope Pius XII . . .

For my part I conceive it my duty to contribute to the task of clarifying and purifying men's judgment on the historical reality in question—so distorted in the representational pseudo-reality of Hochhuth's play—by pointing out that the character given to Pius XII in this play (to judge from

---

This letter from Cardinal Montini to *The Tablet,* an English Catholic periodical, is reprinted by permission of *The Tablet,* which received it an hour after the author had been elected Pope Paul VI. It was published in June, 1963.

the reviews in the Press) does not represent the man as he really was: in fact, it entirely misrepresents him. I am in a position to assert this because it was my good fortune to be drawn into close contact with Pius XII during his pontificate, serving him day by day, from 1937, when he was still Secretary of State, to 1954: throughout, that is, the whole period of the world war.

It is true that the precise scope of my duties did not include foreign affairs ("extraordinary" affairs, as they are called in the language of the Roman Curia): but Pius XII's goodness towards me personally, and the nature itself of my work as "Sostituto" in the Secretariate of State, gave me access to the mind and, I would add, to the heart of this great Pope. The image of Pius XII which Hochhuth presents, or is said to present, is a false one. For example, it is utterly false to tax Pius with cowardice: both his natural temperament and the consciousness that he had of the authority and the mission entrusted to him speak clearly against such an accusation. I could cite a host of particular facts to drive this point home, facts that would prove that the frail and gentle exterior of Pius XII, and the sustained refinement and moderation of his language, concealed—if they did not, rather, reveal—a noble and virile character capable of taking very firm decisions and of adopting, fearlessly, positions that entailed considerable risk.

Nor is it true that he was a heartless solitary. On the contrary, he was a man of exquisite sensibility and the most delicate human sympathies. True, he did love solitude: his richly cultivated mind, his unusual capacity for thought and study led him to avoid all useless distractions, every unnecessary relaxation; but he was quite the reverse of a man shut away from life and indifferent to people and events around him. Rather, it was his constant desire to be informed of everything. He wished to enter fully into the history of his own afflicted time: with a deep sense that he himself was a part of that history, he wished to participate fully in it, to share its sufferings in his own heart and soul. Let me cite, in this connexion, the words of a well-qualified witness, Sir D'Arcy Osborne, the British Minister to the Holy See who, when the Germans occupied Rome, was obliged to live confined in the Vatican City. Writing to *The Times* on May 20th Sir D'Arcy said: 'Pius XII was the most warmly humane, kindly, generous, sympathetic (and, incidentally, saintly) character that it has been my privilege to meet in the course of a long life.'

It is not true to say that Pope Pius XII's conduct was inspired by a calculating political opportunism. It would be just as true—and as slanderous—to assert that his government of the Church was motivated by considerations of material advantage.

As for his omitting to take up a position of violent opposition to Hitler in order to save the lives of those millions of Jews slaughtered by the Nazis, this will be readily understood by anyone who avoids Hochhuth's mistake of trying to assess what could have been effectively and responsibly done then, in those appalling conditions of war and Nazi oppression, by the standard of what would be feasible in normal conditions—or in some hypothetical conditions arbitrarily invented by a young playwright's imagination. An attitude of protest and condemnation such as this young man blames the Pope for not having adopted would have been not only futile but harmful: that is the long and the short of the matter. The thesis of *Der Stellvertreter* betrays an inadequate grasp of psychological, political and historical realities. But then the author was concerned above all to write an interesting play.

Let us suppose that Pius XII had done what Hochhuth blames him for not doing. His action would have led to such reprisals and devastations that Hochhuth himself, the war being over and he now possessed of a better historical, political and moral judgment, would have been able to write another play, far more realistic and far more interesting than the one that he has in fact so cleverly but also so ineptly put together: a play, that is, about the *Stellvertreter* who, through political exhibitionism or psychological myopia, would have been guilty of unleashing on the already tormented world still greater calamities involving innumerable innocent victims, let alone himself.

It would be as well if the creative imagination of playwrights insufficiently endowed with historical discernment (and possibly, though please God it is not so, with ordinary human integrity) would forbear from trifling with subjects of this kind and with historical personages whom some of us have known. In the present case the real drama, and tragedy, is not what the playwright imagines it to be: it is the tragedy of one who tries to impute to a Pope who was actually aware both of his own moral obligations and of historical reality—and was moreover a very loyal as well as impartial friend to the people of Germany—the horrible crimes of German Nazism.

Let some men say what they will, Pius XII's reputation as a true Vicar of Christ, as one who tried, so far as he could, fully and courageously to carry out the mission entrusted to him, will not be affected. But what is the gain to art and culture when the theatre lends itself to injustice of this sort?

With my sincere respects, devotedly yours,

G. B. CARDINAL MONTINI, *Archbishop of Milan*

ROLF HOCHHUTH

Reply to Cardinal Montini

Since His Holiness, Pope Paul VI, has now published an opinion of *The Deputy*, which he wrote shortly before his election, I am unfortunately forced to quote from the appendix to my play those passages which deal with his role as Undersecretary of State during the deportation of Jews from Rome. Legation Secretary Gerhard Gumpert of the economics department of the German Embassy on the Quirinal stated in the Wilhelmstrasse trial at Nuremberg:

> *Later, when I bade goodbye to Weizsäcker because I was being transferred to the Embassy in Northern Italy, he spoke of this incident once more and said in so many words: "That was another stinking mess." In reaction to the reports, he said, they had got cold feet in Berlin and stopped the deportations immediately. He added: "I can also tell you that at the time I spoke very confidentially with Montini (the present Pope; then Undersecretary of State) and advised him that any protest by the Pope would only result in the deportations being really carried out in a thoroughgoing fashion. I know how our people react in these matters. Montini, incidentally, saw the point."*

What we have here is a morass. Weizsäcker's closest collaborator, von Kessel, tries to force the Vatican to drop its reticence. When at least one German bishop takes him up on his suggestion, Weizsäcker temporarily makes the bishop's demand his own. He threatens Berlin with an ultimatum by the Pope; this obviously means that he regards such an ultimatum as a deterrent. But simultaneously he tells the Pope's closest associate that a statement by the Holy Father "would only result in the deportations being really carried out in a thoroughgoing fashion." And Montini, or as the case may be, the Pope, is only too glad to hear that, although they know, although every child in Rome knows, that the first Jews were already being loaded into the boxcars; that the round-ups are going on regardless; and that Weizsäcker's words are therefore—to put it mildly—sheer twaddle.

Finally, by the following weekend (October 25-26), when the Osservatore Romano *reports that "the Pope's universal and fatherly works of mercy . . . know no limits," the first 615 Roman Jews had already arrived at Auschwitz, and 468 of them were already in the crematorium.*

Today, when the present Pope explains that "an act of condemnation would not only have been useless, but harmful; that is all," it only shows he hasn't changed his opinion of 1943, which he formed in agreement with the representatives of Hitler's interests. This assertion is inconclusive. It becomes very questionable in the light of the fact, confirmed by Weizsäcker's representative Dr. Wemmer, that the head of the German Gestapo in Rome, Kappler, at the time hastened to release two Jews from a deportation train which had already left, only because Pius XII had *unofficially* requested it. Would an *official* protest in the presence of the entire world, or even the threat of one, have been completely ineffective? But certainly Pope Paul today could prove that his immediate superior at the time, Cardinal Secretary of State Maglione, had acted justifiably: A few days after the deportation of the Roman Jews Maglione confirmed at the request of Ambassador Weizsäcker in the lead article of the *Osservatore Romano* that German troops in Rome had acted superbly toward the Vatican and the Curia. The Curia's good conduct testimonial for the Nazis was conceivably the most hideous answer to the Allied news bulletins about the terrible happenings in Rome that the Vatican could possibly have given to the world. "Our opponents' propaganda," writes

Weizsäcker, "attempted to picture German troops as desecrators of Rome and the Pope's jailers." With the official "correction" of these circumstances by the Cardinal Secretary of State—which was at the time invaluable to the murderers, who indeed did not destroy Rome, but only the Jews of Rome—once more Christianity, this time its highest authority, paid the kiss of Judas back to the Jewish people. This happened immediately after Jewish families, most of them quite poor, had been herded together in the streets neighboring on San Pietro and had been packed into railroad cars at the terminals without knowing their "destination" (something the Vatican never even forcefully asked about).

Basel, July 1963

ALBRECHT VON KESSEL

The Pope and the Jews

In presenting Albrecht von Kessel's defense of Pope Pius XII, Die Welt *gave its readers the following background material:*

Controversy continues concerning Rolf Hochhuth's play *The Deputy,* which had its world première in Berlin in late February. It sets forth the view that the Holy See did not do all it should—or could—have done to prevent Nazi atrocities against the Jews. On 16 March Father Karl Hard of the Jesuit Order set forth his opinions in these columns. Today we present the opinions of Albrecht von Kessel, a contributor of ours, who at the time of the Nazi occupation of Rome belonged to the staff of Ernst von Weizsäcker, German Ambassador to the Vatican. Von Kessel is mentioned in this scene:

This article first appeared in the United States in the June, 1963 issue of *Atlas,* The Magazine of the World Press, translated by Mary Bancroft. It was originally published in *Die Welt,* Hamburg, April 6, 1963.

RICCARDO (*has turned, aghast, to his father; now speaks softly to the* POPE): Then Your Holiness has already known —for weeks—what the SS here intended to do to the Jews?
POPE (*agitated, evasively*): What are you saying! Father General can bear witness to all that has already been accomplished. The monasteries stand open . . .

The Father General has entered. The POPE *turns quickly toward him . . .*

POPE (*coldly to the* ABBOT): Father General, please inform Us what Bishop Hudal has done in Our name about the arrest of the Jews. Did he conceive this praiseworthy idea himself?
ABBOT: Herr von Kessel at the German Embassy called on me secretly at dawn and asked that His Excellency, the Bishop, threaten the German commandant with a forthcoming protest from Your Holiness.
POPE (*pleased, relieved*): Well, well! A German does that —how gratifying. What times these are, when high treason is the last weapon of the righteous! A German is ashamed of the SS! Well—Kessel is the man's name. We will remember it. Now, then, this letter from the Bishop will do its work and save whatever there is left to be saved.
RICCARDO (*with the bluntness of one who has already lost everything*): That letter will save nothing at all, Your Holiness. Only you yourself . . .

As the discussion about *The Deputy*, the play which recently opened in Berlin, has become quite heated, I feel that I must join the debate, not about the play itself but about its background. I do this reluctantly because all the horrors that took place toward the end of the war cannot actually be put into words. "The rest is silence!"

However, since the silence has now been broken from the other side, I, too, must speak up. Not simply because my name is mentioned in the play, nor in order to defend Mr. von Weizsäcker again, as I already did at Nuremberg. He was one of the most thoughtful and, if you will forgive me for using the word, one of the noblest men that I have met in my long and eventful life. He needs no defense.

I am breaking my silence only because I was attached to the German Embassy at the Vatican during the months with which *The Deputy* deals and because, thanks to my experiences during the twelve year period of the Nazi terror, I believe I can contribute something toward an evaluation of the situation in Rome.

Anyone who has persevered—never mind why—in a diplomatic career under a totalitarian and criminal regime, knows what different levels of credibility can mean.

Written documents should be judged from the purely pragmatic point of view. Their purpose is often the exact opposite of that which the naïve reader assumes. Take, for instance, the lance corporal who served in the unit of one of my friends. This man talked himself practically onto the gallows, but was rescued by a false affidavit from my friend, who swore that the lance corporal, in spite of all evidence to the contrary, had always been a fanatical follower of the Führer. Two years later, on the basis of this false affidavit, the Americans locked my friend up as an influential Nazi. Documents from the days of the terror frequently consist, to put it bluntly, of nothing but lies. One must search for the motives with which a document was written rather than try to draw conclusions from the document itself.

Statements, viva voce, in so far as they are passed on accurately—which happens much less often than the layman believes—come under the same law. They, too, frequently consist of nothing but tactical lies. Only a person willing to appraise a conversation from every angle and put himself psychologically in the position of the individual participants can report such a conversation in a way that has some value. In this respect Professor Carl J. Burckhardt's report of his conversation with Attolico, the Italian Ambassador in Berlin, concerning von Weizsäcker's attitude, is a work of genius.

Having stated the above premises and with all necessary self-limitation and discretion, let me comment on the problems raised by *The Deputy:* When the Italian government signed an armistice with the Allies in September 1943, thus changing sides in the war, German paratroopers occupied Rome. That evening, and even more exhaustively the following day, Mr. von Weizsäcker and I discussed what could be done to help the Jews. It was our conviction—which unfortunately many well-meaning people did not share—that the worst was to be expected. This meant the Jews had to be warned as quickly and as unequivocally as possible and advised to go into hiding or flee. The Italians, even those known to be reliable enemies of the Third Reich, could not be used for this purpose because of their lack of discretion. The familiar saying: "We can protect ourselves from our enemies, but God protect us from our friends!" applied to them.

Finally it occurred to me that the Swiss General Secretary

of the Institute for International Law, whom I knew fairly well, might be suitable for such a mission. With the consent of Mr. von Weizsäcker, I sought him out that same evening at his home. He grasped my position at once and the risk I was taking. I certainly didn't have to caution him to be discreet! I asked him point-blank if he knew any of the leading members of the Jewish colony in Rome. When he said he did, I begged him to look them up immediately and to give them the following advice: They must leave their homes as quickly as possible and seek shelter elsewhere. In view of the chaotic conditions prevailing in Rome, due in part to the aversion that the Roman police felt for the Nazis and in part to the general corruption, it might perhaps be enough for the Jews to go into hiding on the same street or even in the same building by going to the apartments of acquaintances and friends. But it would be better if they could find shelter in various small towns or villages in the surrounding districts. There they would be regarded simply as refugees—of which there were tens of thousands—rather than as Jews. My Swiss acquaintance told me that he would advise the Jews he knew along these lines. Greatly relieved, I returned home convinced that I had done my duty and had, with possibly a few individual exceptions, prevented a disaster.

It is impossible to describe the shock Mr. von Weizsäcker and I experienced some days later when we learned that our warning had gone unheeded and that leading Jews wanted to make an arrangement with the S.S., who had meanwhile entered the city. I sought out my Swiss acquaintance once again. He explained to me—with the naïveté of a man who has never lived under a reign of terror—that there were really no grounds for exaggerated concern: since our last meeting calm and order had been restored to the city and the Germans were behaving extremely correctly. He made the typical mistake of the unsuspecting liberal who believes that terror is identical with chaos and flourishes only in the midst of chaos, whereas the exact opposite is usually the case. I am afraid that at this point I shouted at this sensitive and cultivated man: If the Jews didn't "vanish" at once, every last one of them would be deported. As far as I can remember, I also said: "If they are killed, their blood will be on my head and on the heads of my friends—and we don't deserve that. I implore you to take my advice seriously and use all your influence with the Jews in Rome!" The result is well known. [On the night of 15 October 1943 the Nazis rounded up the Jews in the ghetto of Rome, later deporting them to Germany.—].

I would like to add that everything I did during the months of the Nazi domination of Rome was too little. I feared being tortured by the Gestapo; furthermore what I did often proved futile, and all of it was done at the instigation of Mr. von Weizsäcker or with his specific consent. There were no secrets between us nor even the slightest divergence in point of view, although we had quite different temperaments.

The role of the German Embassy at the Vatican—namely, of Mr. von Weizsäcker and his trusted associates—was, to put it mildly, not simple. It must be reasserted that Hitler, like a beast of prey pursued by a pack of hunters—in this instance the Allies—was capable of absolutely any hysterical or criminal act. The idea of taking the Pope prisoner and transporting him to Greater Germany, had entered into his calculations from September 1943 until the Allied armies reached Rome in June 1944. We had specific information that if the Pope had resisted there was the possibility that he would be "shot while attempting to escape".

We therefore regarded it as our duty at least to prevent this crime from being committed in the name of our people. Mr. von Weizsäcker had to fight on two fronts, as it were. On the one hand he had to advise the Holy See, in other words the Pope, not to undertake anything that was not careully thought through—*i.e.*, not to take any action that might have fatal consequences he could not foresee.

At the same time Mr. von Weizsäcker had to convince the Nazis, in other words Hitler, by subtly worded reports that the Vatican meant well—*i.e.*, that the Vatican was "weak" as far as Hitler himself was concerned. The countless individual cases in which the Vatican had helped Jews were depicted as meaningless in the overall picture and not to be taken seriously.

Finally, all of us—that is to say all members of the German Embassy at the Vatican—agreed on one point. No matter what our other differences may have been, we were convinced that a fiery protest by Pius XII against the persecution of the Jews would in all probability put both the Pope himself and the Curia in the greatest danger, and at that late date—namely in the fall of 1943—would not have saved the life of a single Jew. Hitler, like a trapped beast, would react to any menace that he felt directed at him with proportionate violence.

What we could do, however, was to warn the Vatican, the Curia and the Pope himself not to issue any statements or take any action that had not received very careful consideration. It would have been entirely unsuitable for us Germans, whose nation was led by a criminal, to take any position on a question of martyrdom. Furthermore, no one should expect his neighbor, in the biblical sense of the word, to be a martyr.

Certainly—to repeat—a fiery protest from the Pope in 1943 would not have saved the life of a single Jew. Would it not have been better for Christendom and for the Catholic Church if Pius XII had assumed the martyr's crown—even without achieving any practical results, as the Scholl sisters did in Munich? Perhaps such a politically senseless sacrifice might have sown seeds that would be yielding their harvest today.

Pius XII, whom I had first known when he was Papal Secretary of State and then twelve years later knew as Pope, was a tremendous figure. Nevertheless, I was convinced at the time and am still convinced today, he almost broke down under the conflicts of conscience. I know that he prayed, day by day, week by week, month by month for the answer. No one can take away from him the responsibility for the answer he gave. But who can now maintain, twenty years later, that the Pope found a false answer when he avoided martyrdom? And who dares, if the answer was really a false one, to cast the first stone?

The author of *The Deputy*, whose good faith I acknowledge, expresses decent, even idealistic ideas such as I too would have expressed at the age of thirty. May he be spared, when he has reached my age, from having to say, laconically, because of developments that have taken place in the meantime: "God have mercy on my soul and on my unfortunate people."

ROLF HOCHHUTH

The Playwright Answers

Everyone, no matter what his age, should join in the brief prayer with which Mr. von Kessel concludes his criticism

---

The article first appeared in translation in the June, 1963 issue of *Atlas*, The Magazine of the World Press, translated by Herman E. Weiller. It was originally published in *Die Welt*, Hamburg, April 6, 1963.

of my play. Since the Papal Secretariat of State remembers him even today as an anti-Nazi always willing to help, and since he admits that he dreaded the Gestapo tortures, let me do him justice here and now: I myself would have been so afraid that I could not have helped a soul. But the personality of the author has no bearing whatever on the subject under discussion.

The facts are there—forty crowded pages of documentation in the appendix to my play: is it unimportant that I acted in good faith? Of course, I agree with Mr. von Kessel (and I so stated in the play) that no one, and above all no German, could expect his neighbor—even if he were the Pope himself—to become a martyr.

It is impossible to assume—and no one in the Vatican did, either in 1943 or 1959—that Hitler would have made a "martyr" of the Pope. And it is totally untrue that a "fiery protest" by the Pope, in Mr. von Kessel's words, "would not have saved the life of a single Jew".

I repeat some of the facts quoted in the appendix. Four examples, each taken from a different year, show that help could have been given without danger to the life or limb of any of the rescuers.

1941: Hitler did not make a martyr out of Bishop Galen of Münster, not even when R.A.F. planes started dropping reprints of his defiant sermons on German cities. On the contrary: as a result, Hitler greatly reduced the practice of "mercy" killings.

1942: The Papal Nuncio in Bratislava found out about the gas chamber deaths of Jewish deportees near Lublin. When he requested an investigation, further deportations from Slovakia were halted—for two full years.

1943: Protestant Bishop Wurm, along with the Catholic clergy, threatened to denounce from the pulpit the Nazi racial laws sentencing all Jewish spouses of mixed marriages to deportation. The result: "Since the National Socialist government was afraid of widespread anxiety among the population, doubly dangerous in times of military defeat, the law was never put into effect." (From the *Berliner Petrusblatt.*)

1944: On the day Jewish deportations started in Hungary the Papal Nuncio called attention to the fact "that the whole world is acutely aware of the meaning of this action". But not until six weeks later did he transmit a Papal message to the Regent, Admiral Horthy, which was to be "the beginning of a world-wide appeal to the conscience of the Regent." Even though the Pope was at this time under the protection of the Allies, he did not protest to Hitler when he learned that 380,000 Hungarians had been deported to Auschwitz. The gas chambers continued to work overtime.

Surely at this point Hitler could not have made a martyr of the Pope even if he had wanted to. But Hitler never even considered spreading the news that the Pope had been "shot while attempting to escape." This would have stirred up thirty-five million Catholics and most of his allies, including the Japanese (who had a concordat with the Vatican). This version, Mr. von Kessel, is absurd! It is flatly contradicted by all available German documents: the Goebbels diaries, the von Weizsäcker memoirs and even by the report of Father Leiber on the German occupation of Rome.

Von Weizsäcker tells of his farewell visit to Hitler in the spring of 1943: "I summarized my plan for Rome as follows: 'Mutual non-interference; no discussions on matters of principle; no bargaining.' Hitler agreed. He then talked of Bismarck, who emerged the loser from the *Kulturkampf* because, unlike the priests, he failed to gain the ear of the common man. The only way he would let the Church continue after the war, Hitler said, would be as a tool of the State. Incidentally, Hitler remarked that there were three influential men in Rome—the King, the Duce and the Pope. Of these three the Pope definitely was the most important."

In the appendix to the play I have reported in detail on the Jewish man hunt and on the attitude of the Pope during the German occupation of Rome. Here is just one quotation: Hitler had been infuriated by the arrest of Mussolini and, in discussions with his inner circle, momentarily considered implicating the Vatican while rounding up suspects in Rome. Himmler, Goebbels and Ribbentrop were strongly opposed. "I did not believe that it would be necessary to break into the Vatican, but on the contrary considered that the effects of such action on world opinion would be ominous." On the same day, Goebbels added this entry to his diary: "In any case, everyone, including the Führer, agrees that the Vatican should be excepted from all measures to be taken."

Before the Germans occupied Rome in September the Vatican formally inquired of von Weizsäcker whether its rights and privileges would be safeguarded. Hitler sent an affirmative answer. After the Germans had entered the city, General Stahel, the German commander, renewed communications with the Vatican and posted guards who were under orders to prevent any violation of Papal territory. Rahn, the German Ambassador to the Quirinal, ended his report to G.H.Q.

on the status of the occupation: "Incidentally, I forgot to mention that I have negotiated my own private concordat with the Vatican.

"Bormann, the bitter enemy of the Catholic Church, jumped up, and Hitler looked at me in surprise. In the style of a financial report I then told of the help we had received from the Vatican in re-establishing law and order in Rome, for which the two security companies available to us would never have been sufficient. In exchange, we were of course required to make sure that the person of the Pope, the Catholic clergy and the property of the Church would be protected in every way. I concluded: 'In this business transaction, the balance is at least as much in our favor as in the Vatican's.' I must have hit the right note because Hitler said: 'Yes, sir, when it comes to business, the gentlemen in the Vatican know their way around.' "

In brief: even if the events mentioned above could not be corroborated, one fact cannot be denied: the Pope could have saved innumerable people if only he had warned them. Jews themselves will tell you that of course they could not believe the incredible: they had misgivings about the reports of Jewish persecutions carried by the radio stations of the free world. In the face of the disciplined and largely humane behavior of the German occupation troops in Western Europe, these sounded pretty much like the atrocity tales about cutting off the hands of Belgian children during World War I. But they did have faith in the Vatican radio and in the Pope, the great neutral. He could not know everything, since he was spared many details of the horror. But he did know that the deportees were not being resettled in the East. Not one of his informants could name such a "settlement." By July 1942 he did know that in Poland alone 700,000 people had perished. And if he himself could not ascertain whether these people had perished in spite of the tender care lavished on them by the Nazis or because of a lack of calories, he should have said to the Jews of Western Europe: hide, and if you can't hide, flee! Many, many could have done so, or at least tried. Many more Christians would have helped.

The enormity of the tragedy grips you once again if you look at certain Dutch photographs: the unsuspecting queueing up at the railroad station, reporting for deportation—dutiful, in good faith, unworried, the children clutching toys, the old ladies carefully dressed. . . .

Not once did Pope Pius XII warn them, though the Western allies often urged him to use his authority. The fact remains: if one takes one's religion seriously, if one measures the sincerity of the Church by the claims it makes, the silence of the Pope was a crime.

6 | Comments of Literary Critics and Philosophers

LIONEL ABEL

Rolf Hochhuth's The Deputy

No play as important, as interesting as Rolf Hochhuth's *The Deputy* has been shown for a very long time—and no play as interesting in an important way. I would insist, too, that the importance of the work is due not merely to its subject—as many critics have said—for if the subject were not expressed in the play's action, how would its importance be felt, how could the play hold us? And hold us it does, more and more powerfully, until the tremendous climax of the penultimate scene. So I will not accept the disjunction other critics find tolerable, that this is a poor play with a great subject. It is precisely the play which has made people realize its subject is great. And nobody knew this until Hochhuth had written *The Deputy*.

To be sure, it was known that the Nazis exterminated six million Jews; but this is only the background of *The Deputy*. What was not known generally, and what is dealt with in the play, is the attitude the Vatican took to the Nazis' extermination program. Yes, it was known that Pope Pius XII had done nothing, or very little, in behalf of the Jewish victims; what was not known, and can best be known through seeing Hochhuth's play, is the precise manner in which Pope Pius XII refused to condemn the Nazis or lift his voice in behalf

---

A dramatist in his own right, Mr. Abel is the author of *Metatheatre*. His article is reprinted from *Dissent* magazine, Spring, 1964, Vol. XI, No. 2

of the victims. It has been said that if there is anything great about Hochhuth's work, it is the stupendousness of the historical event which inspired it. Now this is a poor thing to say about a work like *The Deputy*. And it is a false thing to say too. What is stupendous in the play is its action, which consists in the forming of a truly heroic decision by a young Jesuit priest, a decision finally fixed by the unmasking of the moral emptiness of Pope Pius XII. The heroism of the young priest's decision is, of course, not historically authentic: Father Fontana is an invention of the author. Also, the unmasking of the Pope is not historical, he was never unmasked so dramatically, except in Hochhuth's imagination. Instead of talking about how serious and important the subject of this play is and yet how unskilled and crude the devices of its author, let us note that the unmasking of the man who was supposed to be Christ's direct representative on earth is an event of the highest interest, and that the author understood this, which shows him to have the instinct of a true dramatist.

Of course the play has faults. The production is not as skillful as it might have been. I can praise only three of the actors; Fred Stewart as the Cardinal, Jeremy Brett as the young Jesuit priest, and Emlyn Williams, who is magnificent as the Pope. The author can be criticized for not having restricted his play entirely to the struggle behind the scenes among Churchmen over the question as to what the Pope should do or say on the matter of the Jewish deportations. The scenes dealing with the rounding up of Jews and their dispatch to death camps and those in which the Nazi officials express their disgust for the Jews in their power are quite unnecessary and distracting. Moreover, I think Hollywood has presented Nazis better, and in fact there is a certain affinity between typical Nazi methods and typical Hollywood films; the brutality of the Nazis goes very well with the sensationalism of film techniques. But in this play there should not have been a single brute. Nor should there have been a single unwilling victim. The ignominious and debased figures of Jews, the cruel and taunting figures of the Nazi guards and executioners are wholly out of place in a work whose main action is a spiritual one; the decision formed in the soul of the young Jesuit priest, Riccardo Fontana.

But it is one thing to call a play imperfect—most great plays are—and another to call it poor. I submit that I have yet to sit through a modern work, written, say, in the last twenty years, as continuously interesting as *The Deputy*. Moreover, it is interesting without being light or humorous.

There are some moments of humor, as a matter of fact, not many, and these I found rather obtrusive and irrelevant. I would prefer the play to be even more constantly grave than it is, nor would my interest be diminished thereby. I have heard a director say that no modern audience can sit through a play unless there is humor in it. Having seen *The Deputy*, I know this to be false. Most modern plays do have to have humor for us to sit through them, but this, I think, is because those plays are not about anything really important. What is really serious is truly interesting.

Mr. Howard Taubman, writing in *The New York Times* of March 7, 1964, claims to have found this fault in *The Deputy*: the Pope, Mr. Taubman writes, is not permitted by the playwright to justify himself with the brilliance a playwright such as Shaw, for instance, allowed to his priests in *St. Joan*. This is certainly true, and Hochhuth is no Shaw. But the effect at which Hochhuth was aiming in this play would not have been served by Shavian methods, even assuming the playwright capable of using them. Shaw aimed at amusing; and it is very amusing to hear an immoral decision justified by brilliant reasoning. But Hochhuth was not interested in making Pope Pius XII amusing. I think he gave the Pope only those arguments the Pope actually used. Certainly, he did not try to improve on them. But if I have any fault to find with his presentation of the Pope and the Pope's arguments in not intervening on behalf of the Jews, it was rather that the playwright did not show the Pope rendered silent, finally unable even to argue against the crushing force of the young Jesuit's moral appeal.

Pope Pius XII is, as I have said, unmasked by the playwright, an act we must regard as great, both morally and as theatre. But is it only Pope Pius XII, the particular individual, Pacelli, who happened to be Pope at the time of the play's action, who is unmasked by the author? Let me restate the argument as given by Pope Pius XII to Father Fontana for not denouncing Hitler and intervening for the Jews. The situation in Eastern Europe was as follows: the Russians, the victory of Stalingrad behind them, were advancing victoriously into the Catholic communities of Eastern Europe, taking over church properties, and installing Communist bureaucrats in the positions of power once controlled by priests. Against the Russian advance there stood only the armies of Hitler. Was Hitler then the Church's main enemy? Did not the Church have something to gain if his armies held their ground? Was it right in this situation for the Pope to strike at Hitler with a denunciation of his racial policies?

Was it not to be hoped, rather, that the war might end with Hitler still in power and with Catholic properties and the Catholic faithful of Eastern Europe still beyond Stalin's reach? Now the argument, simply as a political argument, is not a poor one, and it was one that any Pope would have been bound to take seriously into account. The question in my mind, though, as I heard this argument put by Emlyn Williams with all the persuasiveness he could give it, was whether it would not have been put by any Pope, and not just the Pacelli of Hochhuth's play. Would Pope John, to take Pacelli's extreme opposite, have reasoned differently had he been Pope at the time? No one can say, of course, and anyone has a right to believe he would have thought differently. It is remarked in the play by the Cardinal that there have been "warm" and "cold" popes, and that since God is the one who determines who will be Pope, then God at that particular juncture of history must have wanted a cold Pope in the Vatican. But was it because Pacelli was "cold" or because he was the Pope that he acted as he did? This question, raised by the play, is certainly not answered by it.

That the question is raised, however, shows that this is a Protestant play. Who but a Protestant would have made the Pope the chief target of a work dealing with the extermination of the Jews by the mainly Protestant Germans? Moreover, the heroic action of the play is an action of *protest,* a protest against Rome on the part of a priest. And the protest is more ringing and challenging when made to the Pope in person than when carried out in Auschwitz, before the Nazi executioners.

This is a modern play, of course. It is not a nineteenth-century play in any sense, and while there is some resemblance in it to certain plays of Schiller, it made me think even more strongly of Corneille. The forming of an heroic decision—was not that Corneille's real subject, was not this the source of the sublimity with which he thrilled the French court? Thinking of Corneille, one can see the immense distance between the seventeenth and the twentieth centuries. Corneille's exalted characters, his kings, his princesses, are not without the spirituality their high positions suggest them to have. Pope Pius XII, in Hochhuth's play, is without the human grandeur required by his office. And Corneille's proud and heroic individuals who set their own moral wills above superior power and station, are further ennobled by the grandeur of their adversaries. Sertorius, in Corneille's play, having turned against Rome, says proudly: *Rome n'est plus dans Rome, elle est toute où je suis.*

Hochhuth's priest, having defied the Pope and placed on his cassock the yellow star Jews were forced to wear, seems overwhelmed by his own action, and is unable afterwards to express any powerful conviction of the rightness of that action. When he goes voluntarily to his death with the Jews at Auschwitz in the following scene, he does not tower over his destiny but seems shrunken beneath its weight. One has the painful impression that in modern times institutional power deprives the individual of spirit, while the defiance of such power by the individual shrinks rather than swells his soul.

Thus it was that during the scene when the priest is merely acting out his defiance before the Pope, his conviction seems more real than in the scene in which acting had to become action and his defiance meant pain to his flesh. This, too, is something quite modern, not conceivable in any seventeenth-century work.

Probably we talk too much about art and do not know enough about it. It is simpler than our aestheticians think. Skill and cleverness are important to art, but not all-important. And a deep seriousness goes a long way toward solving problems too complicated for the unstirred intelligence. The main thing is, as Valéry put it, in a beautiful phrase, that art should "give birth to what gave it birth." Some of the deep seriousness which inspired Rolf Hochhuth's *The Deputy* will remain, I think, with those who see it.

HANNAH ARENDT

The Deputy: *Guilt by Silence?*

Rolf Hochhuth's play *The Deputy* has been called "the most controversial literary work of this generation," and in

---

Philosopher and critic, Miss Arendt is most recently author of *Eichmann in Jerusalem.* This article is from "New York," the Sunday *New York Herald Tribune* Magazine, February 23, 1964.

view of the controversy it has aroused in Europe and is about to arouse in this country, this superlative seems justified. The play deals with the alleged failure of Pope Pius XII to make an unequivocal public statement on the massacre of European Jews during World War II, and concerns by implication Vatican policy toward the Third Reich.

The facts themselves are not in dispute. No one has denied that the Pope was in possession of all pertinent information regarding the Nazi deportation and "resettlement" of Jews. No one has denied that the Pope did not even raise his voice in protest when, during the German occupation of Rome, the Jews, including Catholic Jews (that is, Jews converted to Catholicism), were rounded up, right under the windows of the Vatican, to be included in the Final Solution. Thus, Hochhuth's play might as well be called the most factual literary work of this generation as "the most controversial." The play is almost a report, closely documented on all sides, using actual events and real people, reinforced by 65 pages of "historical sidelights" written by Hochhuth and anticipating nearly all arguments that have been raised against it. The author himself seems at least as interested in literal, factual truth as he is in literary quality, for he says almost apologetically in his "sidelights" that for artistic reasons he had "to advance a better opinion of Pius XII than may be historically justified, and a better one than I privately hold." With this sentence, however, he touches upon one of the really controversial—that is, debatable—points at issue: Is it true, as Hochhuth clearly thinks, that the Vatican would not have been silent "had there been a better Pope"?

There have been few instances in which the Church tried to dodge the grave issues at stake either by imputing a thesis to the play which it does not contain—nowhere does Hochhuth claim that "Pope Pius was responsible for Auschwitz" or that he was the "arch-culprit" of this period—or by referring to the help given to Jews by the local hierarchy in some countries. The fact that local hierarchies did so, especially in France and Italy, was never in dispute. To what extent the Pope initiated or even supported these activities is not known, since the Vatican does not open its archives for contemporary history. But it may be assumed that most of the good as well as the bad done must be ascribed to local and often, I suspect, to strictly individual initiative. "During the deportation of Catholic Jews from Holland," Hochhuth reports, "a dozen members of various orders were actually handed over from Dutch religious houses." But who would dare blame Rome for that? And since another question Hochhuth raises—"How could the Gestapo have discovered that this one nun [Edith Stein, a German convert and famous philosophical writer] had Jewish blood?"—has never been answered, who would blame Rome for that? But by the same token, the Church as an institution can hardly book on her account the few great demonstrations of true Christian charity—the distribution of forged documents to thousands of Jews in Southern France in order to facilitate their emigration; the attempt of Provost Bernhard Lichtenberg of St. Hedwig's Cathedral in Berlin to accompany the Jews to the East; the martyrdom of Father Maximilian Kolbe, a Polish priest, in Auschwitz, to quote only some of the best known examples.

What the Church as an institution and the Pope as her sovereign ruler can book on their account is the systematic work of information done by the nuncios all over Nazi-occupied Europe to enlighten at least the heads of government in Catholic countries—France, Hungary, Slovakia, Romania—about the true, murderous meaning of the word "resettlement." This was important because the moral and spiritual authority of the Pope vouched for the truth of what otherwise could be only too easily dismissed as enemy propaganda, especially in countries that welcomed this opportunity of "solving the Jewish question," though not at the price of mass-murder. However, the Vatican's exclusive use of diplomatic channels meant also that the Pope did not think fit to tell the people—for instance, the Hungarian Gendarmerie, all good Catholics, who were busy rounding up Jews for the Eichmann Kommando in Budapest—and, by implication, seemed to discourage the bishops (if such discouragement was necessary) from telling their flocks. What has appeared—first to the victims and the survivors, then to Hochhuth, and finally through him to many others—as such outrageous inadequacy was the frightening equanimity which the Vatican and its nuncios apparently thought it wise to affect, the rigid adherence to a normality that no longer existed, in view of the collapse of the whole moral and spiritual structure of Europe. At the end of the fourth act of *The Deputy,* Hochhuth uses a quotation from a public statement of Pope Pius, changing only one word: where Pius had said "Poles," Hochhuth has Pius say "Jews," as follows: "As the flowers in the countryside wait beneath winter's mantle of snow for the warm breezes of spring, so the *Jews* must wait, praying and trusting that the hour of heavenly comfort will come."

It is a prime example not merely of what Hochhuth has called "Pacelli's flowery loquacity" but of something more common, a disastrous loss of all feeling for reality.

Still, what the Vatican did during the war years, when the Pope was the only man in Europe free from any taint of propaganda, was considerably more than nothing, and it would have been enough if it were not for the uncomfortable fact that the man on St. Peter's chair is no ordinary ruler but "the Vicar of Christ." Regarded as a secular ruler, the Pope did what most, though not all, secular rulers did under the circumstances. Regarded as an institution among institutions, the Church's inclination to accommodate "itself to any regime which affirms its willingness to respect Church property and prerogatives" (which Nazi Germany, but not Soviet Russia, at least pretended to do) has understandably almost become, as Gordon Zahn, a distinguished Catholic sociologist, has said, "an unchallengeable truism in Catholic political philosophy." But the Pope's negligible secular power—as ruler of fewer than a thousand inhabitants of Vatican City—depends "upon the spiritual sovereignty of the Holy See" which is indeed *sui generis* and wields an enormous, though imponderable "world spiritual authority." The matter is succinctly summed up in Stalin's remark, "How many divisions has the Pope?" and in Churchill's answer, "A number of legions not always visible on parade." The accusation levelled by Hochhuth against Rome is that the Pope failed to mobilize these legions—roughly 400 million all over the earth.

The answer from the side of the Church up to now has fallen into three parts. First, there are the words of Cardinal Montini before he became Pope Paul VI: "An attitude of protest and condemnation . . . would have been not only futile but harmful: that is the long and the short of the matter." (This seems a very debatable point, since more than 40 per cent of the Reich's population was Catholic at the outbreak of the war and almost all Nazi-occupied countries as well as most of Germany's allies had Catholic majorities.) Second, much less profiled but actually the argument that validates the first claim, these legions could not be mobilized by Rome. (This argument has more force. The view that the "Catholic Church [compared with the Protestant Church] bears the greater guilt, for it was an organized, supra-national power in a position to do something," as Albert Schweitzer has argued in his preface to the Grove Press edition of the play may have overestimated the Pope's power and underestimated the extent to which he depends upon the national hierarchies and the extent to which the local episcopate depends upon its flocks. And it can hardly be denied that an *ex cathedra* pronouncement of the Pope in the midst of the war might have caused a schism.)

The third argument on the side of the Church rests on the necessity for the Church to remain neutral in case of war, even though this neutrality—the fact that in modern wars the bishops always bless the armies on either side—implies that the old Catholic distinction between just and unjust wars has become practically inapplicable. (Obviously, this was the price the Church had to pay for the separation of Church and State and the resulting generally smooth and peaceful co-existence of an international spiritual sovereignty, binding the local hierarchy in ecclesiastical matters only, with the national secular authority of the state.)

Even if the Pope had seen in Hitler's wars "the classic example of the unjust war," as Zahn has characterized it—which he evidently did not since, according to one of his secretaries, Father Robert Leiber, he "had always looked upon Russian Bolshevism as more dangerous than German National Socialism" (quoted from the very informative article by Guenter Lewy, "Pius XII, the Jews, and the German Catholic Church," in *Commentary*[1]) — he almost certainly would not have intervened. The point of the matter is rather that despite his conviction "that the fate of Europe depended upon a German victory on the Eastern front" (Lewy), and though very prominent figures in the German and Italian hierarchy tried to persuade him "to declare [the war against Russia] a holy war or crusade," the Pope maintained publicly what another historian, Robert A. Graham, S. J., has called a "significant silence." And this silence is all the more significant as the Pope had broken his neutrality twice—first at the occasion of Russia's attack on Finland, and shortly thereafter when Germany violated the neutrality of Holland, Belgium and Luxemburg.

However one may try to reconcile these apparent contradictions, there can be hardly any doubt that one reason why the Vatican did not protest against the massacres in the East, where, after all, not only Jews and gypsies but Poles and Polish priests were involved, was the mistaken notion that these killing operations were part and parcel of the war. The very fact that the Nuremberg Trials also counted these atrocities, which had not the slightest connection with military operations, among "war crimes" shows how plausible this argument must have sounded during the war. Despite a whole literature on the criminal nature of totalitarianism, it is as though the

[1] See page 195.

world has needed nearly two decades to realize what actually had happened in those few years and how disastrously almost all men in high public position had failed to understand it even when they were in possession of all factual data.

Yet even if we take all this into account, it is not possible to let the matter rest there. Hochhuth's play concerns Rome's attitude during the massacres, certainly the most dramatic moment of the whole development; only marginally does it concern the relations between German Catholicism and the Third Reich in the preceding years and the role played by the Vatican under Pacelli's predecessor, Pope Pius XI. To a certain extent, the culpability of "official Christianity in Germany" has been settled, especially its Catholic part. Prominent Catholic scholars—Gordon Zahn, already mentioned, at Loyola University in this country, the eminent historian Friedrich Heer in Austria, the group of writers and publicists around the Frankfurter Hefte in Germany, and for the early period of the Hitler regime the late Waldemar Gurian, professor at Notre Dame University—have done a remarkably thorough job, fully aware, of course, that German Protestantism would fare hardly better, and possibly even worse, if studied in the same admirable spirit of truthfulness.

Heer notes that it is a matter of public record that Catholics who tried to resist Hitler "could count on the sympathy of their church leaders neither in prison nor on the scaffold." And Zahn tells the incredible story of two men who, having refused to serve in the war because of their Christian faith, were denied the sacraments by the prison chaplains until just before they went to be executed. (They were accused of "disobedience" to their spiritual leaders—suspect, one may assume, of seeking martyrdom and of the sin of perfectionism.)

All this proves no more and no less than that Catholics behaved in no way differently from the rest of the population. And this had been obvious from the very beginning of the new regime. The German episcopate had condemned racism, neo-Paganism, and the rest of the Nazi ideology in 1930 (one of the diocesan authorities went so far as to forbid "Catholics to become registered members of the Hitler party under pain of being excluded from the sacraments") and then it withdrew all prohibitions and warnings promptly in March 1933 —that is, at the very moment when all public organizations (with the exception, of course, of the Communist party and its affiliations) were "co-ordinated." To be sure, this came after the election of March 5th when, as Waldemar Gurian had noted in 1936 in his *Hitler and the Christians,* it had become "clear, especially in Bavaria, that even Catholics had succumbed to the National Socialist whirlwind." All that remained of the former solemn condemnations was a not too prominent warning against "an *exclusive* preoccupation with race and blood" (italics added), in one of the pastoral letters signed by all bishops and issued from Fulda. And when shortly thereafter the help of the churches was enlisted in determining all persons of Jewish descent, "the Church co-operated as a matter of course," and continued to do so right to the bitter end, Guenter Lewy reported in Commentary. Hence, the German shepherds followed their flocks, they did not lead them. And if it is true that "the conduct of the French, Belgian and Dutch bishops" in the war years "stands in marked contrast to the conduct" of their German brethren, one is tempted to conclude that this was, at least partly, due to the different conduct of the French, Belgian, and Dutch people.

However, what may be true with respect to the national hierarchies is certainly not true for Rome. The Holy See had its own policy with regard to the Third Reich, and up to the outbreak of the war this policy was even a shade friendlier than that of the German episcopate. Thus, Waldemar Gurian observed that prior to the Nazi seizure of power, when in 1930 the German bishops had condemned the National Socialist party, the Vatican newspaper, *L'Osservatore Romano,* "pointed out that the condemnation of its religious and cultural program did not necessarily imply refusal to co-operate politically," while, on the other hand, neither the Dutch bishops' protestation against the deportation of Jews nor Galen's condemnation of euthanasia were ever backed by Rome. The Vatican, it will be remembered, signed a Concordat with the Hitler regime in the summer of 1933, and Pius XI, who even before had praised Hitler "as the first statesman to join him in open disavowal of Bolshevism," thus became, in the words of the German bishops, "the first foreign sovereign to extend to [Hitler] the handclasp of trust." The Concordat was never terminated, either by Pius XI or by his successor.

Moreover, the excommunication of the *Action Française,* a French group of the extreme right whose teachings of a *catholicisme cerebral* had been condemned in 1926 as heresy, was withdrawn by Pius XII in July 1939—that is, at a time when the group was no longer merely reactionary but outright fascist. No prudence, finally, and no considerations for the difficult position of local, national hierarchies prevailed when, in July 1949, the Holy Office excommunicated all persons "who were members of the Communist Party, or furthered its aims," including those who read Communist books and magazines or wrote for them, and renewed this decree in April 1959. (That socialism is irreconcilable with the teachings of the Church had been stated before, in 1931, by Pius XI's encyclical *Quadragesimo anno*. Encyclicals, incidentally, are not identical with *ex-cathedra* pronouncements in which alone the Pope claims to be "infallible." But there can hardly be any doubt about their binding authority for the majority of the believers.) And even long after the war, when we read in the official Catholic Encyclopedia in Germany (Herder) that communism "is the greatest and most cruel persecutor of Christian churches since the Roman Empire," Nazism is not even mentioned. The Nazi regime had started violating the provisions of the Concordat before the ink on it was dry, but all the time it was in force there had been only one strong protest against the Third Reich—Pius XI's encyclical *Mit brennender Sorge* (With Burning Care) of 1937. It condemned "heathenism" and warned against elevating racist and national values to absolute priority, but the words "Jew" or "anti-Semitism" do not occur, and it is chiefly concerned with the anti-Catholic and especially the anti-clerical slander campaign of the Nazi party. Neither racism in general nor anti-Semitism in particular has ever been absolutely condemned by the Church. There exists the strangely moving story of the German-Jewish nun, Edith Stein, already mentioned, who, in 1938, still unmolested in her German convent, wrote a letter to Pius XI, asking him to issue an encyclical about the Jews. That she did not succeed is not surprising, but is it also so natural that she never received an answer?

Hence, the political record of Vatican policies between 1933 and 1945 is reasonably clear. Only its motives are open to dispute. Obviously the record was shaped by the fear of communism and of Soviet Russia, although without Hitler's help Russia would hardly have been able or even willing to occupy half of Europe. This error in judgment is understandable and was wide-spread, and the same can be said about the Church's inability to judge correctly the total evil of Hitler's Germany. The worst one can say—and it has been said frequently—is that Catholic "medieval anti-Semitism" must be blamed for the Pope's silence about the massacres of the Jews. Hochhuth touches upon the matter in passing, but, wisely, left it out of his play because he "wanted to keep only to provable facts."

Even if it could be proved that the Vatican approved of a certain amount of anti-Semitism among the faithful—and this anti-Semitism, where it existed, was quite up to date although not racist: it saw in the modern assimilated Jews an "element of decomposition" of Western culture—it would be quite beside the point. For Catholic anti-Semitism had two limitations which it could not transgress without contradicting Catholic dogma and the efficacy of the sacraments—it could not agree to the gassing of the Jews any more than it could agree to the gassing of the mentally ill, and it could not extend its anti-Jewish sentiments to those who were baptized. Could these matters also be left to the decision of the national hierarchies? Were they not matters of the highest ecclesiastical order, subject to the authority of the head of the Church?

For, in the beginning, they were understood as such. When the Nazi government's intention to issue race laws which would forbid mixed marriages became known, the Church warned the German authorities that she could not comply and tried to persuade them that such laws would run counter to the provisions of the Concordat. However, this was difficult to prove. The Concordat stipulated "the right of the Catholic Church to settle her own affairs independently *within the limits of universally binding laws*" [italics added], and this meant of course that a civil ceremony had to precede the receiving of the marriage sacrament in Church. The Nuremberg laws put the German clergy into the impossible position of having to withhold the sacraments from persons of the Catholic faith who according to ecclesiastical law were entitled to them. Wasn't this a matter of Vatican jurisdiction? In any event, when the German hierarchy decided to conform to these laws, which implicitly denied that a baptized Jew was a Christian and belonged to the Church like everybody else, with equal rights and duties, something very serious had happened.

From then on, the segregation of Catholics of Jewish descent within the German Church became a matter of course. And in 1941, when the deportations of Jews from Germany began, the bishops of Cologne and Paderborn could actually recommend "that non-Aryan or half-Aryan priests and nuns volunteer to accompany the deportees" to the East (Guenter Lewy in Commentary)—that is, those members of the Church who were subject to deportation anyhow. I can't help thinking that if there was any group of people during the years of the Final Solution who were more forsaken by all mankind than the Jews traveling to their death, it must have been these Catholic "non-Aryans" who had left Judaism and who now were singled out, as a group apart, by the highest dignitaries of the Church. We don't know what they thought on their way to the gas chambers—are there no survivors among them? — but it is difficult to gainsay Hochhuth's remark that they were "abandoned by everyone, abandoned even by the Deputy of Christ. So it was in Europe from 1941 to 1944."

Indeed "so it was," and against Hochhuth's "historical truth . . . in its full ghastliness" all protests that passivity was the best policy because it was the lesser evil, or that disclosure of the truth comes "at the wrong psychological moment," are of no avail. To be sure, no one can say what actually would have happened had the Pope protested in public. But, quite apart from all immediate practical considerations, did no one in Rome realize what so many inside and outside the Church at that time realized, namely, that—in the words of Reinhold Schneider, the late German Catholic writer—a protest against Hitler "would have elevated the Church to a position it has not held since the Middle Ages?"

It has been Rolf Hochhuth's good fortune that a considerable part of Catholic learned and public opinion has sided with him. Professor Gordon Zahn has praised the play's "impressive historical accuracy." And Friedrich Heer in Austria has said all there needs to be said about truth which, alas, always comes at the "wrong psychological moment" and, in the period under discussion, would have come at the wrong physical moment as well: "Only the truth will make us free. The whole truth which is always awful."

ROBERT GORHAM DAVIS

The Possibility of Individual Choice

When his play was produced in Germany early last year by the aging director Erwin Piscator, Rolf Hochhuth was only

---

A well-established literary critic, Mr. Davis is also Professor of English at Columbia University. This article appeared in *The New York Times Book Review,* March 1, 1964; Copyright © 1964 by The New York Times Company, reprinted by permission.

31. The author of *The Deputy* is of a German generation old enough to have lived through the whole Hitler period, and too young to have played any responsible part in it. Yet he speaks for all those who cannot forget that terrible past or rest until the question of responsibility is completely faced.

The Deputy came at exactly the right moment. Its mood matched the mood of Germany and even of all Europe. People were still deeply stirred by the Eichmann trial. With vigor and increasing popular support, the German Government was at last prosecuting authors of monstrous wartime crimes who had been received back more or less openly, after the war, into civil and even official society.

As numerous, and often quite different, versions of *The Deputy* were produced in Germany, Switzerland, France, England, Greece and Scandinavia, the response became tumultuous. Hochhuth's publishers brought out a volume of comments on it selected from more than three thousand articles, addresses and brochures. The published German text, from which the present translation was made, sold over 160,000 copies in less than a year. The closest parallel is the response after World War I to "All Quiet on the Western Front."

The Deputy did not cause such excitement because of originality in thought or form, or even because of any unusual talent on the author's part. Hochhuth had written little before he undertook this five-act play. It is in many respects the kind of unproduced verse drama on a grand historical theme that ambitious young men have had in their trunks with their juvenilia since the beginning of the romantic movement.

The differences lie in the irresistible immediacy of Hochhuth's materials, and the perfect suitability of his rather old-fashioned, operatic, Schillerian plot to the question of responsibility he so insistently raises.

Three years of research preceded the writing of *The Deputy*. Most of the characters are actual persons under their own names or pseudonyms. In a long appendix, called "Sidelights on History," the author provides documentation for nearly every speech in the play, including the ghoulish jesting of Eichmann's associates. Hochhuth takes liberties only by creating a fictional hero in the person of a young Jesuit priest, Riccardo Fontana, whose wealthy Italian father moves in Papal circles. But his dramaturgy is that of the well-made play of the late 19th century. He brings clearly defined characters of different social types into confrontation at a time of great urgency, and lets the situation work itself out in dialogue directed toward some action or decision. The free verse gives a slight distancing; otherwise Hochhuth has simply presented what was. The facts are sufficiently hallucinatory and macabre not to need any heightening, any metaphor.

In his introduction to the German edition of *The Deputy,* Piscator claims the play for his so-called "epic theatre." But epic requires a very different kind of mediation than Hochhuth performs, for all his documentation. He has none of Brecht's irony, virtuosity and restless sophistication. The play is introduced by a quotation from Kierkegaard, but except for a few speeches by the Luciferian Nazi doctor, there is not much of Sartre or existentialism, either.

The power of *The Deputy* derives from Hochhuth's ability to bring to bear the full weight of mass suffering caused by the Nazi anti-Christ, and yet keep alive a sense of individual option and responsibility. He does this by effects of suspense which the epic theater largely abandoned. Both as a whole, and in most of its individual scenes, *The Deputy* is traditional "rescue-drama."

At the beginning, a young SS officer, Kurt Gerstein, forces his way into the Papal Legation in Berlin to try to bring home to the Pope's representatives the full horror of the mass exterminations in Poland. Gerstein was a historical character, a chemical expert and former activist in the Protestant youth movement who deliberately joined the SS to find out about the euthanasia program, the killing of the insane and chronically ill early in the war. Then he became one of those principally responsible for supplying Cyclon B, the death gas, to the concentration camps.

This extremely ambiguous character is described both in Gerald Reitlinger's "The Final Solution" and in Léon Poliakov's "Harvest of Hate." The most ghastly pages in Poliakov's book, the fullest eye-witness account which we have of the whole extermination process, are quoted from a letter by Gerstein.

In the play, Gerstein makes an irresistible impression on the susceptible young Jesuit, Riccardo Fontana. At Gerstein's apartment, Riccardo helps in the escape of a Jew whom Gerstein has been sheltering. Riccardo just misses betraying Gerstein to the already suspicious camp doctor from Auschwitz who had visited the apartment immediately before him, carrying specimen brains of Jewish children. The doctor, exerting the almost mythic fascination of pure evil, is based on Dr. Hirt, head of the Anatomical Institute of the University of Strasbourg, whose perverse experiments are described in William Shirer's "The Rise and Fall of the Third Reich." A reader of Hegel and lover of Bach's B-Minor Mass, the doctor enjoys testing others by such announcements as, "On Tuesday I piped the sister of Sigmund Freud up the chimney."

Through the rest of the play, Gerstein and Riccardo, in situations of great danger, try to save individuals, but above all try desperately to get the Roman Catholic Church expressly to condemn the mass killings in the death camps. The inescapable occasion seems to have come when the Germans begin rounding up Roman Jews under the Pope's very windows. But the attempts fail, and most of the principals meet once again for the last time in the glow and stench of the human pyres at Auschwitz.

What has, of course, aroused most criticism of the play is its depiction of Pope Pius XII. *The Deputy* is certainly not anti-religious or even anti-Catholic. It is dedicated to Provost Bernhard Lichtenberg of St. Hedwig's Cathedral in Berlin and to a Polish priest, Maxmilian Kolbe. Provost Lichtenberg died in a concentration camp because of his publicly uttered concern for the Jews. When 10 Polish prisoners at Auschwitz were to be beaten and starved to death in reprisal for an escape attempt, Father Kolbe took the place of one of them, the father of a family.

Hochhuth does full justice to the sacrifices and sufferings of the clergy during this period. He knows of the thousand Polish priests at Dachau, and how they were treated. The play itself dramatizes the hiding of Jews in the churches and monasteries of Rome with the approval of the Pope. But there are legitimate moral and dramatic reasons for centering on the Pope's refusal to condemn mass killing, even though the scene in which this occurs has some of the callowness that runs through *The Deputy* as a whole.

The play is about choices. Because he is a noncombatant with vast world influence, and above all because he is the Vicar of God, the Pope is a crucial example of a man choosing. Hochhuth recognizes all the reasons of state, of neutrality, that seemed to dictate the choice, the fear of advantage to Russia and of Nazi reprisals. Moreover, Pacelli had been elevated to the Papacy in part because he was trained to think as a diplomat, because he arranged the Concordat with Hitler.

Yet even as heads of the Church, Popes are men also and men of very different kinds. Hochhuth wonders what choice would have been made by Pius XI, whose encyclical, "Mit Brennender Sorge," in 1937, was such a direct denunciation of the Nazi regime; or by the successors of Pius XII, whose ecumenical interests and attitudes toward the Jews have had such dramatic effect on world opinion.

Much of the debate over *The Deputy* has argued whether an explicit condemnation would have accomplished anything practical so far as the victims of Nazism were concerned. But this is to miss Hochhuth's point. He simply finds it unbearable that from 1941 to 1944 hundreds of thousands of European families, including Catholics, even nuns and monks, went to the gas chambers, "abandoned by everyone, abandoned even by the Deputy of Christ."

The Deputy is a religious play, not a political one. It begins with a quotation from Kierkegaard that asks what God ultimately requires of a man, even of the Pope, as witness to the truth. Riccardo remembers the "suffering and defenselessness of the Fisherman who first held the key." In Auschwitz at the end, sorely though Riccardo's faith has been tested by what the doctor shows him, he is still ready to sacrifice himself even if God alone knows what he has done.

Criticism of individual Popes is, of course, a commonplace in literary history. Hochhuth hardly has to invoke the example of Dante by calling his climactic act "Il Gran Rifiuto." Though he was not critical of the Popes, Paul Claudel wrote two political-religious plays in which modern Popes were characters. One of these, *The Hostage,* depicts Pius VII as the prisoner of Napoleon after he had defiantly excommunicated the French invaders of the Holy See.

Hochhuth does not use the Pope's silence as an excuse for anyone else. He shows fully the criminal complicity of Germans of all classes, the anti-Semitism of Poles and Russians, the indifference and delays of the Western powers. Yet *The Deputy* is nevertheless a drama asserting the possibility of meaningful individual choice, of the categorical act. It is a drama that would take many hours to act in the full text offered us here. Different directors have so selected from it and staged it as to produce very different plays with different political and religious meanings. But as Hochhuth wrote it, *The Deputy* brings back the Nazi period not simply as the dead weight of a terrible, unchangeable past, but in relation to live options in an ongoing history that continues to present tests of the same kind, tests that put the meaningfulness of history itself at stake. However brash and cumbersome it may be, *The Deputy* has evoked throughout the West a passionate moral and religious response that is intensely needed at this time.

KARL JASPERS

On The Deputy

1. Opening Statement

Before making any critical observations I should like to say how much all of us are indebted to you for your play, Mr. Hochhuth. You have summoned great numbers of people to reflection. You were able to impress upon their minds, more than all the documentary reports and books of photographs could ever do, the injury inflicted upon the Jews through uprooting, through humiliation, through torture and finally through mass murder. Hence I consider the high points of your play to be those scenes which affect us deeply through the sufferings of the Jews, as a direct impact or in the horror mirrored on the faces of the audience. The title of your play, perhaps, could have been "The Murder of the Jews" or "The Abandonment of the Jews." Presumably, it would not have enjoyed the enormous success which it has encountered. Jews are not of such great interest. But an attack on the Pope has great drawing power. You did not intend this nor have it in view. In the face of the mass murder of Jews your play poses the question anew: how was that possible? In the first place, it is a question addressed to the German murderers and to their minions. You have merely presented them, but unforgettably. As such they did not become a problem for you.

In the second place, it is a question addressed to the bystanders, to all of us who have remained silent. In the appendix to your play you point out that the Allies did not carry out retaliatory action; they did not bomb the extermination sites, although they were strongly pressed to do so; they did not draw up a public protest, to be ceaselessly repeated, cor-

---

One of the outstanding modern philosophers, Jaspers is also one of the few German professors who, without being either Jewish or left-wing, has a clear-cut anti-Nazi record. This statement is taken from a discussion at Radio Basel about *Der Stellvertreter*. Recorded November 23, 1963, Translated by Salvator Attanasio.

responding to the monstrous character of these events; they limited themselves merely to reporting such news over the radio. They did not set the world in a state of alarm by interpreting this fact so awesomely not only in respect to the idea of humaneness, but as handwriting on the wall in respect to the future of mankind. Why not? I find only one answer: they were afraid, even of the likelihood, that somewhere or other this war could become a war for the Jews. Therefore I do not consider it fair, Mr. Hochhuth, that you should accuse the Pope in particular as the representative of silence. Would not your indignation have been more deeply and truly expressed if the whole general front of silence had been focused upon, if the frightful general abandonment of the Jews had been shown? From the difficulties of their emigration from Germany—increased by the Evian conference, which was supposed to facilitate their emigration but which actually made it even more difficult—up to the prohibition of emigration to Palestine by the English and many other things. If, further, the question about the causes had been revived in historical retrospect through the centuries reaching as far back as the utterance which the author of the gospel according to John (8:44) has Christ pronounce to the Jews: "Ye are of the father, the devil." It seems to me that only a believing Catholic, for whom he is the Vicar of Christ, has the right to demand from the Pope more than he demands from other men. We who in this sense are nonbelievers do not have this right. For us the Church and the papacy are human institutions. They did not behave any better or worse than all the other political authorities. The Catholic faith itself, as we encounter it in individual pious Catholics, certainly deserves more respect than you have allotted to it. Were you justified in dedicating your play to the memory of two Catholics—to Provost Lichtenberg and Father Kolbe? One of them, it is reported, received the blessing sent to him by the Pope as a strengthening of his resolve to face martyrdom. Neither of the two, if we have been correctly informed, ever made any demands on the Pope. Riccardo, whose faith I do not perceive, is your own creation. In the end he wants to shoot the doctor.

In the third place, the question, "How was this possible?" is addressed to God. It is found in the heading of Act Five. Your answers are many. The monologue of the old man at the beginning of the act is grippingly true. It could bring Job to mind. But the old man is a man of our time. He can no longer pray before this awesome God. He can no longer dispute with Him, like Job. He can only entreat Him. The doctor, masterfully created as the absolute nihilist, through his evil deeds aims to force God to answer or, the answer not forthcoming, to prove through his evil deeds that God does not exist. You permit this figure, who is indifferent to and contemptuous of everything, to enjoy his empty independence in the performance of his pitiless rôle. Summing up, I see your genuine indignation, I see your perceptive grasp of the many dimensions of the monstrous question. Who can satisfactorily deal with this question! I see in you a courageous but also—if you will allow me—ruthless naïveté which has the unavoidable drawback of lingering provisional prejudices and blunders. Your work as a whole shows that you are constantly teaching yourself. You make no claim of defending an ultimate position through thick and thin. In the face of one of the greatest questions of our time you have upset our tranquility like a clap of thunder, but you have not given us the answer. You have admirably accomplished an intellectual act—the intellectual act which must be fruitful in order to arrive at pure truth.

2. Concluding Statement

When I think of the future, three points seem important to me in view of the subject that Mr. Hochhuth presents. He has most certainly contributed to impressing the sufferings of the Jews on people's minds in a different way than has been the case hitherto, to spreading this knowledge about the fate of the Jews, and to having it taken seriously. Now that Mr. Hochhuth has opened up these paths it becomes impossible to entertain that state of mind which holds that one should "not talk too much about the Jews, for after all the little people are not so interesting." The second point is that in Hochhuth's play I find a great openness, that is, I do not sense a solidly grounded faith, I do not perceive a position which he aims to defend and assert under all circumstances. Rather, what I see as the center of his concern is the question about God, and this question about God receives no answer through him. That this question is posed so radically, indirectly in view of this monstrous subject matter, seems to be a hope that there will be a continuation from here, that the question will be taken seriously. I come to the third point and to the main thing. Hochhuth's demand is: don't be silent. But the problem does not exist only in totalitarian states, it exists in every state. I mean to say that Hochhuth's demand—don't be silent—applies so intensely to us today that I can almost say there is indeed much, all too much, which is passed over in silence. Not out of fear of death, but out of fear of losing our advantages and comforts. There are so many taboos. Further, we must sight our horizon on the whole earth and not on the limited circles of the powers that are united here. If I think upon that, then I say that the mass murder of Jews was only a beginning. The great prospect is that the event will repeat itself in a grand style, with hundreds of millions being exterminated by atom bombs. I also see perspectives which others may call philosophical phantasy. I do not think it phantasy. Rather, I perceive it as the basic mood of the structure of our age and of the Western world: it is passed over in silence, it is veiled, and we do not see where we are going. And Hochhuth demands from us that we be open, and take questions with complete seriousness, in the face of God, of the Transcendent.

ALFRED KAZIN

The Vicar of Christ

On Easter Sunday, 1943, when all resistance from the Warsaw Ghetto had been crushed, the holiday crowds on their way from Mass "pushed through the streets to catch sight of Warsaw's newest spectacle . . . Batteries of artillery were set up in Nonwiniarska Street, from which the Germans kept up a steady barrage against the ghetto. And everywhere the flame, and the stench of roasting human flesh. The sight was awesome—and exciting. From time to time a living torch would be seen crouched on a window sill and then leaping through the air. Occasionally one such figure caught in some obstruction and hung there. The spectators would shout to the German riflemen, 'Hey, look over there! . . . no, over there!' As each figure completed its gruesome trajectory, the crowds cheered" (Alexander Donat, "Our Last Days in The Warsaw Ghetto").

Author of *On Native Grounds* and other well-known books, Mr. Kazin is Distinguished Professor of English at The State University of New York. This article is reprinted from *The New York Review of Books* of March 19, 1964.

The interest that the spectators took in this carnage was "medieval," in the sense that the public massacre of Jews had in the Middle Ages provided the onlookers with a sense of their own righteousness. It must have been frightful to watch Jews burn, but in the Middle Ages they were feared and marked off with so much holy zeal that to *watch* them burn established your own credit with God. The Poles suffered atrociously at the hands of the Nazis, but at Easter time, a favorite time for pogroms, the average Pole could still attend church, walk the streets, sit in a park, work in an office, get legally married, attend to his children—and thus despise and fear the Jews, who were being hunted down with such raging hatred by a great power already at war with half the world, that it was impossible for the average Pole, growing up in an anti-Semitic society, not to feel disgust and loathing for the Jews precisely because they were so much hated. Just as in the Middle Ages the townspeople of Mainz, Toledo, Worms, and York, watching Jews being burned, could not help despising and fearing people who provoked so much odium, so in 1943 even many a patriot in the resistance was exasperated by the sufferings of the Jews—who were always the same and whose sufferings were the same, and who were so bewildered yet fatalistic as they were mown down in the hundreds, with their babies, by a single machine gunner smoking a cigarette. How could you identify with people who suffered so much and had no friendly Polish neighbors to escape to? How could you help drawing away from what the S.S. professors, watching an "action," fastidiously (and in Latin) called "the asshole of the world?"

Suffering can make people disgusting. The people whose martyrdom was called an "extermination," even to the destruction of a million of their children, made them not objects of compassion, but a disease to stay away from. The Nazis made it easy for the majority to stay away, to look away, to hold their noses, to shrug their shoulders. All very natural—if you gag at the viscera of a dog some passing car has ripped open on the highway, what would you feel at all those mounds of human hair, gold teeth, children's toys smeared with excrement and blood?

The sufferings of the Jews made them unbearable—and this was the war that the Nazis won. Of course there were many individuals throughout Europe, and even a whole people, the Danes, who were not sickened by Jewish suffering, who felt the terror of children as an outrage to Christianity, who saw that "Europe," "the West," "the free world," "the Church," could become empty terms if it were permitted to shovel the Jews out like so much dirt. The Polish priest Maximilian Kolbe took another man's place in one of the "starvation cells" at Auschwitz and died after weeks of agony. Provost Lichtenberg, of St. Hedwig's Cathedral in Berlin, prayed openly for the Jews, asked to accompany deportees to camp, and died on his way to Dachau. A Catholic editor in Bologna, Focherini, lost all seven of his children in a camp because he was active in saving Italian Jews. Many of the lower clergy in France and Holland conspired to save Jews, and saved hundreds. But millions were killed, and it is doubtful that whole communities, towns, districts would have been wiped out if the American government, the British government, the Vatican, had not been able to bear with equanimity the destruction of so many civilians who were not Americans, British, or Catholic. Of course the reasons of state given for their inaction by the heads of state were entirely tenable and normal—as normal as Chamberlain's refusal, as Prime Minister, even to look at the reports of Nazi atrocities sent to him by British diplomats in Germany. Roosevelt had smart diplomatic reasons for not performing any extraordinary action. Pius XII saw no reason to confuse the millions of German Catholics fighting for Hitler. In the face of the total terror against all the Jews—every Jew in the world was marked for destruction—*Realpolitik* paid off. And soon the "normal" world came back. By now many a German civil servant, professor, doctor, policeman, judge, must wonder if it was really he who one day in 1944 drove children into a pit to be shot, who watched the naked women screaming for twenty minutes as the gas came on.

Yet obviously this effort to reclaim "normalcy" and "good sense" has not worked for everyone. Although life is rich in West Germany and Chancellor Erhard fits even better into a Texas barbecue than the late President Kennedy would have done, the Germans don't seem to achieve "normal" status. Herr Adenauer was the very quintessence of a good German mayor, but he was always being embarrassed by associates like Dr. Globke, who did nothing but frame the Nuremberg race laws. The other day it developed that Herr Erhard's Refugee Minister, Dr. Hans Kruger, had been a Nazi judge in Poland. Then the chief of Herr Erhard's own security guard, Herr Peters, who had flown down to the LBJ ranch to guard his boss, was identified as the member of a murder squad in wartime Russia, and took his life to save the government further embarrassment. The Germans would love to get back to "normal" life and to be unequivocally trusted by their allies in NATO, but all sorts of young Germans themselves, like Rolf Hochhuth (born in 1931), are outraged by the claim to bourgeois respectability on the part of so many people who twenty years ago were robbing, torturing and killing all over Europe.

It is rage against the unbearable moral obtuseness of the German philistine, now restored to the complacent gluttony of the good old days plus the self-righteousness of "the free world," that is obviously behind Hochhuth's play. What the author must have said to himself was: How can I attack hypocritical "authority" at its most vulnerable point? How can I shake these symbols of a moral tradition that no longer exists? Who was the one leader during the war whose *Realpolitik* symbolizes more than any other's the moral failure of *Europe* during the war? The Vicar of Jesus Christ on earth, the "deputy" and "representative" of Christ, the Pope . . . Pius XII. Not once did he condemn the massacre of the Jews specifically and by name. He did not speak out even when Italian Jews (many of them baptized Catholics) were being rounded up under the Pope's very windows. He never once ordered priests to pray for the Jews. He never saw to it that spiritual aid was given to the Catholics of Jewish origin (many of them priests and nuns) transported to the camps. He never threatened (as even his predecessor had done before the war) to break the concordat with Hitler. He never threatened to excommunicate Hitler, Goebbels, Himmler, and other Nazi leaders who had been baptized as Catholics.

Hochhuth's calculated provocation has worked. Pope Paul VI, when still Cardinal Montini, was moved to special remonstrances against Hochhuth; his defense of Pius XII was included in each programme at the London production of *The Deputy* and was repeated during his brief stay in Israel. The play has aroused violent protests from members of the Bundestag, the German hierarchy, theater audiences in Vienna and Paris—in Paris some members of the audience, crying *A bas les juifs!,* leaped to the stage and tried to keep the actors from going on—and American Jewish organizations, which sought to dissuade Herman Shumlin from putting the play on after Billy Rose had dropped it. In answer to Hochhuth, whose play charges Pius XII with indifference to the Jews, it has been pointed out that many Jews were given refuge in monasteries, that priests and nuns risked their lives to save Jews, that the Pope once offered Vatican funds to meet the Nazi demand for ransom. None of these points answers to Hochhuth's main charge—he is not attacking the Catholic Church and his work is even dedicated to Father Kolbe and to Prior Lichtenberg. And he rejects Cardinal Montini's claim that Pius XII wanted to protest the atrocities suffered by the Jews, but was silent for fear that he would bring worse down on them. What would have been worse?

Hochhuth offers us both a documented play and a documentary of the times. He makes extremely serious charges in the play and in his historical notes, and so invites the counter-charges that inevitably make up discussion of the play. Yet that is the kind of play it is. It is not a work of art, not a transmutation into imaginative symbols. It is a tract in dramatic form that attempts to humanize what C.P. Snow called "the worst episode in human history"; it is a dramatization of "reality," a vast script out of which different productions can be made and have been made. It is probably impossible, and even intolerable, to fit Auschwitz to the common scale and moral satisfactions of a work of art. Hochhuth's script—humane, polemical, "daring"—was captive to the delusion that anything can be put on the stage and explained on the stage long before he sat down to write. But for a young German writer, there is a spiritual necessity in at least trying to cut through the silence that prevails between the Jews and the Germans. Hitler Germany is the nightmare from which we are all trying to awaken. A German writer who was fourteen years old in 1945 must go down into that hell if he wants to write anything meaningful about his country and his people in the future. I salute Hochhuth for not shirking that journey into hell, for seeking to understand himself in the light of modern German history.

Hochhuth's whole effort here, it seems to me, is to make a dramatic kaleidoscope that will involve people now in the fate of the Jews as it couldn't and didn't involve them before. But as a playwright of the whole Nazi terror, as a documentary maker in dramatic form, he's been too appalled, disturbed and even fascinated by the cruelities of the Nazis even to be able to think of events and people as figures in his own imagination. Piscator, who did the Berlin production, claims in his pretentious preface to the German text that the play has links with Schiller's historical dramas, which Piscator sees as a type of "dramatic novel." And it is true that Hochhuth, whose characters speak in vaguely rhythmic lines that are meant to recall dramatic verse, has put Pius XII and other recent historic personages into some kind of costume drama; he wants to create an effect of historical "art" around the terrible facts. But his play is too eclectic, it is too consciously truth and fiction at once, to suggest anything more moving than his own struggle with these materials.

Hochhuth's "book" has left his producers with so many possibilities and freedoms that it is no wonder that the Berlin and London productions emphasized different sides of it, and that the New York production is sharply different from the others. Shumlin has freely adapted the play, virtually cutting Kurt Gerstein out of it, and has added passages of his own, some of which plainly depart from Hochhuth's own voice. The New York production is bare, crude, and shockingly listless in places; much of it is an anti-Nazi movie of the John Garfield period. If it weren't for Emlyn William's venomously stylized performance in Act II as Pius XII, and the sheer unavoidable horror of the truth as it comes through by the end, the New York production would be amazingly dull. (Most of the excitement opening night came from the American Nazis noisily picketing the play. The audience was asked not to leave the theater during intermission, which was more of a shock than it got from the first act.)

As a "book," complete with sixty pages of historical documentary and stage directions that are understandable assurances that a play about murder factories is possible but should not be taken as "the whole truth," Hochhuth's work lends itself to the most tendentious kind of Broadway production. There are just too many characters, scenes, comments, charges, notes. It opens in the house of the Papal Nuncio to Berlin, when an heroic "spy" in the S.S., Kurt Gerstein (another real person), breaks in to beg the Nuncio to get the Vatican to protest against the murder factories. It ends in Auschwitz, with the unnamed Doctor who assigned the victims directly to the gas chambers debating God's silence with the young Jesuit who, anguished by the Vatican's silence, put a yellow star of David on his soutane and accompanied Jews to Auschwitz. Between these two scenes of direct historical reference, we are taken to Berlin for rapid glimpses of Eichmann living it up in the company of a Rhineland industrialist, mapping Krupp's future holdings in Russia, a Nazi "scientist" who collects Jewish-Bolshevist skulls for his anatomical collection, and other such charmers out of a horror film; we are in Rome to hear a Cardinal defend the Pope's silence to a Papal count; we attend as Pius XII heatedly defends his policy while Jews are being rounded up in Rome by Nazi policemen who are now amiable bureaucrats in Bonn.

So all the oppressors and victims and onlookers are represented in the play, and everything is made—how Hochhuth would like to make it—believable, actable, dramatic, moving. If in design Hochhuth's play *is* costume drama (Rome: a palace . . . The Vatican: the Pope's chambers), in language it is very like the "living theater" of the 1930s. The "rhythmic" lines are *not* prose only in the sense that they allow a character to give us information in "spoken" form—

One million eight hundred thousand Jews
in Poland alone
have been murdered already—and since this figure
was given officially to the Papal Legate
in Washington this July by the Ambassador
from Warsaw to the White House . . .

But the tone is not right: *no* tone is right for this kind of thing on the stage. Hochhuth moves up to Auschwitz, in the last act, full of fear and trembling for his own presumption; but he does think he can put it on the stage and make it dramatically swallowable. So we can hate "The Doctor"—based on Joseph Mengele, who made the final selection of the victims, and who is still at large—as this mad scientist boasts about "whistling Freud's sister up the chimney," or shows the brains of a pair of Jewish twins, or tells the Jesuit that he has put endless Jews to death so as to "provoke" God to answer.

Of course Hochhuth doesn't really understand this "Doctor," who in Elie Wiesel's memoir of Auschwitz, *La Nuit,* is remembered as pointing out his victims with a *conductor's baton.* These Auschwitz scenes, with their attempt to give the Doctor a pseudo-theological and very "German" rationale in philosophy for his frightful crimes, are pretentious and false. The bitter truth, the ultimate humiliation for us humanists and anti-Nazis, is that the "Doctor" was not a theologian, not a false theologian, not even an anti-theologian, but a sadistic clown, a frivolous maniac and gangster. That is the horror for us, who for thirty years now have tried to make Hitlerism accountable to our humane culture—the horror is that so many frivolous, hysterical, ignorant, *trivial* people could have captured the hearts of millions of Germans and have killed millions of human beings for reasons no more "significant" and "historical" than their own murderous vanity and rage. One is now supposed to honor Napoleon for the millions of deaths he caused because he was the vehicle of historical progress. In the case of Hitler and his gang, no delusion is possible. Like the boy who stabbed an enemy in a gang war and as he took the knife out, said to the corpse, "Thanks very much!," Hitler operated on the weakness of his victims and the fear he inspired in the onlookers. He had no serious historical ideas, no tenable hopes. All those millions died to the frenzy of murdering gangsters. They died *meaninglessly.* And how do you make art out of what is inherently meaningless, was never a contest? Nowhere has totalitarianism as a climate, or totalitarianism as a subject, been able to produce a work of art. What it does provoke, from the millions ground down in our time by the Moloch of "History" or "Race," is occasional personal testimony. The victims alone can testify to the power of these murderous abstractions. Their own existence is the moral authenticity they have saved from the encompassing conformism and cruelty.

Hochhuth's polemic is irrefutable on one point. If it was all for nothing, if this was a massacre of the helpless and the innocent that in the end became as horrible in its felt insignificance as any industrial process, shouldn't those who believe that God is present in history, that He once came to earth as man—shouldn't they have protested against so much frivolity and meaninglessness—not in love for the Jews, but in defense of Christianity itself? On August 23, 1942, Archbishop Saliège cried out in Toulouse—"Why does the right of asylum no longer exist in our churches? Why are we a vanquished people? Lord, have pity upon us! Our Lady, pray for France! These Jews are men, these Jewesses are women; these aliens are men and women. All is not permissible against them, against these men and women, against these fathers and mothers. They belong to mankind. They are our brothers, as are so many others. No Christian can forget that."

What would have happened in Europe in 1943, 1944, 1945, when Jews were being killed at the rate of a thousand an hour—how many children would have been saved from the fire—if the Vicar of Christ on earth had said that?

JOHN SIMON

The Deputy *and Its Metamorphoses*

When the gifted German novelist and playwright, Martin Walser, hailed *The Deputy* as "a legitimate offspring of the

---

Mr. Simon is drama critic for *The Hudson Review* and film critic for *The New Leader*. This article is reprinted from *The Nation* of March 16, 1964.

long overdue marriage of Sartre and Brecht," he was only half right. Though *The Deputy* owes much to Sartre's skill in casting political and philosophical polemics in highly stageworthy molds, it has nothing of Brecht's alienation and epic theatre or even didactic satire. Erwin Piscator, who gave the play its first production (in Berlin), was nearer the mark when he called it "a historic drama in the Schillerian sense."

It is certainly true that Hochhuth has all the moral fervor of Schiller, the disciple of Kant, and that the ethical criterion of the play is a categorical imperative that will have no truck with relativist notions of comparative good or comparative evil. However, Schiller's use of the historic in drama is not Hochhuth's. Most patently in *The Maid of Orléans,* but also elsewhere, Schiller was willing to alter historical facts radically to suit his purposes, whereas Hochhuth is at great pains to include all possible historical data and limit his invention to the interstices—sometimes to the detriment of his play.

Actually, among Hochhuth's artistic forebears, two other great German historical dramatists figure more prominently: Kleist and Hebbel. It is Kleist's Romantic passion that largely informs *The Deputy;* its idealistic young Jesuit hero owes something to the Prince of Homburg and even to Michael Kohlhaas, figures whose noble passion makes them politically or socially culpable, but who are more troubled and complex than, say, the hero of Schiller's *The Robbers*. And it is Hebbel's notion of historical drama, based on Hegel rather than Kant, in which protagonists become symbols of their society, their age and the workings of history, that importantly affects Hochhuth's dramaturgy.

This inevitably leads to the question of the role of historicity in historical drama. Does *Richard III* fail as a play because it is unfair to Richard? Does the fact that Anouilh makes his Norman hero into a collaborating Saxon invalidate *Becket?* Does Shaw's cramming *Saint Joan* full of twentieth-century hindsight and Shavian philosophy disqualify it as a historical play? Clearly historic drama can emphasize either half of its name: it can make history subserve the ideas and effects of drama, or use the drama as a vehicle for momentous historical truths. Though either approach is valid, the former is more likely to produce a work of art, the latter a tract in dramatic form. But the importance of the literate tract in the theatre should not be too readily dismissed, whether it is called *The Cradle Will Rock* or *The Exception and the Rule.*

It is equally clear that a major stumbling block is the question of contemporaneity. It is all right to be fiercely critical or freely inventive, or both, where a figure of the distant past is concerned—where our own world and memories are not incriminated and the plea of insufficient evidence can be advanced. Thus *Becket* may grossly caricature a twelfth-century pope and elicit no more than the arching of an isolated eyebrow, whereas *The Deputy* may make a twentieth-century pope less unsympathetic than its author personally considers him and yet provoke outcries of "Caricature!" from critics all over, regardless of race, creed or competence.

Let us consider the main artistic charges (as opposed to political ones) that have been leveled against Hochhuth's Pius XII. We are told that this Pius is not a worthy antagonist for the idealistic hero—in other words, the "caricature" argument in more sophisticated form; and that *The Deputy*, asserting as it does its historical authenticity, has no business imputing motives of a damaging yet unprovable sort to the Pope. Now if you believe in a categorical imperative to do right, as Hochhuth does, Pius can no longer be an equally convincing defender of an antithetical position as Kleist's Elector or Antony in *Julius Caesar* can be. Absolute morality compels a pope to speak up in behalf of six million human beings, dead, dying, or yet to die—even if the consequences, to himself and all Catholics, were more manifestly dangerous than they may have appeared to be. By keeping the Pope as close to absolute silence as dramatically feasible, Hochhuth is actually lending the greatest possible dignity to a position he considers untenable. What makes Shakespeare's Iago a greater figure than Verdi's and Boito's is that, despite minor and inconclusive clues, he remains silent on his ultimate motivation.

Now for that motivation. Hochhuth has indeed put forward all conceivable reasons for the Pope's silence; the safety of Catholics, business and financial considerations, ecclesiastical politics (danger of schism), European politics (Hitler as bulwark against Stalin and communism), a kind of aristocratic hauteur and lack of human warmth, failure of nerve. Hochhuth does not insist on the equal relevance of all—indeed, he allows directors, actors, audiences and readers to consider some of them as irrelevant. If, however, it is objected that the particular juxtapositions are misleading, I reply that the need for compression makes them inevitable. And if it is maintained that there is still too much invention involved, I answer with the words of Lessing from the *Hamburgische Dramaturgie:* "Whoever reasons correctly also invents, and whoever would invent must also be able to reason. Only those believe in the separability of one from the other who are by disposition incapable of either."

Here we come to the crux of the matter. If Hochhuth had written a play about Pius XII and only about him, it is entirely probable that the play would have been, by accepted standards, more dense although not necessarily more substantial: much polemical material that is relegated to the "Historical Sidelights" of the play's appendix could have been set forth in greater detail in the play itself. Hochhuth, however—and here lies what is both the glory and the foredoom of his undertaking — is after something bigger: a historical fresco of the entire complex of events that begat and tolerated Auschwitz. No matter how important the Pope may be to the play, other elements are of equal importance: the Germans, the Nazi Party, big business and science gone mad, the Catholic Church, other churches, individuals everywhere, and the metaphysics of evil as embodied in the play's one predominantly mythical character, the Doctor. What ultimately drags the play down to some extent is the very opposite of insufficient historical data: the excess of usable, and used, documentation.

We should note, then, that the Catholic Church, for example, is seen in the play not only as the Pope, but also as the Apostolic Nuncio to Berlin (who is a historic figure), the Cardinal (who, I suspect, also has a historic basis), the Abbot, three quite different monks, an important lay adviser to the Holy See, and, above all, the young Jesuit, Riccardo Fontana, who stands for not only the two priests to whom the play is dedicated, but also, in Hochhuth's words, "for those priests, mostly nameless, who instantly set love for their neighbor above all utilitarian considerations—ultimately at the price of their lives." It is thus that the entire spectrum of clerical reaction to the plight of the Jews is represented.

So the deputy—or vicar, or representative—of the title is not the Pope, who shirks his duty, but Riccardo, who takes on the Pope's burden and dies for it. Riccardo is a profoundly religious figure, and it is largely because of him that the play can justly call itself "a Christian tragedy." Indeed, it is the only major religious play written since the last war that I know of, and it is perhaps a fitting piece of worldly irony which would brand this one, of all plays, as irreligious. What makes Riccardo into a Christian tragic hero is not only the fact that he assumes the guilt of his Church and unsolicitedly becomes the vicar's vicar. It is the fact, too, that Riccardo's magnanimous desperation forces him toward two of the gravest sins a priest can commit: insubordination to his spiritual superiors, climaxing in the contemplated political assassination of the Pope; and an attempt to murder the villainous Doctor of Auschwitz. But something prevents him from committing either of these—perhaps salutary—sins: is it Providence in its wisdom, or just the weakness of the spiritual arm of this world? In his final despair, Riccardo is forced into something graver yet: doubting the very decency of God. (None of this, by the way, remains in the preposterous Broadway version, to list all of whose omissions would require another historical appendix.)

Riccardo's counterpart is Gerstein, who represents the secular hero and the lay sacrifice: the man of moral action who must, in time of assassins, besmirch himself by ostensibly joining with evil in order to undermine it, and who, presumably, dies a death which is as anonymous as, but less expiatory than, the priest's. As opposed to these two, there are the two poles of culpability: the scientist whose evil knows no bounds, and the Pontiff whose goodness, unfortunately, does; or, to put it more abstractly, the sado-satanist doctor whom metaphysical silence drives to unconscionable crimes, and the high-minded trimmer whom unconscionable crimes leave physically silent.

Alfred Kazin has criticized Hochhuth's characterization of the Doctor for not having the horribly vulgar reality of Josef Mengele, the bestial doctor of Auschwitz. And this is, precisely, Hochhuth's problem. There is so much fact in his play that whenever he transcends it into fiction, into art, he seems fated to be immediately pounced upon by one group of partisans or another. Thus Kazin ignores the fact that there are several other characters in the play who quite sufficiently body forth the "sadistic clown and frivolous maniac" one might miss in the Doctor.

But if *The Deputy* is too multifariously ambitious to be a complete success, it does not flinch from attempting to pursue a theme into most of its terrible ramifications. In fact, the construction of the play is by no means unskillful in the way it manipulates characters through various scenes—dropping them and picking them up again—toward a final, perhaps somewhat disappointing, showdown. The suspense leading up to the Pope scene is ably handled, and there is also an effective contrapuntal construction: scenes involving individuals alternate with scenes involving larger groups or their typical representatives. (Nothing of this, either, on Broadway.)

Where the play really fails—aside from a certain weakness in some of the characters, partly a consequence of their numerousness—is in its language. Though it is written in free verse, this free verse makes very little sense in its line breaks, and its rhythms are far from compelling. In truth, it might as well be written out as prose, though even as prose it would be no more than adequate. The one exception is the trio of monologues by representative victims in a freight car on the way to Auschwitz, where the style becomes more unabashedly poetic — not, however, with unqualified success.

What is much less successful, though, is the English translation of the complete text by Richard and Clara Winston. That they were unable to cope with the profusion of juicy dialects enlivening the language and making it ecumenical is understandable and forgivable, although their haphazard attempts at dealing with it are less pardonable. Thus they will Americanize a Nazi doctor who now experiments on "critters," or Eichmann, who now recalls the first "date" he ever undressed, and will turn an ironic reference to the Gestapo from "your friend in need" to "mother's little helper." They can likewise be unidiomatic or overliterate, as when a bowler is told "Take your stance!" or when an importunate visitor is urged by a Bavarian monk "Now, please, take yourself off," or when "stir-craziness" emerges as "cabin-fever" and "easier said than done" as "easy to say, but hard to do."

The unfortunate truth is that the translation abounds in errors of taste and judgment, and, every once in a while, even misunderstands the text. Here are a few examples taken from one passage alone. The Winstons, in their prolixity, will turn Gerstein's simple statement, "The souls of the bystanders are also at stake" into a wordy bit of Sunday Christianity: "Those who keep silent are accessories to murder/and they imperil their immortals souls" (p. 80). They will miss a piece of *humour noir* (p. 79), "people cremated on the family plan," by translating "whole families pushed into the ovens." They reveal ignorance when they refer to "St. Loyola" (p. 76), which is rather like saying "Sir Churchill." When Riccardo (p. 84) uses the conversational *now,* "now don't you go giving up God as well," the Winstons translate it as temporal: "you don't want/to give up God as well, not now," as if the young priest might condone giving up God later. More serious is the mistranslation of Gerstein's pregnant words (p. 90), "Both of us will not survive this war" (i.e., either Nazi Germany or Western civilization must perish) as "Neither of us/is going to survive this war."

Some of the worst excesses of the Winstons occur when, for no good reason, they persist in veering toward blank verse: "If you insist on it, you'll die here/like a snail crushed under an *auto* tire — /die as the heroes of today do die, *namelessly*,/snuffed out by powers they have never known,/let alone can fight. In other words, *meaninglessly*." (Italics mine.) But they are fully capable of still more mysterious lapses. Thus when the Pope makes the important statement that he leaves protest against the Nazis to the *Oberhirten* ("chief shepherds," i.e., the episcopate of the respective countries), the Winstons translate, "We leave it to the local parish priest." Again, when the Doctor jeers at a young Jewess who has managed to survive "our recent Feast of Tabernacles, the great autumn wine pressing" (i.e., bloodletting), we read "the Feast of Tabernacles, our harvest-home," which is meaningless. And when Riccardo exclaims, in abhorrence of the Doctor, "What sort of . . . of a devil are you?" we get "What a devil you are!"—straight out of Edwardian farce.

But at least the Winstons try, however clubfootedly, to keep up with the text and respect its integrity. No such thing can be said for the Herman Shumlin-Jerome Rothenberg adaptation we are treated to on Broadway. These two men have cut out, completely or in large part, any scenes of or references to utter horror, Jewish collaboration, Protestant indifference, Catholic inadequacy other than the Pope's. Thus no mention of Himmler's modeling the SS on the Society of Jesus, Cardinal Spellman and Catholic power in the United States, the Holy See acting as bankers for the Italian royal house while also doing business with Mussolini, the Pope's concern with liquidating the Church's Hungarian assets before the Russians march in, the callousness of the German bishops and their active support of the Nazis, and God knows what else. Almost anything beyond a decorous suggestion of Jewish suffering and Papal insufficiency, anything that might really draw blood or tears, is cut. Similarly, finer discussions of philosophy, theology, politics, history, literature—or even just passages where the style is a little more complex and poetic—are all ruthlessly cut.

Thus, for example[1], the Jew Jacobson, an ordinary middle-class person, a teacher perhaps, is turned here into a violent proletarian type continually complaining about his fleas: "They're killing me, the bastards. Look, my navel is raw from them!" and about "pee stains on my underwear . . .

[1] The *Nation*, by whose permission this article is printed stipulated that an omission of 56 words be made at this point. E. B.

what a mess!" The Doctor is reduced to a *Playboy* magazine fan, "You spread their legs apart and read a textbook: hot confessions in the curls of hair," which does not even make sense. Poor Gerstein is obliged to chant incessant litanies—Rothenberg evidently considers the refrain a highly poetic device — and keeps repeating in two separate scenes, "My name is Gerstein!" and "No matter!"

Here are further examples of Rothenbergian poesy: "By the hair and teeth of God! By the plundered hair and teeth of God!" or "Take the star, priest. The light is in the star. The pain is in the star," chanted antiphonally into Riccardo's ears by Jacobson and Gerstein. This at least might stand as a parody of Christopher Fry; but what of "I supplicate, I beg, I grovel, I beseech, I whimper, I demand!" which can only be taken as a parody of Roget's *Thesaurus*. Again, when a young Italian girl is questioned by a Nazi about her fiancé, the text has her reveal that he died fighting in Africa. Here, however, he is made merely a prisoner of war, so that Rothenberg can let the girl scream: "He's blonder than you are! His hair is blond all over his body. It shines in the light." And so it goes. *The Deputy* on Broadway is like one of those comic-strip versions of a literary classic ("My name is Julien Sorel. I just got here!" framed in a balloon above a head) and as the characters bestride the stage you can virtually see the balloons coming out of their mouths.

What makes *The Deputy,* as Hochhuth has written it, important, however, is not so much the political revelation it may have made. Nor technical devices such as having the same actors enact several contradictory parts, to convey that in our age it is merely a matter of "military conscription . . . whether one stands on the side of the victims or the executioners." Nor the elaborate stage directions which bitterly project certain characters into the future, describing, for example, such and such a Nazi as a solid citizen of postwar Germany. What *is* momentous is that in an age which has progressively convinced itself that its significant dramatic form is dark comedy, that, to quote Dürrenmatt, "our world has led to the Grotesque as to the atom bomb, just as the apocalyptic pictures of Hieronymus Bosch are grotesque, too"—that in this era when "the death of tragedy" has become a literary commonplace, *The Deputy* stands as a valid tragedy: not great, but good, and anything but commonplace.

SUSAN SONTAG

Reflections on The Deputy

The supreme tragic event of modern times is the murder of the six million European Jews. In a time which has not lacked in tragedies, this event most merits that unenviable honor for reasons of its magnitude, its unity of theme, its exemplariness, and (not least of all) its sheer opaqueness. For no one understands this event. The murder of the six million Jews cannot be wholly accounted for either in terms of passions, private or public, or of error, or of madness, or of moral failure, or of overwhelming and irresistible social forces. Some twenty years after, there is more controversy about it than ever. What happened? How did it happen? How could it have been allowed to happen? Who are responsible? This event is a wound that will not heal; even the balm of intelligibility is denied to us.

Yet, if we did know more, that would not suffice. In saying this event was "tragic," we allow other demands than those for factual historical understanding. By tragic, I mean an event—piteous and terrifying in the extreme—whose causation is super-charged and over-determined, and which is of an exemplary or edifying nature that imposes a solemn duty upon the survivors to confront and assimilate it. In calling the murder of the six million a tragedy, we acknowledge a motive beyond the intellectual (knowing what happened and how) or the moral (catching the criminals and bringing them to justice) for comprehending it. We acknowledge that the event is, in some sense, incomprehensible. Ultimately, the only response is to continue to hold the event in mind, to remember it. This capacity to assume the burden of memory is not always practical. Sometimes remembering alleviates grief or guilt; sometimes it makes it worse. Often, it may not do any good to remember. But we may feel that it is *right,* or fitting,

---

Novelist, author of *The Benefactor,* Miss Sontag is also a critic and teacher. Her article is reprinted from "Book Week," the Sunday Book Review of *The New York Herald Tribune,* March 1, 1964. Permission of Susan Sontag and Farrar, Straus & Company, Inc.,

or proper. This moral function of remembering is something that cuts across the different worlds of knowledge, action and art.

We live in a time in which tragedy is not an art form but a form of history. Dramatists no longer write tragedies. But we do have works of art (not always recognized as such) which reflect or attempt to resolve the great historical tragedies of our time. Among the unacknowledged art forms which have been devised or perfected in the modern era for this purpose are the psychoanalytic therapy, the parliamentary debate, the political rally, and the political trial. If then the supreme tragic event of modern times is the murder of the six million European Jews, the most interesting and moving work of art of the past ten years is the trial of Adolf Eichmann in Jerusalem in 1961.

As Hannah Arendt and others have pointed out, the juridical basis of the Eichmann trial, the relevance of all the evidence presented and the legitimacy of certain procedures are open to question on strictly legal grounds. But the truth is that the Eichmann trial did not, and could not, have conformed to legal standards only. It was not Eichmann alone who was on trial. He stood trial in a double role: as both the particular and the generic; both the man, laden with hideous specific guilt, and the cipher, standing for the whole history of anti-Semitism, which climaxed in this unimaginable martyrdom.

The trial was thus an occasion for attempting to make comprehensible the incomprehensible. To this end, while the impassive bespectacled Eichmann sat in his bullet-proof glass cage—tight-lipped, but for all that like one of the great shrieking but unheard creatures from the paintings of Francis Bacon—a great collective dirge was enacted in the courtroom. Masses of facts about the extermination of the Jews were piled into the record; a great outcry of historical agony was set down. There was, needless to say, no strictly legal way of justifying this. The function of the trial was rather that of the tragic drama: above and beyond judgment and punishment, catharsis.

The very modern feeling for due process which the trial appealed to was also genuine, but the ancient connections between the theater and the courtroom went deeper. The trial is preeminently a theatrical form (in fact, the very first account in history of a trial comes from the drama—it is in the third play, "The Eumenides," of Aeschylus' trilogy, "The Oresteia"). And as the trial is preeminently a theatrical form, the theater is a courtroom. The classical form of the drama is always a contest between protagonist and antagonist; the resolution of the play is the "verdict" on the action. All the great stage tragedies take this form of a trial of the protagonist—the peculiarity of the tragic form of judgment being that it is possible to lose the case (i.e., be condemned, suffer, die) and somehow triumph nonetheless.

The Eichmann trial was such a drama. It was not the tragedy itself, but the attempt, dramatically, to deal with and resolve the tragedy. It was, in the profoundest sense, theater. And, as such, it must be judged by other criteria in addition to those of legality and of morality. Because its purposes were not simply those of a historical inquest into the facts, an attempt to determine guilt and affix punishment, the trial of Eichmann did not always "work." But the problem of the Eichmann trial was not its deficient legality, but the contradiction between its juridical form and its dramatic function. As Harold Rosenberg has pointed out, "The Trial undertook the function of tragic poetry, that of making the pathetic and terrifying past live again in the mind. But it had to carry out this function on a world stage ruled by the utilitarian code." There was a fundamental paradox in the Eichmann trial: it was primarily a great act of commitment through memory and the renewal of grief, yet it clothed itself in the forms of legality and scientific objectivity. The trial is a dramatic form which imparts to events a certain provisional neutrality; the outcome remains to be decided; the very word "defendant" implies that a defense is possible. In this sense, though Eichmann, as everyone expected, was condemned to death, the form of the trial favored Eichmann. Perhaps this is why some feel, in retrospect, that the trial was a frustrating experience, an anti-climax.

It remains to be seen if art of a more easily recognizable type—art which need not pretend to be neutral—can do better. By far the most celebrated of all the works of art which take up the same functions of historical memory served by the Eichmann trial is *The Deputy*. Here we have a work of art as we ordinarily understand it—a work for the familiar theater of 8:30 curtains and intermissions, rather than for the austere public stage of the courtroom. Here there are actors, rather than real murderers and real survivors from hell. Yet it is not false to compare it with the Eichmann trial, because *The Deputy* is first of all a documentary work. Eichmann himself and many other real persons of the period are represented in the play. The speeches of the characters are drawn from historical records.

In modern times, this use of the theater as a forum for

public, moral judgment has been shunted aside. The theater has largely become a place in which private quarrels and agonies are staged; the verdict which events render upon characters in most modern plays has no relevance beyond the play itself. *The Deputy* completely breaks with the private boundaries of the modern theater. And as it would be obtuse to refuse to evaluate the Eichmann trial as a public work of art, it would be frivolous to judge *The Deputy* simply as a work of art.

Some art—but not all—elects as its central purpose *to tell the truth*; and it must be judged by its fidelity to the truth, and by the relevance of the truth which it tells. By these standards, *The Deputy* is an extremely important play. The case against the Nazi party, the SS, the German business elite, and most of the German people—none of which is slighted by Hochhuth—is too well known to need anyone's assent. But *The Deputy* also stresses — and this is the controversial part of the play—a strong case for responsibility against the German Catholic Church and against Pope Pius XII. This case I am convinced is true, and well taken. And the importance—historical and moral—of this difficult truth at this time cannot be overestimated.

The Deputy is a documentary play, rather than a historical play. In a preface to the German edition of the play, the famous director Erwin Piscator, who gave "The Deputy" its first production in Berlin, wrote that he saw Hochhuth's play as a successor to the historical dramas of Shakespeare and Schiller and the epic theater of Brecht. All questions of quality aside, these comparisons—with classical historical drama and with epic theater when it deals with historical subjects—are misleading. It is the whole point of Hochhuth's play that he has barely transformed his material. Unlike the plays of Shakespeare or Schiller or Brecht, the play of Hochhuth stands or falls by its fidelity to the complete historical truth.

This documentary intention of the play also indicates its limitations. The fact is that as not all works of art aim at educating and directing conscience, not all works of art which do have a moral function entirely satisfy as art. I can think of only one work of art of the type of *The Deputy* —an act of historical memory of the tragedy of the six million—which satisfies equally as a moral act and as a work of art. This is the film "Night and Fog" *(Nuit et Brouillard)* by Alain Resnais.

"Night and Fog" is short, highly selective, emotionally relentless, historically scrupulous, and—if the word seems not outrageous — beautiful. *The Deputy* is not a beautiful play. Nor does one necessarily ask that it be. Nevertheless, if I can assume the immense interest and moral importance of the play, the aesthetic questions need to be faced. There is the matter of length, for example. I don't find *The Deputy*'s length objectionable. Probably it is, indeed, one of those works of art—like the novels of Dreiser, the operas of Wagner, the plays of O'Neill—which positively benefit from their outlandish length.

Nevertheless, whatever *The Deputy* may be as a moral event, it is not playwriting of the highest order. One reason is the style—a colorless but correct German arranged in free verse form on the page. The language of the Winston version is flat, neither formal nor truly idiomatic. ("The Legation is extraterritorial—be off with you/Or I'll send for the police.") Hochhuth may have put his lines in free verse to emphasize the seriousness of his subject, or to reveal the banality of Nazi rhetoric. But I can't imagine any plausible way of *speaking* these lines which convey the effect (either one) that Hochhuth intended. A greater fault is the thick chunks of documentation which Hochhuth has piled into the play. Much of the play as written reads as an elaborate casebook in dramatic form. It is clogged with exposition.

There are, to be sure, a number of extremely powerful scenes, particularly those involving the demonic SS Doctor. Yet the fact remains that one of the principal and recurrent —and almost, by nature, undramatic—reasons for characters confronting one another in a scene is that of *informing each other of something*. Hundreds of names, facts, statistics, reports of conversations, items of current news are crowded into the speeches. To read *The Deputy* — I have not yet seen it performed—is an exhausting, an overwhelming, and a tremendously moving experience. But this is, I believe, because of the supreme importance of its content — not because of its style or dramaturgy, both of which are extremely conventional.

I imagine that *The Deputy* could, of course, be completely satisfying on the stage. But its effectiveness on the stage places an unusual burden upon the director. A good production of *The Deputy,* I would think, must be tense and stylized and modern—not overly realistic or ideological. Hochhuth himself has provided one of the best ideas for stylization. In listing the characters in the play, he has made certain groupings of the shorter roles; all the roles in a single grouping are to be played by the same actor. Thus, the same actor is to play both Pope Pius XII and Baron Rutta of the

Reich's Armament Cartel. In another grouping the same actor is to play a Father in the Papal Legation; Witzel, an SS sergeant, and a Jewish Kapo. "For recent history," Hochhuth explains, "has taught us that in the age of universal military conscription it is not necessarily to anyone's credit or blame, or even a question of character, which uniform one wears or whether one stands on the side of the victims or the executioners." I can't believe that Hochhuth really subscribes to this facile, very modern view of the interchangeability of historical and personal roles (his whole play precisely contradicts this view) but it is an excellent theatrical idea. Along the same lines, in Peter Brook's production of the play in Paris, the actors all wear identical blue cotton suits, over which, when identification is needed, are slipped the cardinal's scarlet coat, the priest's soutane, the Nazi officer's swastika armband, and so on.

A final point. The play has caused riots in Berlin, Paris, London, almost everywhere it has been performed, because it depicts (not just reports) the late Pope Pius XII refusing to use the influence of the Catholic Church and oppose, either openly or through private diplomatic channels, the Nazi Final Solution.

There is reason to believe such protests by the Church might have had some efficacy. When the German Catholic Church strongly opposed Hitler's euthanasia program for the elderly and incurably ill Aryans—the trial run for the Final Solution of the Jewish Problem—it was stopped. The Vatican had made strong pronouncements on such public issues as the Russian invasion of Finland. And there are documents which indicate that the Pope, like many conservative European rulers of the time, did approve of Hitler's war against Russia and for that reason did not want to actively oppose the German government. For this scene in particular, Hochhuth's play has been slandered by many Catholics as an anti-Catholic tract. But either what Hochhuth reports is true or it is not. And, assuming that Hochhuth has his facts (and his notion of Christian courage) right, a good Catholic is no more bound to defend all the actions of Pius XII than he is to admire the libertine Popes of the Renaissance. Dante, whom no one would accuse of being anti-Catholic, consigned Celestine V to hell. Why may not a modern Christian—Hochhuth is a Protestant—argue that it is not the Pope but the Berlin provost, Bernard Lichtenberg (who publicly prayed for the Jews from his pulpit and volunteered to accompany the Jews to Dachau), or the Franciscan monk, Father Maximilian Kolbe (who died hideously in Auschwitz), who is the true Deputy, the true Vicar of Christ.

In any case, the attack on the Pope is scarcely the only subject of *The Deputy*. A great deal depends on the selection that a director and adaptor will make from a printed text, which would run some eight hours if performed in full. The Pope appears in only one scene of the play. The story is centered on the two heroes—the Jesuit priest Riccardo Fontana (mainly based on Provost Lichtenberg, with something of Father Kolbe) and the remarkable Kurt Gerstein, who joined the SS in order to gather facts to bring to the attention of the Papal Nuncio in Berlin. Hochhuth has not placed Gerstein and Fontana (Lichtenberg) in any "grouping," lumping them with other persons to be played by the same actor. There is nothing interchangeable about these men. Thus, the main point that *The Deputy* wishes to make is not a recriminatory one. It is not an attack on the hierarchy of the German Catholic Church and the Pope and his advisors, but a statement that absolute honor and decency—though it may entail martyrdom—are possible, and mandatory for a Christian. It is precisely because Hochhuth shows us persons who have chosen, that he has a right to accuse the others who refused to choose, to speak out, of an unforgivable cowardice.

ROLF C. ZIMMERMANN

Drama or Pamphlet: Hochhuth's The Deputy *and the Tradition of Polemical Literature*

I

In the discussion on *The Deputy*, the historians chiefly have held the center of the stage till now. Even the author, who

---

Rolf C. Zimmermann is a distinguished Swiss scholar who teaches German literature at Hamburg University. This article is reprinted from *Der Streit um Hochhuths "Stellvertreter,"* copyright © 1963 by Basilius Presse Basel. Translated by Abe Farbstein.

provided his drama with an extensive historical postscript, has confronted his critics in the armor of an historian. It soon became clear he was not only presenting the public with a play, but also meant to offer it a lecture on contemporary history. When an historian arrogantly rejected the play from the superior heights of his profession and began to criticize it in a rather *ex cathedra* fashion, a dramatic scene developed: Hochhuth rebelled as an indignant deputy against an unmoved profession, against an entrenched authority that seemed to him to have fallen in error because it had been partly blinded by its dulled feelings.

This is not said just to make a point. With the postcript, "Sidelights on History," Hochhuth renounced his play's artistic autonomy. He deliberately renounced the enduring alibi Lessing's essays on drama gave to writers of historical plays: his material was not intended to be merely a useful story, exempt from reality and historical truth so as—in Lessing's sense—to better serve human potentialities and philosophic truth. On the contrary, his material was explicitly meant to present the historical truth in an artistically useful dramatic form. He will soon learn what is meant by "useful." With his entry into the discussion of the play, Hochhuth again emphasized and showed he would be the last person to want to wave historical arguments aside as irrelevant to his work. But why not, then, focus the discussion on "Sidelights on History" alone, since it does deal with the historical events involved? He supplies the answer through Riccardo in his audience with the Pope-historian. He accuses the latter of blasphemy, cold indifference toward historical events. What if historians and the contemporaries they teach were incapable of seeing the truth because it didn't agree with their vision of the world? This is Hochhuth's question and protest against the science of history. Hochhuth's deep distrust of history peers through "Sidelights on History." We can sense his reasoning between the lines: let history endow the meaningless facts with meaning but let it not dare argue away millions of slaughtered people. And isn't this just what it is doing?

It is not by chance that Hochhuth's text combines a drama with historical notes. In both forms we must recognize the major common denominator: Hochhuth in both attacks what he once called "Hegelian detachment." Pius is its representative, just as Hochhuth believes other representatives are to be found among historians. It is this "detachment" he distrusts and fights, opposing to it an "undetached" vision of the Nazi persecution of the Jews, of suffering without name or number. This suffering has enough weight to determine for the future the human—not historical—value of important historical individuals, from Hitler to Eichmann, from Pius to Weizsäcker But to do this we must be able to see the suffering, be able to empathize with it, and then relate it to the behavior of those who held power. Hochhuth is not concerned in "Sidelights on History" only with historical judgments he finds fitting. He is concerned with seeing to it that this suffering plays its part in the process of judgment. He presents it to those who judge as he himself sees it. This is why he moves beyond a purely historical presentation, beyond historical sidelights, into the play itself. The playwright's medium, the drama seeking to represent reality, the presentation of the historical situation, is deliberately employed to create the perspective from which history is to be viewed. The outraged heart turns to the concrete impression that has wounded it and tries to re-create it, to objectify it. The drama becomes an imaginary and imaginative on-the-spot investigation without which judgment must not be rendered. Hochhuth puts his faith in the reality of suffering in order to indict "detached" historical writing as well as the detached coldness of the powerful figures whose praises it sings.

That which arouses indignation must be set before our eyes, and in doing this Hochhuth gives his artistic means full range. This formula, in fact, explains a great deal when we examine the literary form of Hochhuth's *The Deputy* more closely. That we should see the outrageous is—as we shall show immediately—the very principle on which the scenes are constructed. From the beginning of the play, in the very first scene, when Gerstein wants to report to the Papal Nuncio, he sets it before us. In the second scene, after the more indirect report, the direct representation of the outrageous unfolds: the doings of the "Jägerkeller" are pilloried with the "photographic perfidy" (Hochhuth) of satire. In the third scene, the two types of presentation are combined: Gerstein reports on the horrifying (Cyclone-B gas, two thousand kilograms of which have been ordered for the killing of more Jews); the doctor shows his revolting exhibit (the brains of Jewish twins in a glass jar). In the second act, Riccardo reports to his father; in the third, reports and direct presentation visualize for us the shattering round-up of Jews in Rome; in the fifth, Auschwitz finally appears in its red glare. There is not one scene that does not aim at provoking the reader's or spectator's indignation.

With our formula we can also explain how the characters are drawn. It is striking that we cannot tell from their tenor whether the scenes take place in Berlin, Rome, or Auschwitz. There is no play and counter-play of scenes, there is no external "camp."[1] The figures are grouped according to an inner principle. If we ask what it is, we find it is again the principle of indignation—the inclination to indignation which is either present or absent, whether it involves the Germans or the Pope's retinue. Just as every scene is something of a human test, an experimental arrangement, so, too, the figures who appear are experimental objects, individuals to be tested. Will they reveal that they have a heart and grow angry, or will they remain cold? Will they make excuses, or reveal themselves to be wholly monsters? Hochhuth arranges his characters, both historical and invented, in an overall pattern of this kind. On one side is the outraged group: Gerstein and Riccardo. On the other side the anger-provoking group: the bowlers in the Jägerkeller, the SS soldiery and its helpers, and the Cardinal as well, whose conviviality in this situation represents outrageous irresponsibility. Between these two groups are those who have eyes in their heads and hearts in their bodies, but who abstain from courageous outrage against the criminal events. The test of these vacillating people is how much they see and feel. It determines their stature and responsibility—and accordingly—their function in Hochhuth's work. Indignation drives Hochhuth to include the Pope in his play, not pleasure in scandal or the motives of a Herostratus. The Pope saw everything that happened and his heart should have been the one most open, most outraged at the extermination of a whole people, the people of the Old Covenant. Hochhuth's treatment of the other deniers is less intense: since they lacked feeling they had a much narrower understanding of the events and therefore cannot really be held responsible. Such figures as Colonel Serge or even Riccardo's father belong in this category: basically well-meaning but unspiritual men engaged in active life. The other people who appear are mere victims of events, without spiritual freedom or the practical possibility of expressing their feeling of outrage. Consequently, they merely embody that unlimited demand which the cowardly and the heartless, the silent and the sophistical, have abandoned, a demand that can only rend the hearts of those who see and feel. If we fail to grasp the meaning in the pattern of Hochhuth's characters, we will ask—while shaking our heads—why Pope Pius is presented on stage as an eccentric, emotionally impoverished to an almost pathological degree, and not as a cool diplomat. In the vision of a "detached" historian Pius will not appear more abnormal than other cerebral figures. It is different in the vision of the out-

[1] The reference is to the warring camps in Schiller's play, *Wallenstein,* in which external trappings mirror the personal qualities of the antagonists. (Trans.)

raged heart. It knows no "normal" characters and types, but only experimental individuals, experiments, and the two factors crucial for the outcome of the experiment—knowledge and conscience. It rejects psychological relativism just as much as historical relativism. Its starting point is an intact conscience and intact knowledge which spontaneously, indeed, reflexively revolt against this flood of injustice and murder, and —if only to preserve themselves—stop the raised arm of evil. For this vision Pius was necessarily a monster of cold intelligence and apathy. There is a reason why Hochhuth carefully draws a circle around the factor of conscience just as he does around knowledge of the facts. He believes there is hardly a need to be concerned any longer with documents. All we need do is watch how this or that conscience responds to a challenge. To an unequivocal challenge, of course, thus he precipitates a crisis in the Pope's relation to Hitler's annihilation of the Jews in the notorious fourth act: not only does Pius know everything, but in Riccardo's eyes at this moment he is being put to the test not just as Christ's deputy, but also as Bishop of Rome and as a human exemplar for other men. His Christian duty, professional duty, and human duty lay siege—externally projected in the scene—to his heart. The magnitude of the crime and the nearness of its execution—in space as well as time—no longer permit him to ignore it or wallow in indecision. There are no longer any interceding factors, any sources of error in this experimental situation, any refraction of morality through the prism of his own conscientiousness. If Pius has a conscience he must grow angry in this situation, "curse" as Riccardo curses, act as Riccardo acts; he must at least decide as Riccardo has decided. History, as it actually occurred, may never have known such a sharpening of the situation. Yet all the elements of this fourth act were potentially embedded in the historical situation. This enables Hochhuth to recognize his test case in history, to recognize in the historical Pius his bloodless esthete and sneak before he angrily and relentlessly presses home his attack on the real historical qualities of the latter.

Of course, this angry vision does not permit that development of character which different critics have routinely and superficially demanded of *The Deputy*. We have already indicated that history is being presented on stage from the viewpoint of the moral, not psychological, imagination. For Hochhuth the only issue is the responsiveness of the human heart and conscience. The standard of good is constant, the vision undimmed. He does not want his public to recognize human subjectivity; he wants it to judge historical events with its heart. And inversely, what is of interest in the depicted historical events is no longer human finitude, as would be the case in a character drama, but human infinitude; that is, the capacity—driven by insight into the good—to renounce the finitude of the instinct for self-preservation and its aims, and to obey the will of objective law, whether it is called God, the Good, or love of humanity. Rather than place the individual, with his relative limitations, stage center, Hochhuth, to the contrary, focuses on the residue of the absolute within each individual, the universal piety of the heart that abrogates all distinctions — including that of character — when it begins to speak. Here nothing can develop because such matters of the heart never come fully to consciousness, but emerge in the spontaneous and momentary conquest of feeling by an unequivocal and massive evil that defies discussion. The striking shortcomings of the characters and the transposition of the historical-real into an abstract-intellectual discussion both lead us back again to outraged indignation as the true germ cell of this play. To preserve the unconditional power of this anger, Hochhuth must choose the clearest situation which the Hitlerite annihilation of the Jews could offer the moralist. He had to avoid every problematic character and situation since it was a question of putting the heart to the test. Is this a lazy evasion? "Sidelights on History" had to be written and appended to the play in order to dispose of such objections. With a much better instinct than his critics. Hochhuth kept his play free of all discursive modifications of its unconditional demand. When the play does lapse into discussions of practical possibilities of action (in the second scene of the third act and parts of the last act), it clashes with its own essence and is at the furthest remove from the basic principle involved in the imaginative reproduction of judged history and materalized indignation. So, too, the figures of Riccardo and Gerstein are just substantial enough to serve as vessels of outrage. They are not characters, but avowers of a faith. It is pointless to attribute individualized situations and individual traits of character to mystery plays and morality.

Hochhuth's Pius is meant to appear as a moral individual, which is why he cannot develop. This means that in dealing with him, the limits of the experimental moral situation must not be transgressed and the sphere of psychological and pragmatic motives entered. The latter are of interest—and then only as substitutes—when dealing with lesser challenges to humanity and conscience, with spiritless figures, not here. Hochhuth, in full control of the historic *fait accompli,* wants to put the palpable evasions of the Pope on his dramatic pillory. He does not have to understand because he does not have to forgive. Should he try to understand, he is immediately threatened by the spirits of the innocent murdered, by justice and truth.

It sounds paradoxical, but it is proven by Hochhuth's minor figures: the author endows the figure of his Pope with dignity, and defends the dignity of man by never putting into the Pope's mouth all the petty arguments of physical fear, the fear of violence, which show the unspiritual man his finitude, arguments thrown into the debate by the Pope's defenders. Man's situation between finitude and infinitude is not decided here—as it is among other, pettier and unspiritual souls—by fear or courage. Hochhuth's Pius is not simply cowardly, just as Riccardo is not simply courageous. More is at stake here. The morality play does not demand heroes but saints. What is involved here is the avowal: "I cannot do other, God help me." In its identification with a truth that demands avowal, the self no longer knows either dangers or prospects of success, because in the moment of avowal and crisis it feels duty-bound to serve with all its powers and possibilities. This readiness for self-denial is the heart of the matter for Hochhuth when he focuses his outraged vision on the figure of Pius XII. It is such readiness which had already decided for Hochhuth the historical stature and worth of this Pope. His only problem in the play, therefore, is to show Pius XII's impassivity, i.e., his incapacity to be fired by the need for avowal inherent in truth. This is no longer a question of fear or courage but of a kind of constitution. It is just these spiritually eccentric traits of impassivity, and egocentricity of the narcissistic esthete which Hochhuth depicts in Pius XII. The entire argumentation on stage is meant to sketch the character type. For Hochhuth the dramatist—not the historian!—the real trial records were already completed before he put the first stroke of pen to paper. This is really a crucial point in understanding the text. In every character drama it would be interesting if the traits of a type had been concretized in an historical figure. But it is different with Hochhuth. For him it is a question of the traits of a type—to the degree that they will evoke outrage under the given circumstances, according to attitude and situation. This is precisely what Hochhuth is after: to sharpen the spectator's conscience through indignation and expose the injustice of the "detached" historian. The angry vision, refusing to focus on individuals and employing only the suitable or less suitable instruments of truth or justice, explains the portrait of Pius XII. We are immediately struck by how definitively this technique—the moralizing description of types—shapes Hochhuth's play. Not just Pius is cast as a human type, whose satirical complacency is posed in the moralistic stage-setting of outrage. Typicality and satire play exactly the same role in the case of the Cardinal, setting this type of portly *bon vivant,* so highly prized in everyday life, against a background of apocalyptic events and thereby blackening him as a useless instrument, a contemptible denier. Satire serves even more plainly in the moralistic exposure of everyday human types represented by Hitler's retinue. The serious gentlemen who are relaxing in a bowling alley, and behaving accordingly, seem to belong in a comedy. It is the proper artistic locale for an awareness of petty, all-too-petty humanity; our attention is captured completely by the comic disproportion between subjective claim and the objective failure of this claim, between deliberate action and duped suffering, between small profit and the price of great absurdity. Comedy, too, can approach satire when the discrepancies depicted refer to a type, not the limitations of an individual. Can we say that Hochhuth's "Jägerkeller" scene is a satirical interlude in the manner, for example, of Auerbach's cellar in Faust? But just this comparison makes plain the lack of one element in Goethe's scene on which Hochhuth obviously builds his satire—with the Cardinal, and here too: the element of horror. Officers, industrialists, scientists and administrators are all drawn into the satirical sketch: whether it is dealing with an allied bomber squadron ending the bowling game instead of an increasingly impatient host, or the "doctor" pursuing the barmaid Helga for a very human private entertainment that is to take place nowhere else but Auschwitz; whether the subject matter of the usual idle shoptalk is the famished children in the Krupp labor camps or the scientifically instigated murder of Jewish Soviet commissars. And always, the reader is hardly given time to complete the comic contrast before it is lifted to the moral plane. What Bert Brecht in his *Threepenny Opera* could still deflect into the esthetically enjoyable and comically inoffensive is here made palpable in its full weight and macabre extremity. These serious burghers are criminals even if the word is not applied to them; these representatives of a human state are beasts, no matter how human and jovial their appearance. The money they spend is blood-money, the decorations they wear, the mark of Cain.

The satire on *Gemütlichkeit!* There are well-known situations in which joviality spoils language. Hochhuth wants to depict just this. Satire is good enough to provoke the spectator to reflection, but only if he then immediately abandons satire because he sees the dimensions of the moral contrast. From this point of view note how Hochhuth never lingers over the all-too-human. The petty is no longer the human; the human misery of the satirist turns into the inhuman misery of the moralist. This is most obvious in the figure of Helga, perhaps the one person we would like to dispose of as quickly as possible with the grim smirk literary satire inspires. In the entire comical cuckold relationship, the element of Auschwitz raises a question of honor and conscience that transcends the natural inconstancy of Eve's daughter. Thus, it is experimentally demonstrated that honor and conscience, spirit and dignity, cannot be imputed to this girl. In the fifth act the coffee and silk stockings of a spoiled mistress cannot be linked in satirico-comic fashion to the war, but must be treated moralistically in their relation to the inferno of Auschwitz. It is not that these people have or do not have something (as in war), but that creatures with silk stockings are beasts and the cattle ready for slaughter in the freight cars are human beings. Helga fails as the Pope fails. That Hochhuth does not emphasize her failure is connected with her human stature. The test of her humanity can be made unmistakably clear only in the situation. Helga's low level of spirituality merely provides a moralistic side-theme, yet Hochhuth does not ignore it. The moralizing background of Auschwitz continues to have its effect in the stage directions where Hochhuth notes that Helga will deceive her next lover. This deception is not related to manly jealousy, so dear to satire. Rather, it appeases a purely human jealousy, that of a Jewish occupation officer who cannot believe a woman who is his mistress knew of the Auschwitz gassings and even helped as best she could. Again, the background deprives satire, here a lover's deception, of all enjoyment. Witzel is a figure very similar to Helga. In his case, too, satire—that "photographic perfidy"—presses to the limit where the pleasure of recognition abruptly changes into angry revulsion because of equally recognizable injustice and the inhuman misery bound up with it—the misery that leads the terrified Jews to believe they are only being sent to the Apennines for road labor. Pleasure turns into revulsion at sight of this lack of conscience raised to the highest power, deceiving the innocent destined for death, denying them the truth, and not daring to look at itself in order to maintain the "smoothness" of the operation.

Hochhuth is so much more than a mere moralist, belonging in hidden fashion to Apollo's train. The gentle melancholy, always present when he is putting the finishing touches to figures like Helga or Witzel, reveals this. In the brilliant stage directions for the second Auschwitz scene, he writes "that 'human' is a far too equivocal word to be useful any longer." He even speaks of Helga's "warmheartedness." He lets the reader know he would much rather keep these people —the Cardinal, Witzel, Helga—under the satiric lens in their colorful humanity. In the indestructible capacity of these figures to change, he is charmed by nature's naive, unspiritual "innocence" and power, an unreflective nature which he praises in his use of stereotypes and dialects. But this finitude of the unreflective is just one extreme; it comes into contact with the other extreme, the finitude to be found in the *purely* reflective. Both the naive person and the esthete have their own distinctive qualities and, moreover, can claim a part as human beings in determining the concept of natural humanity. This is just how they appear to the writer. And yet, the writer, with his spirit and reason, knows that humanity is also a normative, a demanding concept; that in every epoch the spirit has put natural man to the test and commanded him to renounce his half-heartedness. With his gifts as a writer, Hochhuth feels himself put to a truly ascetic test, just as he sees all his characters and all historical figures subject to the same test. He cannot simply draw types as a satirist, even if as an objective artist he is under no compulsion to draw complex individuals and characters. Against an egotistical humanity destructive of man, spirit demands that he criticize those human qualities that tell man to forget nature itself. It is as if the sun were to enter a cathedral whose stained-glass windows it ordinarily endows with poetic radiance and suddenly approach so closely to the windowpanes that only their scorched outlines remained visible. Hochhuth is well aware of the finitude and limitations of his historical and imaginary people—their concrete traits suffice for that—but as spokesman of spiritual humanity he is forced to curse them, because in the most unequivocal situation, before the most gripping challenge, they have failed to pass the test as examples of human spirituality, fearlessness, and absolute conviction.

Why do Hochhuth's figures fail? How does he compose those characters in his play who do not fail? Are they grouped in terms of belonging or not belonging to an organization? Have those who fail sacrificed their human dignity to the interests of their profession? To the state, the church, industry, even the family? We need only recall the cynical quotation from Talleyrand used by Hochhuth in his stage directions for the fifth act. Who else remains? Two deserters and lone wolves: Gerstein and Riccardo. And a semi-private person, Riccardo's half-indignant father. Hochhuth's play shows those people who are duty-bound to uphold their own human dignity in the degrading clutches of legitimate, yet autonomous, social institutions, which, as a result of their autonomy, are always predisposed to inhumanity. This element in the play gains weight against the requirements of the raw material, so that it seems as if Hochhuth had functionally related this conflict of spontaneous conscience and group duty. It alone can elucidate what piety, today as always, must defy. The inhumanity unconditionally challenged by Luther, Voltaire, and Thomas Mann has other names today. Yet, resistant inertia, intent on blocking the absolute challenge, the prison of finitude and limitation, always remain the same. It is the social discipline to which each individual first submits for the sake of his own welfare and those nearest him. Yet, beyond this rationale, it can become the prey of tyranny, take irrational and capricious forms. It is the Antigone conflict which can occur ninety-nine times in nontragic circumstances against the one tragic occasion. (As we know, Hochhuth also dealt clearly with this conflict in a prose drama—*The Berlin Antigone*—and indignantly denounced it.)

Let us return to the form of Hochhuth's play, to its originality and the suitability of its dramatic means. We still have to localize the Achilles' heel in a drama of outrage and a sequence of scenes consisting of experimental moral tests. The keen critics of the original presentation have not overlooked it. How can a play that limits itself to representation, to demonstration—in the two-fold meaning of the word—how can such a play give birth to more than an episodic drama of a prophet cut off and expelled from the world and finally "sent into the desert?" Especially since the constellation of characters is to be tested by their hearts and bitter passions, and forbidden to find consolation in mind and philosophy? How can a more profound dramatic process take place here, not only pointing to external events, but also imparting a sense of necessity and insight because it expresses the play's essence? The classic drama of catharsis was based on the concurrence of character and reflection on character. Here, on the other hand, the absence of both these factors is emphasized. Even Gerhart Hauptmann's naturalistic drama, radically excluding the reflection on character that precedes catastrophic episodes, needed the internal and external immobility of its figures to give a sense of inevitability to the tragic defeat of the soul as it fell into the unavoidable trap of finitude. Hochhuth, of course, introduces some minor figures who are conceived naturalistically. But how far removed his major figures are from the blindly functioning characters of naturalism! It is true that intuition rather than reflection ignites the divine spark of outrage in both Gerstein and Riccardo, but in both the spark is ignited in a state of fully wakeful, not blind, humanity. A spirituality, a moral mobility, enables both angry men to identify with the suffering of strangers, and it is just this spiritual humanity that makes Hochhuth's figures so extremely mobile in external form as well. Like Ahasuerus, Gerstein incites agitation from place to place; Riccardo is driven by his spirit to Rome, to Lisbon, to Auschwitz. No net can be drawn over Riccardo's head. He enters the catastrophe as a completely free agent and thereby affirms once more that the victim is not being strangled by the naturalistic entanglements of causality in his own life. Only the Jews, as a horrifying variation of the naturalistic hero, pursue the path of suffering taken by Hauptmann's characters: helplessly blind victims of their natural humanity—driven wild by the dog packs—they conform to Hauptmann's favorite image. But just as Bert Brecht rebelled against this situation for man, so Hochhuth turns even more clearly against naturalism's scene of tragedy. A type of indignant drama originates with him to accuse spiritual humanity for the victim's helplessness and blindness. Hauptmann lulls himself with the tragic, "This is how everything must be." Brecht stirs things up with the untragic denunciation of what in changed form could have prevented the naturalistic tragedy. Hochhuth is even more radical: he denounces as universally guilty the conscience that will not allow itself to be agitated by anything.

The cohesion of drama achieved by linking the problem of character and reflection on character, the progressive clarification of the relation between the individual and his environment, is already lost in Hauptmann's tragedies. Its absence in Hauptmann, as in Brecht and Hochhuth, gives rise to the episodic drama. What then gives cohesion to their dramas? Hauptmann rounds out his tragedies by drawing together a catastrophic net of events. Brecht dispenses with this. His plays are held together by a concept of discussion set in motion during the play which should be continued after the last curtain falls. And Hochhuth's drama? Does it have the same goal, but other means? Does it want to challenge the contemporary audience to the factual discussion it has universally instigated? Appearances deceive. The "Sidelights on History" may provoke discussion, but the play has a different goal. No theses are advanced, and we need only compare the wealth of scenes in a play by Brecht with the quite limited number in *The Deputy* to realize they have a quite different function here. They are not meant to set in motion the dialectic of an actual human situation, with all its implications. We already know their function: Hochhuth's scenes are meant to evoke indignant anger; they have been written with an eye to making them unequivocal and unchallengeable, so that a discussion of the facts is well-nigh impossible. It is not the mind that is appealed to in the play or by it, but the responsive power of conscience, piety, the heart—in a word, feeling. For this reason, as with Brecht, the play is unrounded, open; it attempts to arouse agitation beyond itself which, however, unlike Brecht, is emotional in nature. It was not

Hochhuth's intention to start a discussion with the play. According to all newspaper accounts, the Berlin theatregoers went home in a shattered, silent mood, not at all eager for discussion.

To what conclusion do we come? The Hauptmann tragedy robbed of its "necessary" catastrophe? The Brechtian sequence of scenes deprived of its red thread? Hochhuth has to give his scenes a different sort of continuity. Of course, there is one major character who draws all events concentrically around himself in constituting his own situation: Riccardo. Actually, Goethe as a dramatist anticipated this style in his *Götz von Berlichingen.* He leads his indignant hero through a loosely connected number of typical situations, an angry man who always seems to get entangled in shortsighted, morally ambiguous, spontaneous actions and who finally, overwhelmed by circumstances and muzzled, must die tragically. If the succession of scenes and episodes lacks the economy and necessity on which structure is built, the same cannot be said about its power of representation. The dramatized biography is here transformed into an accurately grasped problem of character. Hochhuth's play resembles Goethe's first drama in many surprising respects: its excessive length, the almost epic breadth of the situations depicted, the indignant hero, the lack of reflection (Emil Staiger called *Götz* Goethe's most unintellectual play), and, finally, its success. But in Goethe the individual character is a self-sufficient element and, accordingly, the readiness to anger in *Götz* is made relative and treated ironically in relation to character. The exact reverse is true in Hochhuth: the theme is treated from an absolute point of view; everything of a relative nature is sacrificed for the sake of the action. Irony is present and seems to take the form of individuality: the outraged man is a Jesuit, a diplomat, the favorite of those who are not outraged. But for Hochhuth the succession of scenes does not serve to characterize his hero; instead, it must provoke indignation. How are we to understand this?

Goethe's Götz acts. But by his actions he makes clear the limitation of spontaneous conscience. Because his anger has an impure source, is too quick and shallow, it loses the absolute quality of its spiritual pretentions by which he believes himself favored. The reader or spectator can no longer be convinced of its absolute nature, and there is no reason why he should be. But in Goethe it is not at all a question of the morally unequivocal, in the light of which this anger and the readiness to act on it must lose their typical and symptomatic meaning. Götz's situations are never general test situations of heart and conscience. Because the situations are morally twisted—he attacks Nuremberg merchants, violently abducts a friend of his youth, places himself at the head of incendiary peasants—the knight can count on the sympathy of reader and spectator, but not on any understanding of his primitive feelings and behavior. The public is involved esthetically, never morally. But this is just what is meant by self-sufficiency in the representation of character. Hochhuth's Riccardo would like to see action take place, and, along with his character, Hochhuth would like to see the public morally decide as Riccardo does. But quite unlike *Götz, The Deputy* makes completely clear that not every feeling of outrage must be translated into spontaneous actions. Neither Gerstein nor Riccardo is a monomaniacal fanatic or an anarchistic desperado. Both are intelligent and know precisely, along with their outrage and absolutism, the duties people must perform. They only consider themselves obligated by their consciences to pass the torch of truth on to those from whom redress may be hoped. With his life at stake, Gerstein informs the Nuncio. Scorning all Curial customs and laws, Riccardo appeals to the Pope's conscience. To do more is forbidden by their spiritual humaneness, that very rational refinement of the heart which, in its turn, guarantees the righteousness and genuine character of their anger. Unlike Götz, they both preserve the purity of their flames. That is, they do not allow their sacred indignation to turn into mindless rage. Riccardo goes to his death in complete possession of himself after he has seen to it that the only person who could provide redress has been reached and informed. *Dixi et animam salvavi.* The last act could, of course, seem an unholy and spiteful reaction. But when Riccardo enters the murderous reality of the gas chamber it is only a last attempt to arouse the Pope. At the same time, it is a summons to indignation, even if now a silent one.

The play's cohesiveness must also be approached from the perspective of anger. Hochhuth wants to establish this in every scene, in every figure. His purpose in making Riccardo his major character is to have him personify outraged anger. He intensifies this anger, letting it find its way to inevitable self-consciousness in truth's clarity and impotence because the truth was clear and impotent in Pope Pius' historical situation. With his reference to the unsuspecting willingness of the Dutch deportees, Hochhuth calls attention in "Sidelights on History," as in the newspaper discussions, to just this point. No accident that he speaks so passionately about it! We see him first employ the figure of Riccardo as the personification of both an infinite moral demand and finite anger, and then, step by step, clearly transform him into the symbol of the infinite alone, that impotent truth in the period when Hitler was persecuting the Jews. It is no longer Riccardo whom the Pope surrenders to the executioners but the truth. Let us examine Riccardo's end closely. Here no pathetic sell-out betrays the classical hero, who still manages to save the dignity of his own finitude as he perishes. The play is very much damaged because Hochhuth in the last act does not simply send Riccardo to his death as a mute victim with all the others. Measured by its symbolic value to the dramatic process, the final discussion is theatrical and lacks sense because the representation of the shocking is fused with Riccardo's fate, his personal fate, which should no longer be of interest at this moment. For he is no longer the shocked individual; he is the presence pure and simple of desecrated truth and her infinite demands. Then, too, he is placed on the far-removed plane of a Gerstein and Jacobson. To have him meet these figures of the drama's beginning is a way of rounding it out externally, but it is achieved at the expense of a far more important internal consistency.

II

Given all this, the reader will believe Hochhuth's drama is a simply and crudely constructed partisan play. The obvious skill with which poetic means were concentrated on a goal did indeed produce an effective text, but this effectiveness is not esthetic in kind. Accordingly, the text does not deserve to be considered by literary criticism.

We will attempt to remove this question from the reach of pretentious and impertinent commentaries, which are always influenced by the latest period in literature or the prevailing tendency and—concerned wholly with esthetic sensibilities—are as uninterested in new spiritual beginnings as they are in satisfying old, habitual tastes. Let us not forget that taste and culture are always the passive materialism of an active, spiritual attitude. Goethe's *Götz von Berlichingen,* clumsy and monstrous, opens the epoch of autonomous personality and with it a period of drama that improves esthetically at a rapid pace. And yet, so competent a critic as Lessing considered this first-born child of classic German drama to be a fraud. Hochhuth is certainly no Goethe, just as no Lessing is to be found among his critics. But in quite similar fashion there are people today who view *The Deputy* scornfully. People approach it with a consciousness that has been refined through a long period of eclecticism, and condemn it instead of observing and understanding what spirit is groping for expression here. Will this spirit some day succeed in shaping a body for itself? Will it, perhaps, even initiate a new literary taste with its poetic means, a new esthetic domain? What is the nature of the seed and the nascent impulse?

We will immediately give it its name: it is the pathos of an unconditional feeling that demands the absolute. *The Deputy* is permeated by a mind that no longer accepts being split by the traditional dialectic of individual right and the necessity of the whole, nor does it accept the idea of balance and resignation. It is just this absence of a balance that is so characteristic.[2] Riccardo must turn his own reason into the mouthpiece of a collective reason, sacrifice his subjectivity to the objective from the very outset. The dramatic movement does not arise from the dialectical conflict of a reason split into two equally justified parts, but from the distress of reason overwhelmed by the concrete. The autonomous individual no longer has any self-sufficient dramatic meaning. The main character becomes a mere figure of demonstration. The entire weight is laid on the situation and the theme. But how can this interest and excite us? Certainly not as invention, as fiction, where esthetic pleasure takes the emotionally exciting individual claims of the classic hero, so repugnant to higher reason, as the chief aim. The situation can no longer be chosen arbitrarily, can no longer be merely instrumental (means to an end) or esthetic (the probable semblance of some reality). It must be a concrete, real situation which shocks reason and calls for change. Because of this not only is a balance between feeling and reason thwarted from the very outset, but a movement is sought that will breach the framework of the play. Simultaneously, the material must have documentary immediacy. And just as it must no longer remain a fiction, just as the main figure must no longer have a self-sufficient individual character, so too, the public is not to be appealed to in its esthetic capacity. It is to follow the play as contemporaries, as spectators in an imaginary courtroom. Its mood is not to be swayed but defined. It would

[2] This is what distinguishes *The Deputy* so basically from Goethe's *Götz von Berlichingen,* where the tragic dialetic, the polarity of individualized and all-embracing reason, makes intelligible the framework within which autonomous human dignity works out its destiny. Goethe himself formulated the spiritual basis of his first play when he wrote — simultaneously with *Götz* — in his "Speech for a Shakespeare Festival": Shakespeare's plays all turn around the same point "in which the distinctive trait of our ego, the supposed freedom of our will, clashes with the necessary working of the whole" — a formula, which modified, continued to be operative up until Hauptmann's tragedies.

be nonsensical and impossible to do this with a detached semblance of reality.

Subjective feeling and objective reason become identical in Riccardo. They can no longer be reconciled, maintain the balance, and consequently concentrate all interest on the esthetically "beautiful" and the humanly "significant." However, this absolutism, which makes reason and feeling identical, fundamentally transforms the meaning of the dramatic material and form. It robs the representation of the qualities of "distance" and perfection which are imminent in all higher art. In terms of his own understanding as well as our analysis, Hochhuth's play is not tragic but polemical. And this is why it acquires representative significance for the present literary situation.

The appeal to the human heart, to its yearning for absolute truth, for absolute justice and the beauty of feeling reconciled with reason, and because of this, the appeal to the dialectic of individuality and the whole which is bound up with the individual's dignity yet brings into view a transcending objective order—this appeal to the public is found for the last time in Gerhard Hauptmann's tragedies. Rose Bernd's natural exuberance is as much a divine right as the rights on which she tramples in that exuberance. And once again appears the tragic circle which admits no lasting excitement of feeling beyond the play and moving to possible action, which admits not even a moral decision. Sympathy and rational consciousness are in equilibrium because it is known they both are held in balance by dialectically split truth and necessity. This tragic *"nihil contra deum nisi deus ipse"* appears for the last time in Hauptmann. For the last time, too, it is possible for him to link and balance reason and feeling; it is possible for a self-contained form to emerge, externally complete and truly balanced internally. The dramas written in Germany after Hauptmann surrender this balance along with their faith in a rational order.

The truth of individual human right, which Hauptmann easily discovers in the reality of simple, kind people and presents in the inherent conflict with the right of the whole—only relatively more rational—merely needed human understanding, the kindness of the heart, for its legitimation. In Wedekind, Sternheim, Kaiser and the young Brecht, this right of the individual requires an ideology, just as in turn the surrounding order cannot be understood except ideologically. The dialectic of the individual and a hostile whole is no longer derived from an esthetically intelligible human nature, whose unconditionality may issue from a divine reason that also gives credibility and rationality to the whole. The dialectic is now a product of the individual and his rights, and he complements the injustice of the surrounding order. Thus, this order becomes concrete and documentable, and that means—contemporary. The whole art of drama must now increasingly tend to burden esthetic representation with the weight of depicted injustice, the satirically "inverted" world. As a consequence, it demonstrates even more how little the critical individual need trouble himself about the whole subject of criticism. The result is destruction of the balance of subjectivity and objective reason: in the writer's vision, in the dramatic story, and in the effect on the public. The order binding on consciousness no longer has access to the depths of compliant feeling, the feeling of individual autonomy no longer has the clarity of consciousness disciplined by reason. Drama becomes one-sided, striving for witty or spectacular effects; mysticism and art for art's sake spread; the public diminishes to a handful of experts and professional dilettantes.

The appeal to the heart in which the subjective need for happiness dwelt as much as the feeling for justice and injustice, the appeal that allowed the individual to feel his own dignity and first made esthetic means necessary for this self-reliance, this appeal vanished increasingly after Hauptmann's dramas. With it not only human responsibility left the drama, but the possibility of tragic (and comic) effectiveness. What remained was a superman seen through ideological glasses and set upon the pseudo-reality of the stage, whose appearance largely went to serve as an alibi for the grotesque. If one knows nothing of Wedekind's human beast, Sternheim's super-burgher or Kaiser's ego-monomania, one can innocently enough find just diversions of the understanding and wit[3] in their plays, that is, esthetic effects. The deep emotion springing from the integration of all spiritual capacities in the self-reliance on the *"condition humaine,"* still to be found in

[3] It is obvious that I have deliberately used the title of the Gottsched Journal (1741-1745). The pre- and post-classical literary periods correspond to each other in a rather remarkable relationship. The classical synthesis of reason and feeling in both the autonomous personality and its poetic medium appears either not to have been reached yet or to have been again lost. The field is dominated on one hand by a dry utilitarian understanding, and on the other by a "feeling" subservient either to religious dogma or ideology. Of course, post-classical periods preserve the possibility of individually producing anew what was achieved in the past—their people *and* their poets.

Hauptmann's tragedies, occurs less and less. By and large, it is now the ideologically conditioned mind that is at work. This puts an end to the internal perfection and balance of the medium's dramatic form because its source was feeling disciplined by reason. What remains is a predetermined conflict between the hero and his environment, in which both sides lack the necessity of truth. The features defining the picture of German drama after Hauptmann's great naturalistic art are: rarefied conflicts, points of view in a reality already distorted by interpretation, the boredom of everything intellectually relativized, the quickly outdated justifications of the individual whose reason knows no limits, and satirical attacks on the surrounding order that has become concrete and thereby emptied of sense. Now drama seeks to be ideological on one hand, and on the other to provide a satirical demonstration. It is not based on the excitement and, simultaneously, on the restraint of a deep feeling for dignity and the right to individual action. On the contrary, it is based upon the mind's preoccupation, which yearns for concrete, existing problems or causes, or immerses itself in psychological, philosophical, or even theological problems. The weightless fiction of the reality of a higher, instrumental art solidifies into the invented model of genuine reality which is a problem or annoyance to the understanding. The drama becomes a "statement," if not the vehicle of a "thesis." What it flees as a relic and dire reminder of its former faith in meaning is feeling, since it can no longer fulfill the latter's demands—having become skeptical and immoral—for the unity of the true, the good, and the beautiful. It is no longer acquainted with a human dignity that can be represented in pure esthetic form because it is not reconciled with the latter's conditional nature.

As a consequence of this skepticism toward any type of world reason, which was for individual autonomy a postulate of both heart and reason, pathos must vanish completely from post-naturalistic German drama while expressionism—again skeptical toward reason and ideological—calls for a "new pathos." Satire, lashing out at the horrible-philistine society about it, follows the hymn to unlimited man. It, too, is incapable of producing great drama. Only with lyric poetry does expressionism succeed in creating art of stature. It is obvious: a lost belief in a world reason counterposed to the individual cannot be rediscovered through an act of will or an esthetic program. Yet, a symptom of inadequacy is evident in the Expressionistic call for a new pathos. A vague cry for a new faith—still heard—goes up, it alone can reconstitute art. The basis for poetry and literature was felt to have grown too narrow, its reasoning valid only for man's concrete present. A recurring demand is made on surviving poetry that it influence the whole of human existence. (Correspondingly, art too, in the long run, will be unable to orient itself toward human existence in the syncopated Stone Age or kindergarten.) Literature can exclusively satisfy one aspect of the human—feeling, mood, critical understanding, metaphysical impulse—only in the opening or closing stages of periods of great art. Where such a stage is sociologically favored over a longer stretch of time (a not unusual case) the neglected force grows underground and brutally seeks itself to restore an equilibrium that is just as one-sided as art's at that moment, and is inhuman only in other respects. (The iconoclastic fanatics, the Puritan enemies of poetry, anti-Romantic Young Germans, the Nazi and Stalinist persecutions of art—all these movements otherwise so different have one thing in common: in the name of a primitive concept of religious, social, or national human dignity, they condemn the increasingly tortuous practice of art by an ever-contracting elite. And this at a moment when the dreamers and visionaries among the artists are already moving toward them; even individually winning back the integrity of the human as a whole—Grünewald, Milton, Büchner, Brecht. . . .)

Another spiritual phenomenon equally characterizes these periods of crisis when a one-sided practice of art is as little capable of realizing art's nature as the individual is of believing in his own dignity: the polemics of pathos. The yearning for the integration of all human powers, the new concept of human dignity, seek expression in the pathos of polemical literature. Of course, polemical literature at first is no less a headache than the most intellectual art can be. But through its pathos the polemic of Luther, Lessing, or even Karl Kraus represents the whole man. The medium that sets the polemic into motion before the public is certainly not poetry. It lacks the creative freedom to shape a pseudo-reality in which human meaning can be embodied. But to the degree that poetry itself renounced this pseudo-reality and chose to mirror the concrete reality of a concrete human existence in an attitude of struggle, the poetic medium transformed itself via a cold road—unpathetic, ideological, and satirical—into a polemical medium.

What is the medium of the polemics of pathos? It is the cause of justice and truth fallen into crisis through a concrete constellation of concrete reality—fallen into crisis, however, because in the period encountered by the polemic all absolute postulates have either become uncertain or been lost. While art had to become playfully irresponsible, the polemic draws an absolute pathos from suffering and indignation which must immediately move every person's heart. The eternal reason of the heart, namely, the feeling for the true, good, and beautiful that belongs to every human existence, which seems to have perished long ago in the forgetfulness of historical relativism or resignation before the concrete, this feeling is conjured up again in the unbearable burden of exposed suffering—just as the eye reflexively reproduces a complementary color after looking at a bright light. Human consciousness also has its own hygiene. It cannot endure an assault of feeling without a reflex of the spirit. Against unlimited injustice it decrees for itself an absolute duty to justice; in doing so it requires an ethos that can issue only from the movement of the heart and is made objective in conscious demands. The polemic, keeping pace, produces its own distinctive variation of that integration we already know. It is not a question here, as in great drama, of a mutually conditioning balance, but of an integration of the subjective and objective in the absolute. It is not the tranquility of balance, but the tranquility present in the tension of all forces, which finds its analogy in the mystical moment or in every other form of visionary enthusiasm. Just as Luther, when he polemicizes, "feels moved not only in the heart but from head to toe," so in every polemicist the feeling of objective justice in his cause unites with the feeling of subjective power derived from knowledge and exposure. The person draws dignity from self-confidence in his function. And this feeling of new dignity is communicated to the public which takes sides.

But—as said—the medium of poetry cannot be the polemicist's. If the polemic can mobilize all the individual's power, insight, and will, it is only to restore the form of responsible individuality to the person. But it cannot give the text to the objective form of a plot enveloped in an esthetic aura, in which the irrational movement must not seek any concrete outlet—while the public calmly enjoys its own awakened integrity and sensibility unbound by any purpose. What does the text signify, what poetic means remain to the polemicist? His entire effort is inexorably dedicated to open demonstration: a demonstration that draws its pathos only from the absence of ambiguity and, therefore, is concerned to endow the unambiguous with intelligence against the prejudice and conspiracy of silence inimical to it. By its very nature, then, the polemic is drastic. It wants, with all means, especially those of satire, the grotesque and the *reductio ad absurdum,* to display what will unconditionally "stand firm." Everyone, including the dullest and the most hard-boiled, must understand how dear is the defended cause and how infamous its enemies and those who patronize them. But when a polemicist writes works that no longer feel obligated to seek immediate redress, direct the public not to the dignity of the cause but to the dignity of personal decision, the medium immediately begins to approach poetry and, in the main, is logically inclined toward a lyrical form of expression. Many of Luther's chorals fall into this category in contrast to his genuine polemics. Most recently, the work of the distinguished polemicist and lyric poet, Hans Magnus Enzensberger, oscillates between these poles. However, the "Buch des Unmuts" in the *West-östlicher Divan* shows there are great examples of this affinity between polemics and poetry. Thus, too, in the earliest times of prophetic wrath there was a connection between the polemics of pathos and lyric poetry.

As we know, lyric poetry rests on the unique esthetic weight of language and is so independent of a pragmatic continuity of story that it is only a question of linguistic condensation as to whether a polemical content can raise itself above its concrete occasion to the level of an imaginative textual form.

But first and foremost, the language of the polemicist is an instrument of demonstration, not one that mirrors itself and its author. The polemicist is not an artist but a demonstrator. It is almost inevitable—when a dramatic form of demonstration is involved—that he will allow his main character to become a demonstrator too. Hochhuth's Riccardo is quite plainly one. In the most polemical of Brecht's plays, Joan Dark, the saintly Joan of the stockyards, is no less a demonstrator. This play should generally be viewed as the closest existing relation to Hochhuth's *The Deputy*. Joan, too, is a deputy. Joan, too, is involved in a confrontation between religion and suffering. By this measure Hochhuth's play is hardly an accident in our literature and compels us to take this *"scandal de succès"* seriously from a literary point of view. The satirical and socio-critical literature based on contemporary events, toward which present-day criticism is so indulgent, has awakened needs it is no longer capable of satisfying. It is time again for the spirit to consider an absolute, no matter what objective form its demands take. The comparison with Brecht's *Saint Joan* is interesting in still another respect. It reveals that Hochhuth's difficulties had in the main already been confronted by Brecht. This is particularly true, perhaps, for the most striking features of both plays: the avoidance of a tragic solution and the avoidance of naturalistic language. It must be admitted that

Brecht dealt with both points more thoroughly, with greater consciousness. This is why Hochhuth's play is filled with a greater and purer pathos. Brecht, in all consistency, turns his *Saint Joan* into an anti-tragedy. Let us recall that Joan finally has to protest and demonstrate against that tragic resignation which is exploited by the unscrupulous and hypocritical lease-holders of God to further hush up the polemical truth. No-where can it be made clearer that polemical literature lies beyond the traditional rational faith in the tragic structure of the world, and, simultaneously, that its faith in reason grows out of pathos. The hour of the polemic is untragic. The polemicist does not want the movement toward the absolute to pass through tragic limitation. Understanding and limitation do not exist in unequivocal situations. Therefore, no reason exists to demand tragedy from Hochhuth if we do not want to join those who criticize his play. Were Brecht's Joan tragically limited, Mauler and Cridle would have their excuse as well; were Hochhuth's Riccardo a tragic hero, Pius XII would certainly be one too. Nothing remains after outraged anger and absolute humanity. The polemic, therefore, must deny and avoid all tragedy for the sake of its goal, which is to continue to influence men in their real life.

Equally, the different treatment of language in poetry and the polemic is due to the difference in goal and medium. Language becomes a factor of man's limitation in the higher drama. To know people through their speech means to understand them in their tragic dignity. This is why stylization in high drama signifies the elimination of the accidental in every-day language so that every word can attain necessity in the relation of character and reflection on character. Post-classical drama, up until the *Family Selicke,* with its insight into man's limitation, increasingly renounced stylization in favor of *concrete* speech. But stylization as such was abandoned only individually because it remained a postulate of the economy of meaning. We must keep this in mind if we want to understand that polemical drama, concerned with man's unconditional nature, could not admit a naturalistic language based on man's limitation. Hidden in the naturalistic attention to the gestures and interjections of a dull consciousness is *"tout comprendre c'est tout pardonner,"* so loathesome to the moral polemicist. Moralism and naturalism exclude each other basically and irrevocably. A verse speech in which every word has its own esthetic value (just as every classical hero has a human value) is forbidden the polemicist, and all the more so, because every moment of narcissistic speech would allow the movement of meaning borne by the language to drain away.

Both Brecht and Hochhuth find themselves in this situation. Brecht solves his problem with satirical language. By having Mauler and Cridle, whom the play's ending so mercilessly exposes, speak in the accents of high tragedy, he demonstrates the connection between tragedy and language. But while employing this tone satirically, i.e., in the wrong place, he has already substituted "understood" for "understandable" language in the commentaries on the figures that flow from his angry vision. Brecht's choice of language for his minor figures strongly resembles Hochhuth's in *The Deputy*. There is no sign of naturalistic plasticity or motivation to be found in either Snyder or Frau Luckerniddle. They are officials in the exhibited machinery of justice and injustice. How, as human beings, they could reach the point of fulfilling their functions is not considered. It makes no sense, therefore, to provide them with naturalistic speech. It would require elements that would introduce confusion into Brecht's moral picture. Hochhuth prides himself on having dared experiment with rhythmic prose. But what appears most remarkable is that the author sensed a naturalistic language would have been completely contrary and repugnant to his polemical freedom of movement. Not the person, but the tool either of conscience or institutions is to be exhibited. The individual source of individual forms of action must not enter the reflective consciousness. Above all, Hochhuth's stylization leads to a de-subjectivization of the dialogue, if the word may be permitted. The figures have no right to arouse understanding and sympathy for their own particular situation in face of the great pathos of the theme. The monologues at the beginning of the last act take effect all the more powerfully because they are directly contrary to this principle.

This does not mean Hochhuth has not written any dramatically effective speeches. But they are scenic effects, theatrical. They are not the result of an individual human exhaustion, defending itself. Hauptmann and Schnitzler are nowhere in sight. The stereotype of the Cardinal makes him a satirical type, not an individual with his own subjective life. The different dialects no longer concretely show the consciousness of simple people. They want to place the "joviality" bound up with dialect in painful contrast to the horrors around which everything moves. On the whole, therefore, Hochhuth's play is characterized by a language closer to a light social comedy than the author would probably admit. Neatness and superficiality of stylized sociability—but in the service of polemics. It is the language of the thesis play, though no thesis is announced. Still, a "cause" is present, and in order to push it into the light, language is also present.

III

After analyzing the play and defining its literary position, we can turn to the most striking and discussed point of its public career: its effect. The reader will immediately understand that the effect of polemical literature may claim for itself a significance quite different from that of purely poetic statements. We ordinarily distrust widespread influence when it is a question of poetic claims. But we can hardly ignore the fact that the widespread effect of *The Deputy* is not poetic and not even that of a "hit." Neither the one nor the other expands its audience through discussion, but steals its way into favor on soft shoes quite unlike the polemic. Quarrels about taste are short-lived, those about a "cause," on the other hand, go on forever. And while with poetry the extent of its effect is irrelevant, with the polemic—precisely for the sake of the cause—it is a sign of its quality. Certainly only a small stratum has read or seen the play while the broadest circles discuss it from mere hearsay. But in no sense does this widespread effect run contrary to the intentions of polemical writing as long as the continuing discussion follows the tracks laid down by Hochhuth's text. We repeatedly saw that the polemicist is most profoundly concerned first with his cause and then with the medium of his text. Hochhuth has demonstrated the primacy of his theme with his public appearances in a number of round-table discussions. In this respect, too, he follows the tradition of polemical literature. Luther often avowed his "little book" could readily disappear if the cause of "pure doctrine" had triumphed. Lessing expressly wrote: "I hope to see the time when people will scarcely remember that a Lange translated Horace. My criticism, too, will be forgotten and that is just what I wish." Of course, there is no question that both Brecht and Hochhuth look upon their works as authors and poets. But the polemical nature of both their plays acquires so great an impetus that its effect negates the authors' self-interpretation. They are plays of transition, of an interim literary period. Brecht added to the form of his mature drama a scarcely veiled but surreptitiously introduced tragic view, with its new twofold belief in the individual and the lawfulness of the whole. What develops from Hochhuth's beginning is a question of spiritual energy in which the pathos of the heart must undergo a metamorphosis. And it is in no sense certain that Hochhuth will again succeed, as Brecht succeeded, in extracting from the drama as a literary species that inner form which does not remain a mere means to an end, or a platform, or a figurative vessel of opinion, but becomes a symbol for the whole of the human.

At the start of his career Hochhuth already has the glory of having shown literature the way out of naturalistic irresponsibility and esthetic narrow-mindedness into a realm of spiritual humanity, of spiritual demands that lie beyond all ideological relativity because they become immediately intelligible. It was an unpretentious reader's letter, with its allusion to one of Albert Camus' remarks that provided the appropriate motto for Hochhuth's play, the dedication now printed at the beginning of the book. The play actually appeals to all those who want to represent the spirit, and to whom, therefore, the absolute demand of the spirit (once more understood as *spiritus, pneuma,* not just mind) need not be alien. The overwhelmingly positive reception of the play is not at all self-evident and almost a small miracle in a country where from Nietzsche's and Ibsen's time the demand of the ideal [4] was forbidden and *sacro egoismo* took on ever more vulgar and nasty forms. Hochhuth, on the contrary, postulates that there are principles higher than the interests of the individual and society. A fundamental axiom of all civilized morality prevails anew. And if civilized morality is something different from a work of poetry, still, a road leads from human dignity to the dignity of art that is far more promising than all philosophy of the machine age.

[4] The motto in Ibsen's *The Wild Duck.*

7 | And of Journalists, Social Scientists, Historians

CARL AMERY

The Harassed Pope

In quick succession, two plays about popes have appeared on German stages: Reinhard Raffalt's *The Successor* and Rolf Hochhuth's *The Deputy*. Even the plays' titles seem to have been attuned to one another—which, of course, was not the case. What is this duplication all about? Is it sheer chance resulting from a shortage of ideas? That seems hardly likely or at least hardly likely to be the only reason. *The Successor* and *The Deputy* are two jagged peaks of a single large iceberg which floats along beneath our cultural-political water line. And this iceberg, which in the future may become rather dangerous, merits a little thought.

Let me start with a negative observation: the iceberg has relatively little to do with current theological discussion. In fact, almost nothing to do with that. Until around 1918 virtually the only emotional points of reference that existed for German Catholics were their own rights and the pope in Rome; while Catholic theology, since the Twenties at the latest, has been busy creating other points of reference. The old discussion on the nature and scope of the primacy of the Papal See, which reached its climax in 1870, has yielded to other concerns.

But—and here we are coming closer to our iceberg—religious problems, in the theological areas in which they are

---

Mr. Amery, author of *Die Kapitulation, oder deutscher Katholozismus heute,* wrote this article for *Süddeutsche Zeitung,* Munich, March 2-3, 1963 issue; translation by Richard and Clara Winston.

engendered, are in any case rarely felt to be urgent problems of cultural politics; as an iceberg is not dangerous as long as it is connected with the great central polar icecap. Just as there are submerged cultural values, so also there are emotional floes from other eras of theology drifting about in our cultural landscape—submerged religious values, if you will. Literary themes and subjects which yesterday engaged the attention of the greatest spirits trickle downward in two to three generations, gradually pass, by way of lending-library readers and the film-makers, into decay and disrepute, and ultimately can no longer be used except in parody. Granted, theology and discussion of internal church problems are not subject to fads to quite such an extent; but it may nevertheless be observed that subjects which would agitate an editor of the *Neue Bildpost* [an illustrated mass-circulation magazine] are unlikely even to appear in magazines such as *Hochland* or *Stimmen der Zeit* [Catholic periodicals].

The ecclesiastical topics which stir big winds and big waves among the larger public are not today's but yesterday's topics. Today's ecclesiastical topics are largely still connected to their central theological "icecap," that is, they represent no danger to general cultural commerce on the seas of secular society. The consequence is that all the "church problems" that bob to the surface and are discussed in the general flurry will usually strike the Catholic (or Protestant) "insider" as quite old-fashioned—in spite of which the churches themselves will register their own favorable or unfavorable reactions to the fray. Our two papal plays are cases in point.

It would be idle to attempt to compare them. Raffalt's play is written with considerably more knowledge of the papacy, and is dramaturgically more skillful. Hochhuth's play is several literary notches higher, and (to my feeling) several Christian notches higher as well. But let us leave aside literary blame or praise; let us deal with both plays to the extent that they are evidence for the existence of the above-mentioned iceberg, that is, evidence for a specific cultural-political situation in which we now find ourselves.

On the basis of my negative review of *The Successor*, I recently received an invitation to discuss the play with young Catholics. That was not easy. Finally I was able to formulate the principle which I felt struck at the heart of the matter: No dramatic situation is really dramatic unless it is a boundary situation. The choice of a good pope (and that is certainly the question involved in the choice of Raffalt's Cardinal Bologna) is therefore not a real dramatic problem. Far more exciting would be the choice of a bad or mediocre pope—and a Catholic writer's dramatic confrontation with this theme.

Well, this Catholic writer has not come forth. Instead we have Hochhuth. His *The Deputy* starts at precisely this point. He postulates that Pius XII was a mediocrity, if not a bad Pope; he charges him with having forborne to take possible and practical steps for the rescue of Europe's Jews—and offsets this unforgivable passivity with an example of a truly Christian Catholic. In doing so, he is fair enough to deputize a priest to die in Auschwitz (although one never quite escapes the feeling that inwardly Father Fontana has only come on a visit to the crematorium).

Unfortunately, Hochhuth is no Catholic, and that becomes evident. A Catholic might not have ventured to attack the papacy itself; but he would have exposed the guilt of church bureaucrats more boldly and cruelly than the Protestant author. For the rest, Hochhuth deals with the same thematic material that fascinated Reinhold Schneider for a lifetime: the dilemma between power and grace. Schneider chose Innocent II and Celestine V as examples: popes who had considerably more power at their disposal, at least potentially, than Pius XII. But Pacelli's power was the power of a tremendous moral "credit," as Hochhuth explicitly stresses; and the charge he hurls against him is that he did not invest this credit for the sake of the Jews.

I really cannot regard this proposition as wicked and anti-Catholic. Hochhuth dealt seriously and thoroughly with the documents; I agree with the reviewer of the *Süddeutsche Zeitung* who made the point in her discussion of the book that the documentary section is often more exciting than the play itself. But as long as the documents do not flatly contradict him, a historical dramatist has the right to represent his characters in line with his thesis. Why may or might a pope not be such a character? Why should a Christian dramatist not be allowed to write a tragedy about Gregory XVI and Lammenais, about Celestine V or Julius II, in which a pope comes off badly or is judged unfavorably? Is there an interlude during which popes are protected from attack, as a writer's works are protected by copyright from infringement?

Ridiculous as that sounds, it does exist, *hic et nunc* in our particular cultural-political situation. The furious outcry against Hochhuth has its reasons, and we shall now have to discuss these in somewhat greater detail.

The "term of copyright" begins around 1870, at the latest around 1900. That is no accident. The following four factors have contributed to establishing it: 1) the disintegration of the pope's secular rule; 2) the proclamation in 1870 of the dogma of infallibility; 3) the growing religious indifference and secularization of public life; and 4) the fact that the popes from Leo XIII to Pius XI were men of unusual stature.

The most important of these four facts is the growing secularization of public life. In a self-assured Christian world —let us say, the world of the sixteenth century—the dogma of infallibility would have been discussed far more hotly than it was in 1870; but everyone would have realized quite clearly that it had nothing to do with the person of the pope reigning at any given time. Only in a world increasingly indifferent and blind to the real questions of Christianity, increasingly ignorant even of its vocabulary, could there arise the disagreeable possibility of building up the popes not as holders of the office, but as celebrities. (I beg forgiveness for this press-agent's word—but it describes the situation only too exactly.) To such men, the argument more or less went, the vessel of St. Peter (and consequently the wielding of the instrument of infallibility) can be entrusted without anxiety.

Of course this argument is false, and can lead to the most unfortunate consequences. Infallibility, in the sense of the dogma, cannot have anything to do with human qualifications; that was and is patent to anyone capable of clear thinking on theological matters. But nevertheless, as secularization took its fateful course, the "building up" of great papal personalities went merrily on. Each pope in turn was provided with a tremendous "moral" credit, a credit which (we repeat), he would never have needed in a preponderantly Christian world. This papal press-agentry has been directed at the millions upon millions of the indifferent—in order to bind them to their faith, while within the church it has served to strengthen peripheral feelings of personal loyalty toward the reigning head of the church.

In no case, however, did this outwardly directed propaganda, meant to affect surface emotions and to reach the masses on the fringes of the church, attain such proportions and such intensity as in the time of Pius XII.

Let us admit it: Today it is virtually impossible for a Catholic who does not live in Rome to obtain any personal ideas of his Pope. He must depend for his picture on the communications work of those intermediaries whom Hochhuth maliciously calls "publicists." Only by *discretio*—that power to distinguish among minds, which has been praised as a gift of the Holy Spirit—can one discover the person of the Pope behind the almost invariably vulgar and banal phrases of the publicists. (John XXIII seems to have more talent than his predecessor for making this person visible.) It is nowadays of prime importance whether these intermediaries are interpreters or pure advertisers; whether, in other words, an "image" of the reigning Pope is projected or his actual person and personality are brought forth. Here, in this potential discrepancy between the image and the real person lies the problem of Hochhuth's play for Catholics—and not so much in the charge actually pronounced. Hochhuth is compelling us to examine more closely and to revise a projected publicity image of the deceased Pope. But over and beyond that (whether Hochhuth's accusation is correct or not), his play raises the question of whether it would not be better to put aside the propaganda methods of the ad writers and to return to real, essential emotions about the papacy too.

But if we did that, we would shake up the whole system. In our secularized western world of today, the system, of which the "moral," i.e. personalistic exaltation of the Pope is only a small part, is based upon lip-service to "religion" by those who are indifferent to it; that is, upon the operation of a shamanistic concession by the professional "servants of religion." The modern unbeliever, the subject of so much lament, is extremely generous in making possible the administration of this concession. He is much farther from being a Christian than his forefather who read Haeckel and regarded himself as a militant atheist. He is so far from having any feeling at all for divine presence that he has officially recorded his incapacity to concern himself with it. He confesses *e silentio* that it would be utterly pointless to discuss ultimate questions with him. He lacks both the passionate Greek delight in the pursuit of speculative theological truth and the Franciscan-Protestant bent for "living religion." What he desires and what he approves is a neat and competent administration of divine matters by the franchised shamans. Once this aspect of the divine is taken care of, he regards everything as fairly equal in worth: the Trinity and the Pope, the defense of the West and of personal property. Our western average citizen (who of course is never found in the pure state) leaves all that to the appropriate authorities.

This situation has been recognized and openly discussed by clear-sighted men of all churches. Below a certain academic level, however, it has not yet been converted into the hard cash of action, because the price is determined not by the thing itself, but by the demands of the indifferent. To my mind it is idle to attempt to change this state of affairs by setting up such organizations as the Humanistic Union.

Those militants who have gathered around Dr. Szczesny do not, after all, want to help the man who is indifferent to religion — on the contrary. They want to compel him to determine his own position in the world of divine things (or against divine things, if need be). But that is the last thing the indifferent man wants to do. His own central interests are to be found in entirely different fields—whose boundaries may have been drawn by Adam Smith or by Karl Marx, as the case may be. That this situation may in the long run be fatal to the church also, likewise does not interest him. What he demands are "religious services"—and he demands them at those "frontier posts" of his life which are still not governable by economics and civilization: at birth, marriage and death. It is most significant that public rebellions against "clericalism," at least in Germany, are usually sparked by inadequacies of the churches in such matters: by refusals of church burial, say, or a church marriage. Ironically enough, therefore, "clericalism" is fairly well tolerated in the very places where it seems a dubious matter to perceptive Christians, and is reviled in the very places where fundamentals of Christian life are actually at stake. (This is not to say that a good many aspects of canon law may not well stand in need of change.)

The personalistic and "moral" upward revaluation of the papacy fits well into this pattern. Here at any rate, the propagandists would have it, is the figure to whom we can safely entrust our needs with regard to divinity, or rather, who will act as deputy for the divine part of our existence. It would be fruitless and senseless to attempt to explain to the indifferent the real basis of this doctrine; equally fruitless and senseless as to explain the Ninth Symphony to a deaf man. The statement has to be made on a "human," that is to say, in the final analysis on an irreligious basis.

Hochhuth's play strikes directly at this sore spot in the publicistic argument. It shows us that this man, the man in white, who is so photogenic and telegenic, is not in every case the ideal personal deputy for our distresses, needs and responsibilities. All those officials, therefore, whose function it is to keep the indifferent (on whom the concession ultimately depends) convinced of the qualifications of the concessionaires—must feel cut to the quick. And they have reacted accordingly.

With that, we return to *The Successor*. If we stay within the complex of problems we have outlined, *The Successor* represents the ideal counterpoise to *The Deputy*. On the broadest possible wave band, it has broadcast the preeminent qualifications of the Roman Catholic Church to serve as shamanistic administrator of our requirements in the field of divinity. The play proves, or is intended to prove, that there's something to Rome. I chose this vague expression deliberately; for it seems to me that *The Successor* does not actually convey more than that. There's something to it for the lover of art (verse, Michelangelo's Last Judgment, etc.), for the timelessly noble man, for the modern man (the Cardinals' debates, the role of Reverend Scott). It proves, as Catholics have repeatedly pointed out to me, that the church is so very human. And (I don't know whether anyone has noticed this), in the final scene of *The Successor* there is imposed upon the Pope precisely the burden and precisely the part that Dostoevsky's Grand Inquisitor claims for his "church": the part and the burden of representing Christ against Antichrist, that is, against the possibility that the anti-divine will burst from the unfamiliar numinous sphere into history.

In addition, the new Pope, Cardinal Bologna, must be an altogether likable man. Even the candidates whom he replaces were certainly no Borgias or incompetents—at most we might predict that Cardinal Palermo would reign in a somewhat reactionary manner. But these rivals are eliminated by the direct intervention of the Holy Spirit, namely, by the death and dying speech of the Cardinal of Toledo before the assembled College of Cardinals. Dramatically speaking, this death and this speech are a trick. They communicate to the audience the secure feeling that here in the administrative realm of the divine things always take place, and always will, which ultimately guarantee the moral and human qualifications of the successor to the throne of Peter. All of us, believers and unbelievers, actually know better; we have all heard of Alexander VI. But as I have said, those were embarrassing incidents which took place in times that are in the public domain, to which the historical copyright does not apply.

Comparison of these two plays about popes has thus, in the final analysis, brought to light a paradoxical situation: that the play by Hochhuth, the Protestant, does much more to help Catholics understand the problems of their own church than Raffalt's *The Successor*. But as things are here and now, Hochhuth's play is being attacked, must necessarily be attacked. It must be attacked because it radically questions an axiom of our present religio-cultural situation, the axiom of shamanic authority. Yet we Christians (no matter whether we are Catholics or Protestants) must strenuously combat this very axiom, if we do not want to end up with a church fashioned on the ideas of Dostoevsky's Grand Inquisitor.

Thus the fronts are reversed in the battle that is being waged in Germany. Granted, Hochhuth has undertaken a little too much. For he not only attacks the attitude of the Pope on the Jewish question; he also hints at shady transactions with Hungarian railroad securities; he asserts that the Society of Jesus sold Spanish mercury to Stalin in the midst of the war—and similar compliments. These points have naturally also been noted and forcibly "repudiated" (although, to be sure, we see no signs of unequivocal counter-documentation). But only the attack upon the Pope himself has been felt to be crucial.

"Nothing is taboo any more!" the *Neue Bildpost* moans. Well, the fact is that nothing has been taboo any more since Christ walked upon this earth and Paul wrote his epistles (there should be no room for the concept of taboo among Christians!). But above all, one taboo should and must be violated: the taboo that the church is, as it were, automatically qualified and deputized to administer the realm of divine matters.

Yet even the intrepid taboo violators are scarcely convinced of that, as may be seen from all the fuss over the Piscator production. Piscator's vigorous cutting of the play was a technical necessity. But that in the final sentence (". . . the last prisoners in Auschwitz were freed by Russian soldiers") he chose to cut the Russians was not a matter of necessity. Yet I regard those three words, "by Russian soldiers," as the most important in the play—in terms of Hochhuth's intentions also. They confront us, Catholic and non-Catholic Christians alike, with the inescapable fact that the most frightful form of inhumanity for many thousands of years was stopped not by Christians, but by the "red hordes." By those very hordes whose existence then and now serves all too many Christians as grounds for the most profoundly un-Christian thoughts and actions imaginable. May we ask Piscator whether these three words cannot be restored to their rightful place?

We have rowed around the iceberg, so to speak. Its true dimensions cannot yet be measured. Above all we have not been able to go into a highly important question of detail: the question of the actual limits of the Pope's, or as the case may be the Church's, credit in a world indifferent to religion. Hochhuth's appraisal of this credit is very high, astonishingly so. I am afraid he is deceiving himself. As I have said, what the world primarily wants is religious *services*. It does not want moral teachings. It does not want to be bothered with a reality which it does not recognize as such. It is quite possible that the Pope's voice—in that unique situation, in the retreat stage of Hitler's war, when Hitler's men were caught in the dilemma between opportunism and murder on principle—that the Pope's voice would have sufficed to save the lives of several hundreds of thousands of people. But let us be clear about one thing: the best advertising, the hardest sell, is useless when nobody is any longer interested in the product. In other words, if the church adopted the practice of consistently drawing on its credit in all questions that affect the world, the credit would be exhausted fairly quickly. It is my firm conviction that, for example, in 1933 the majority of German Catholics would not have obeyed had the German bishops insisted on their rejection of Nazism. The German Catholic milieu was ripe for capitulation, and nothing, literally nothing, not even the voice of the bishops and the voice of Rome, would have prevented this capitulation.

At any time the voice of the church is decisive only for a minority. This number grows steadily smaller the more resolutely the church turns against its profane vital interests. In the conflict between principle and self-interest, self-interest will always win. Rome's wisdom in the course of the centuries has consisted in no small part of never forgetting this fact. But—says Hochhuth and so must we all say if we think seriously about it—there may come times and situations in which a clear choice must be made between principle and self-interest. And then the chaff is separated from the wheat. Anyone who resists this separation, and moreover resists it in the alleged interests of the church, is fighting on the wrong front.

ARTHUR C. COCHRANE

Pius XII: A Symbol

Unless the symbolic character of the play is recognized, not only will its salutary message for all men everywhere, and

---

Author of *The Church's Confession Under Hitler,* Mr. Cochrane is visiting professor of systematic theology at Yale Divinity School. The article is reprinted with permission from *Christianity and Crisis, A Christian Journal of Opinion,* March 30, 1964.

especially for the Church of Jesus Christ, be woefully misconstrued, but — quite unintentionally — it will have the effect of impairing good relations between Catholics and Jews and between Catholics and Protestants. The symbolism of the play, if rightly grasped, could contribute to that solid foundation upon which genuine ecumenical relations can be built.

If the symbol of the "deputy" is not also applied to the whole Christian Church as the vicar of Christ, as the ambassador for Christ to whom the message of reconciliation has been entrusted, and if the guilt imputed to Pius XII is not recognized and confessed as the guilt of Christendom toward the Jews — not only in Germany during 1933-45 but in every age and in every country since 72 A.D. — then *The Deputy* will be seen and heard in vain. Then it can only give rise to bitter accusations and counter-accusations, self-righteous protestations of innocence and mutual recrimination.

No church, especially in our age, can expect to be taken seriously as the "representative" of God on earth unless she acknowledges her solidarity with the sin of the world and puts her hope in the forgiveness of *her* sins. And how can the Church ever hope to be reconciled with Israel without confessing her transgressions against God's chosen people?

Indeed, what is at stake here is the very possibility of faith in the face of man's frightful inhumanity and the Church's indifference. The last scene of the play is entitled "Auschwitz, or Where Are You, God?" Realizing that the neutrality of the Vatican is bound to continue, young Father Fontana decides to become a "real substitute" and joins a group of Roman Jews who are arrested under the windows of the papal palace and are carried off to the gas chambers of Auschwitz. There, as he watches Jewish men, women and children being "led as sheep to the slaughter," a cynical Nazi doctor taunts him: "Now, Father, after all that you have seen, do you still believe in God?" Riccardo Fontana replies: "I am in a narrow room. I am suffocating . . . and no one cares. O God, help me! Help me!"

For Protestants *The Deputy* is a challenge to re-examine the record of *their* sins of omission. Perhaps in the light of the actual aid that the Pope rendered the Jews — which Hochhuth fully acknowledges in his play — and in the light of the murder of 3,000 Catholic priests by the Nazis, Protestants will be less inclined to cast stones in the direction of Rome.

When the Council of the Evangelical Church in Germany welcomed representatives of the World Council of Churches to its session in October 1945, it issued the now famous Stuttgart Declaration. It read in part:

> We are all the more thankful for this visit in that we are not only conscious of oneness with our nation in a great community of suffering, but also in a solidarity of guilt. With great pain we say: Unending suffering has been brought by us to many peoples and countries. That which we have often witnessed to our congregations we now proclaim in the name of the whole Church: We have in fact fought for long years in the name of Jesus Christ against the spirit which found its terrible expression in National Socialist government by force; but we accuse ourselves that we did not witness more courageously, pray more faithfully, believe more joyously, love more ardently.

It should be remembered that this Stuttgart Declaration of guilt was signed by men who had done more than others in resisting Nazism: Asmussen, Niemöller, Niesel, Lilje, Heinemann and others. Yet they were first to acknowledge that their own witness and that of the Evangelical Church with respect to the plight of the Jews was lamentably deficient.

Whether one regards a theory of the superiority of the "Aryan" race or anti-Semitism as the basic principle of National Socialism, the fact remains that from the very beginning the Nazis looked upon the Jews not merely as an inferior race but as the *Gegenrasse* (misbegotten race) that had to be exterminated. In Hitler's *Mein Kampf* and in all the party literature the Jews were singled out for attack. Thus the Church can in no sense plead ignorance.

Yet few people, in Germany or elsewhere in Europe, took Hitler's program seriously. When it began to be implemented after Hitler's accession to power, the Church repeatedly protested against the application of the Aryan paragraph of the party program within the Church. *But never did the German Evangelical Church make a public and explicit protest against the treatment of Jews outside the Church by the Nazi Government.*

The Church's silence was not broken until June 4, 1936, when the Provisional Board and Council of the Confessing Church sent a lengthy memorandum to Hitler. It not only called attention to the pagan character of the Nazi State but also condemned anti-Semitism, racialism, concentration camps, secret police methods and the perversion of justice in the courts. But even this otherwise excellent and courageous document failed to speak specifically of the persecution of the Jews.

Moreover, the ten brave men who, without any security whatever, signed the memorandum (among whom were Asmussen, Niemöller and the layman von Thadden-Trieglaff) had to put up with being forsaken, disavowed and maligned by many of their fellow church leaders. The Lutheran Council dissociated itself from the action of the Board, and the churches in Hanover and Württemberg ignored it.

In his book *Der Nationalsozialismus. Dokumente 1933-45* Walter Hofer has distinguished four stages in the development of the severity of the Jewish persecutions: 1933-35 when isolated measures were taken against the Jews on the basis of emergency orders and the "enabling law"; 1935-38, the period of the Nürnberg laws and the decrees based on them; 1938-41 the pogroms and the first mass deportations to the Polish camps; 1941-45 mass exterminations by gas chambers and shootings.

During the first two periods Jews were excluded from public office, from the arts and from schools and universities. Jewish shops were forced to carry a sign: "This is a Jewish store." There is no record of the Church having protested against this frightful discrimination, nor is there any record of the Church having publicly denounced the pogrom of November 9-10, 1938 when hundreds of Jewish stores, houses, schools and 250 synagogues were burned to the ground, and thousands of Jews were arrested and beaten, and scores killed. Of course, individual Christians, notably Helmut Gollwitzer and Heinrich Grüber, raised their voices in protest and came to the succor of the Jews. But the Church, Christ's "deputy," was silent while there was still time to prevent the mass murders that followed in the later stages of persecution.

Particularly depressing is the fact that as late as May 31, 1939 leading bishops of the Lutheran Church, among them Bishops Marahrens, Wurm and Meiser, actually supported Hitler's policy. On that date a conference of church leaders sent a message to the Reich Minister for Church Affairs that stated: "In the realm of faith there is a sharp opposition between the message of Jesus Christ and his apostles and the Jewish religion. . . . In the realm of our national life a serious and responsible racial politics is necessary for the preservation of the purity of our people (*Volk*)."

Prior to this the Erlangen Theological Faculty issued a statement signed by such leading theologians as Paul Althaus and Werner Elert. It read in part: "In the struggle for the renewal of our people the new State excludes men of Jewish or half-Jewish origin from leading offices. *The Church has to acknowledge the basic right of the State to take such legislative measures*" (italics added).

What about the attitude of the peoples outside Germany? As early as December 27, 1935 Sir James G. McDonald, in his letter resigning as the League of Nations' High Commissioner for Refugees Coming from Germany, called attention to the enormity of the problem and insisted that "the efforts of the private organizations and of any League organizations for refugees can only mitigate a problem of growing gravity and complexity." He concluded with these words:

> When domestic policies threaten the demoralization and exile of hundreds of thousands of human beings, considerations of diplomatic correctness must yield to those of common humanity. I should be recreant if I did not call attention to the actual situation and plead that world opinion, acting through the League and its member states and other countries, move to avert the existing and impending tragedies.

In spite of a wave of protests by individuals and religious groups, Sir James' plea fell for the most part on deaf ears. Allied governments continued to maintain friendly diplomatic relations with Germany and to look upon Hitler's policy toward the Jews as a German domestic affair.

Only a relatively small handful of Jewish refugees was permitted into Western countries. The British Government's White Paper of May 17, 1939 limited and eventually stopped Jewish immigration into Palestine. The S.S. "Strumma," with 769 Jewish passengers aboard, sank at sea after having been refused entry into Palestine and into a Turkish port. Rabbi Abraham Feinberg of Toronto complained bitterly and truthfully: "The immigration bars of Canada admitted such a tiny trickle of Jewish refugees that 1941 saw a smaller proportion of Jewish Canadians than 1931."

One poignant illustration of the desperate situation is found in *Report on Survey — United Service for New Americans:*

> In the Spring of 1939, the desperate plight of the Jewish refugee was dramatized for the world by the odyssey of the S.S. "St. Louis." Its cargo of 900 men, women and children in flight from the Nazis had obtained Cuban visas and had set sail from Hamburg for Havana. The "St. Louis" made port, but the Cuban government canceled all visas and turned away the 900. In quest of asylum, the "St.

Louis" sailed on. From country to country it sailed, its entry refused at port after port. Desperation aboard mounted. Finally, the Joint Distribution Committee (then engaged in a valiant rescue operation in Europe) persuaded the governments of Belgium, France, Great Britain and the Netherlands each to accept a portion of the "St. Louis'" cargo of 900. Subsequently, many of them were deported back to Germany and killed. They could have been saved by asylum in the West. (p. 6)

Yes, Pope Pius is a symbol. He symbolizes the truth that "the way for evil to triumph is for good men to keep silent." To accuse him is to accuse ourselves. Pius XII was not only God's "deputy": he is our "representative" — the representative of our inhumanity!

DESMOND FISHER

The Dilemma of Pope Pius XII

Rolf Hochhuth's *The Representative* comes to London under the auspices of a company which has earned the respect and gratitude of British theatregoers. It comes preceded by much favourable criticism for its Berlin production and much censure for its treatment of Pope Pius XII.

It is right that Christians—and men of all religions and none—should be made to examine their consciences about the Nazi massacre of the Jews, surely the worst crime man has ever committed against his fellow-man. To some degree, the blame falls on us all for our sins of action or inaction.

For Hochhuth, the sole villain is Pius. His thesis is that the Pope had it in his power to stop Hitler—by publicly condemning the "final solution" policy of exterminating the

---

Mr. Fisher is editor of the *Catholic Herald*, London, where this article originally appeared on May 7, 1963.

Jews—and that, for the most unworthy of motives, he chose to remain silent.

Hochhuth depicts Pius as a vain, greedy and unprincipled man who wanted Hitler to win the war in order to halt Bolshevism, who did nothing to stop the hostilities because he was profiteering from them and who harboured the conceit that eventually, if he remained neutral, he would be called on to mediate.

The Pope of *The Representative* is more than a *dramatis persona.* He is treated as an historical figure, fact and fiction, real and imaginary people being skilfully interwoven so that the audience does not know where history ends and imagination takes over.

Thus the play presents an historico-moral judgment and the Catholic objection to it is based on the ground that if Hochhuth presents his thesis in the form of history, it must be judged by the criteria applied to history. By this standard, they argue, Hochhuth cannot support his case.

Was Pope Pius silent? The first encyclical of his reign, *Summi Pontificatus,* was a condemnation of Nazi totalitarianism and racism. Then, and on many subsequent occasions, he condemned Nazi policies and called the persecution of the Jews to the attention of the world's conscience.

Using the word *stirps* (race) to identify the Jews, he pleaded, as in his Christmas 1942 speech to the Cardinals, for "the hundreds of thousands who, personally without guilt, sometimes only because of their nationality or descent, are condemned to death or exposed to progressive misery."

It is true that he avoided specific condemnations, speaking, as he customarily did, in general terms. But his meaning was quite clear and if Hitler and the Nazis did not heed his words it was not because they did not understand their significance. The argument that world leaders listen to the Pope and obey does not survive the most cursory historical examination.

Local representations, made through Papal Nuncios and Bishops, did sometimes succeed in helping the Jews. But these were cases where, because of local conditions, orders from Berlin might be ignored or circumvented. In Berlin itself repeated protests were fruitless; in Holland a protest against the deportation of Jews was immediately followed by the rounding up and extermination of all Catholic Jews, including Edith Stein. And in Poland, Cardinal Sapieha repeatedly pleaded with the Pope to stop protesting as it only made things worse for his people.

Why didn't Pius break the Concordat with Germany? Because a Concordat is not a friendship pact. It is an arrangement, in times of Church-State tension, designed to protect the Church's basic interests and give it a *locus standi* for negotiations with the Government. To have broken it would only have roused Hitler to further fury against the Jews and probably against the Catholics as well.

Could Pius have appealed over Hitler's head to German Catholics?

In the first place, the mechanism of ruthless political control would have prevented the dissemination of his message. Even if it did get through, would Germans, fighting for their lives, have heeded it? And would it not have, in German eyes, put the Pope squarely in the Allied camp?

Was Pope Pius the cold, calculating diplomat Hochhuth depicts, lacking humanity and pastoral feelings, ready to sacrifice millions of people for the sake of fame, money or to save the world from Bolshevism?

He did, indeed, give the appearance of being withdrawn, ascetic, ill-at-ease in company. But those who knew him—among them Pope Paul VI, Sir D'Arcy Osborne, former British Minister to the Holy See, and others—have effectively refuted this picture. The real Pius was a very human man, sensitive, conscientious, anxious above all to act in the way which would do the most good.

This is the key to his decision not to make a public protest against Hitler. Hochhuth argues that such a denunciation would have stopped Hitler. In the view of such people as the Jewish historian, Leon Poliakov, of Baron von Weizsäcker, the German Ambassador to the Holy See during the German occupation of Italy, and other key witnesses, the effect would have merely been to drive Hitler to worse excesses.

Pope Pius himself recognized this. In his correspondence with Bishop Preysing of Berlin, he said that he had restricted his pronouncements against Nazism *ad maiora mala vitanda*—"to avoid greater evils."

Speaking to his Cardinals on June 2, 1943, he declared: "Every word spoken by us with this end (to help the Jews) in view to the competent authorities and every reference in public by us have had to be most seriously pondered and weighed in the interests of those who were suffering in order not to render, unwittingly, their situation more grave and unbearable." Further on, he spoke of finding himself "sometimes before doors which no key could open."

"Doors which no key could open." This phrase explains the nature of the great dilemma in which Pope Pius was placed. On one hand, he was filled with horror and sorrow at the persecution which so many millions were suffering. His most ardent wish was to do what he could to alleviate or stop it.

On the other hand, he had to decide for himself, for the agonising decision was his alone, whether public condemnation of the Nazi atrocities was more likely to open the doors which he sought to open or whether the means he had been adopting were not the best ones. They had kept the door slightly ajar; they were doing some little good; was it wise to risk having the door slammed altogether and ruining the good that was being achieved?

Could Pope Pius have been wrong in his decision to keep silent?

Catholics do not hold that Popes are infallible in matters like this and many eminent people, including some Catholics, believe he was wrong. It is possible that a public protest would have forced Hitler to modify the persecution. And even if it did no positive good, was it not what the world expected of the Pope, the head of Christendom?

This is legitimate criticism though the evidence is against the judgment on which it is based. But this is as far as legitimate criticism can be pushed. It faults Pius XII's judgment, which is a matter of opinion, but it does not question his honesty in arriving at a judgment.

In presenting his case, Hochhuth has contravened an elementary principle of justice—that a man is innocent until he is proved guilty. He has put Pius XII in the dock and condemned him without being able to put forward any real evidence, which would show that the charges were either baseless or unprovable. As a prosecutor, the onus of proof is on Hochhuth. He has not discharged it.

It is true that a play presented on the stage is not a trial in a court of law. But the dramatic impact of *The Representative* is likely to be so great that large audiences will, inevitably, be left with a false picture of the "culprit" unless the charges and the evidence for and against them are put in their proper perspective. Insofar as Hochhuth's attack on Pius faults the Pope's judgment, it can be refuted with evidence of at least equal weight, some of it from experts with first-hand knowledge of conditions at the time. And where Hochhuth makes personal attacks on the Pope and specifically attributes to him cowardice, avarice and total insensitivity, he is making a subjective judgment which is not alone unsupported by evidence but which, in fact, contradicts all the available evidence.

Catholics will find Hochhuth's thesis distasteful, unseemly and contemptible. But their rejection of it is based on the fact that, as well as this, it is *wrong*.

FRIEDRICH HEER

The Need for Confession

No play since the end of World War II has scored such a direct hit as Rolf Hochhuth's *The Deputy*. Catholics, Protestants, Jews and "neutrals" have vociferated against the play and its staging. Catholics, Protestants, Jews and "neutrals" have also supported it. But the loudest and most violent protests have come from Catholics, including Catholic journalists, who have neither read nor seen the play but who are mesmerized and shocked by its theme. The play, they feel, is a monstrous insult to the Holy Father and to our Mother, the Church; anti-Christ has stepped before the footlights!

But Hochhuth's play, which dares to violate some of the most cherished taboos, is neither anti-Christian nor anti-Catholic. Hochhuth, a young German Protestant, made an exhaustive study of the question, not least in Rome, where he was advised by an elderly and experienced German-speaking bishop. Moreover, *The Deputy* is dedicated to the memory of two Catholic priests: Father Maximilian Kolbe, prisoner No. 16670 at Auschwitz, and Father Bernhard Lichtenberg, provost of St. Hedwig's cathedral in Berlin—two courageous opponents of Hitler who suffered martyrdom. Thus we have to realize, in this connection, that many of the Catholics of German-speaking regions who attack Hochhuth are actually defending not so much Pope Pius XII as themselves, their own attitude, their collaboration with Hitler to the—literally—bitter end. Two Catholic writers—Gordon Zahn in *German Catholics and Hitler's Wars* and Carl Amery in *Die Kapitulation—oder deutscher Katholizismus heute* [*The Surrender—or German Catholicism Today*]—have shown the well-nigh total integration of a certain type of German Catholicism in Hitler's war machine.

Hochhuth was interviewed by the editors of the *Züricher Woche* (27 September 1963) at the time his play opened in Basle. He was asked: "You are accused, for instance, of anti-

---

Professor Heer is a Catholic historian who teaches at the University of Vienna. This article is reprinted from *Commonweal* of February 20, 1964.

clerical bias . . . Do you personally have any anti-clerical sentiments? Do you perhaps bear some personal grudge against Catholics?" To which he replied: "My best school friend is a Catholic. In fact, so strict a Catholic that his parents were very much afraid that he would enter the priesthood. He is now in the Federal Department of Justice at Bonn. He is also my son's godfather. That would not indicate anti-clerical or anti-Catholic bias on my part, though I make no secret of the fact that I find the silence of the higher clergy about what happened absolutely reprehensible—in contrast with the lower clergy. Three thousand European Catholic priests fell victim to Hitler, without the Pope so much as raising a finger on behalf of any one of them."

Now let me quote the letter which a German Catholic cleric wrote to Mr. Hochhuth and which expresses openly what a number of distinguished Catholic theologians and high-ranking churchmen have admitted to me in private conversation, but without making their sentiments public:

"Since I consider the attacks made upon you by certain groups of Federal German Catholics on account of your play as exaggerated and unjustified, I feel impelled to take this means of expressing to you my appreciation and admiration for your work. I rejoice that you have dared to scatter the artificial mists which had been raised in order to obscure the past. The Pope's silence about those crimes was and remains painful to me. On 12 July 1943, at a clerical conference, I sharply criticized the Pope's silence, after an eyewitness had given me an unforgettably detailed description of the mass execution of Jewish persons. After the war, therefore, I could never understand how the Catholic press could positively idolize Pius XII. Your work has a cleansing and liberating effect, and gives grounds for hope for the future. Those who think it harms the Church are mistaken. Moreover, I could complete and confirm your 'historical sidelights' in certain points from my own experience, and I am sending you today the photostat of an English leaflet which the RAF dropped over northern Germany in the summer of 1943. The original is in my possession. I wish you every success in your further labors. Do not lose heart in the face of the massive attacks launched against you."

This letter, written by Dr. Gökhen of Lingen/Ems on May 18, 1963, appears on pages 81-82 of the miscellany entitled *Summa Iniuria, oder: Durfte der Papst schweigen?—Hochhuth's Stellvertreter in der öffentlichen Kritik* ["Summa Iniuria, or: Should the Pope Have Kept Silence? Hochhuth's 'Deputy' in the light of public criticism"]. This work, together with the volume put out by the Basilius Presse of Basle, *Der Streit um den Stellvertreter* ["The 'Deputy' Controversy"], constitutes a good introduction to the discussion of Hochhuth's play in German-speaking Europe.

Dr. Gökhen hopes that Hochhuth's Christian tragedy will have a cleansing and liberating effect—precisely on Catholics. But this calls for an important qualification: the play can have such an effect only on Catholics who have acquired a certain degree of twentieth-century consciousness.

American Catholics are reproached—unjustly, in my view —for cultivating an immature, infantile Catholicism, informed by a primitive group egotism, incapable of so much as perceiving spiritual problems. They are alleged to be incapable of discussion, of objective argument with friend or foe; to be vain, egocentric, wrapped up in themselves, nationalistic, inclined to react with annoyance to anything they do not like. Personally I do not believe that these characteristics apply to American Catholics; but they do apply to many European Catholics, who now sit in judgment upon Hochhuth.

This is where one has to take a personal stand. Pius XII treated me, personally, with the greatest friendliness, kindness and cordiality. It was in the consciousness of that fact that I wrote, in my frequently quoted statement on *The Deputy* of 17 March 1963:

"Anyone who ever approached the impressive figure of Pope Pius XII and looked into his careworn features, his bloodshot eyes, anyone to whom he extended his hand, finds it hard to 'judge' this Pope. I cannot do it, I do not want to do it, but I have to confess that all Catholics, from the highest to the lowest—priests, chaplains, laymen (anti-Semitic to this day) — are co-responsible for the mass-murder of the Jews. Not only the thousands of baptized, confirmed and religiously wedded Christians who took a direct part in the mass murders . . . Not only bishops who, as in Poland and Hungary, drew up anti-Semitic pastoral letters and permitted their publication . . . The frightful failure of Rome from 1933 to 1945 is fresh in our memory. There were many reasons for this. One of the principal reasons for the terrible error of Pope Piux XII should be looked for in the circumstance that this Pope — who was not well disposed toward democracy, as he himself admitted to Heinrich Brüning, and not a few members of the Curia, more unconsciously than consciously — regarded Hitler's war against Russia as a possible liberation from Communism."

I concluded that statement with the following lines: "One word more as a Catholic. For years I have been haunted by the thought of the confession of sins—*Confiteor Deo omni-*

potenti—recited by millions of Catholics in thousands upon thousands of Holy Masses . . . The Confiteor is ritualized thoughtlessly, without understanding, mechanically; whereas if it were actualized, it could mobilize tremendous energies and powers of the soul. The great potential of inner powers —the real armament which is needed within the Church and throughout Christendom—will be released only when the daily confession of sins is in the best sense of the term politicized, actualized, concretized. Then it will mean: 'I confess to God the almighty Father . . . that I have sinned . . . through my fault, through my most grievous fault in the persecution of the Jews . . . (for "Jews" you can substitute, as occasion arises, the next best hated "enemy").' Rolf Hochhuth's *The Deputy* is a clear invitation to such an actualization of the Confiteor."

That seems to me the chief point, for Catholics, about this provocative play. I am using "provocative" in the positive sense of a call, a challenge, a calling forth to personal responsibility. Catholicism will become believable again, in the family of man, only when it takes its place squarely in the world's solidarity in guilt. We Catholics do not live in the beyond, but right in the middle of this world, and we are united in multifarious ways with all our brethren, black, red, yellow, brown. The preconditions for Hitler's "solution" of the Jewish question were, on the one hand, a thousand-year Christian, and also Catholic, anti-Semitism, and, in the nineteenth and twentieth centuries, a close alliance between leading churchmen and authoritarian, totalitarian, Fascist men and powers.

Pope Pius XII was a prisoner of the nineteenth century. The promulgation of papal infallibility made the Pope a prisoner of the integralist party. The integralists locked the Pope up in the Vatican and raised him—for the masses—to the position of a fetish surrounded by taboos (hymns to the Holy Ghost, for instance, were directly applied to the Pope). The Pope, "the Holy Father," became a protective shield for the intrigues of the "officials," as Lord Acton and Friedrich von Hügel called similar men in their day, who loudly invoked the authority of the papacy in their hard struggle for mastery over the Church and over those objectionable Catholics whose views differed from their own. They were always talking of the Holy Father, but they listened to him only when his words suited them. What is the function of the Holy Father for these integralists? Quite simply to defend the fortress of the Church against anti-Christ, in the person of the bad liberals, etc. How is he to do this? By concluding agreements, pacts, concordats with princes, kings, emperors, statesmen, by issuing pastoral letters and encyclicals fulminating against innovators and modernists. In addition, there must be no conversation with the "enemy," no dialogue, no sober and objective discussion with adversaries.

The nineteenth-century popes sought alliances with the Czars, and sacrificed Poland to them—Poland, the ancient bastion of Catholic Christendom in eastern Europe. On the eve of Hitler's invasion of Poland, Pius XII made arrangements with Hitler's Government through his nuncio in Berlin for the protection of the rights of the Church in Poland after the occupation. Shortly before the outbreak of the Second World War, at the Eucharistic Congress in Budapest (near Vienna, already under Nazi occupation, where a good number of Catholics were imprisoned), Cardinal Pacelli, as the legate of Pope Pius XI, made a statement which at the least could be interpreted as a call to arms against the godless Bolsheviks. On the eve of the German invasion of the Soviet Union, and during that invasion, Pius XII made arrangements concerning the ecclesiastical "new order" in the occupied territories. Pius XII, prisoner of the nineteenth-century curial mentality, concluded agreements with Hitler, Franco, Mussolini. . . . The many thousands of sheets of paper which constitute the encyclicals, addresses and radio messages of Pope Pius XII contain no reference to the Jews—nor to the thousands of Orthodox Serbs murdered by the Catholic Croats.

This leads us to an extremely important conclusion: up to the time of Pius XII it was not considered self-evident that the Catholic Church should champion the rights of those outside its fold—Jews, Protestants, and others were "overlooked." Suffragan Bishop Kampe, discussing the Hochhuth play, emphasized the point: "It is not customary," he said, "for ecclesiastical pronouncements explicitly to take up the cause of groups adhering to a different philosophy." But that is precisely where Catholics who believe in an open Catholicism come in: for them it is intolerable not to be responsible before God and man; for them, the *Pontifex maximus,* as chief shepherd and bridge-builder, must identify himself with all the persecuted, with all who are threatened with extermination.

The great Copernican revolution in the Church set in only *after* Pius XII. Under John XXIII and Paul VI the Church has begun to see itself as involved in discussion, in dialogue: discussion among Catholics of greatly differing viewpoints on politics and spirituality; and discussion between the Church and the rest of the world. A Council under Pius XII would have been unthinkable; so would a statement by the Church about its share in guilt for what has happened in the twentieth century; and so would a statement by the Church on a matter which has long been necessary—a new encounter between Christians and Jews. It is no accident that to this day, in Rome, integralist Catholics can campaign against the presentation of a schema to the Council which would reformulate the relations between Christians and Jews—after fifteen hundred years of Christian murder and persecution of Jews.

Pius XII himself was neither a friend of Hitler nor an enemy of the Jews, but his political ideas were such that he considered it more important not to "stab Hitler in the back" by diplomatic means (diplomatic negotiations, *in camera*, would have sufficed to postpone Hitler's "solution" of the Jewish question to the day of victory!) because he regarded the Wehrmacht as the strong bulwark against Bolshevism. He was therefore opposed to the policy of unconditional surrender. Father Robert Leiber, S.J., who for many years served as his confidant and secretary, expressed it thus on March 27, 1963: "The Pope regarded the policy of unconditional surrender declared at Casablanca in January, 1943, as a calamity."

Yet the abandonment of the principle of unconditional surrender would have meant a peace treaty with Hitler! And that would have meant the elimination of all "objectionable" Christians and Catholics, or at least their deportation to the East (the plans had already been worked out).

The *Neue Jiddische Zeitung* of Munich stated on March 8, 1963: "Pius XII's attitude is a sad historical reality, confirmed by secret diplomatic papers which the American Department of State has made public. These papers tell of Washington's efforts to alleviate the plight of the European Jews by soliciting the support of the Vatican on their behalf. The American ambassador in Switzerland approached the Vatican on a number of occasions to urge the Pope to protest publicly against the horrors committed by the Nazis—in vain. A similar intervention by Brazil was equally unsuccessful. Nevertheless, the United States Secretary of State, Cordell Hull, ordered his ambassadors to continue their efforts. Finally, on October 16, 1942, Cordell Hull was officially informed that the Vatican had rejected America's diplomatic endeavors. Mr. Myron Taylor, President Roosevelt's representative at the Vatican, reported to Washington that the Vatican was seeking to circumvent the problem on the grounds that it was impossible to verify the accuracy of the documents concerning the murder of Jews. This answer was made after Myron Taylor had presented to the Vatican documents containing precise details of that frightful murder."

We know now that Hitler, Himmler and the S.S. were very careful to show regard for the Pope, at least until the day of "final victory." Pius XII did not once protest when in Rome itself, literally at his doors, thousands of Jews were herded off to extermination. This is attested by a Catholic member of a resistance group in Rome, Hans Kühner-Wolfskehl: "A public appeal should have been made at the latest on the day when the first thousands of Jewish Roman citizens departed for their agonizing death. The death trains, as we believed at the time on the basis of our immediate knowledge of the situation, would not have left Rome, with all that that entailed, had the Pope personally intervened, and the arrests would, in addition, immediately have been called off.

"When he wished, as in connection with the two bombardments of Rome, Pius XII could act astonishingly fast. But in the case of the deportation of the Jewish citizens, we of the resistance waited in vain for the appearance of even a single cardinal. It must be clearly stated today—and in this respect Hochhuth is right—the threat of an interdiction and the denunciation of the ill-starred concordat which bound up papal history with Hitler Germany and which Hitler constantly violated, would have had a not insignificant effect. During the difficult months of terror prior to the liberation of Rome, we repeatedly discussed this with responsible personalities."

The editors of the *Züricher Woche* also put this question to Hochhuth: "Have you not been accused of attacking a Pope for an individual failure, and thereby by implication of attacking the whole Church?" Hochhuth answered: "No, I wish people would finally understand. But they don't. Pius is not regarded as one of 260 pontiffs; people identify themselves so completely with Pius, or rather, they identify Pius with the Catholic Church, with the whole institution of the papacy, as though there had been no other popes, as though there were no other possibilities, as though all this had not taken place eighteen long years ago. And I believe that a change will come. Recently, here in Basle, a Jesuit father visited me. He told me that in a group of clergy in Cologne an old, very distinguished Jesuit had said that what Hochhuth said about Pius was not so important after all. Pius was a historical figure, he was not the Church. This surprised me very much. It was the first time anyone had reacted in that way. Yet that is how people should react. This old Jesuit in Cologne was much more concerned about the reference to God in Act 5 of *The Deputy*."

The controversy about *The Deputy* leads, for Catholics, to the very heart of the necessary discussion of the firmly-entrenched tradition of the Church: Should the Church continue to regard itself, as it has since the Counter-Reformation, as a fortress which, in defending its own "holy interests," ignores the life, suffering and death of people of different views? Or should the Church—Mother Church—be conceived of as the matrix of mankind, open, protective of all the children of men, Buddhists, atheists, Negroes, etc.?

There is something else which Rolf Hochhuth's creative provocation should and could call forth among Catholics: a really adequate presentation of the life and suffering of Pope Pius XII. Thus far he has been surrounded by taboos, glorified as a plaster saint, dehumanized—and thus made to appear inhuman. But this would be a task for a truly Catholic investigation and historical writing, conscious of the duty of the *Pontifex Maximus* since Auschwitz, Maidanek, Mauthausen and Hiroshima: to portray the Pope bearing the cross of human guilt, of common guilt, up until his frightful agony, his solitary death, deprived of human communication.

To such a pope, bearing the cross of human guilt, Christians and non-Christians would not give a false aura of holiness, but neither would they deny him a crown—the crown proper to a mortal man who, in times of Copernican revolution, where Catholicism seeks to shake off the shackles of centuries, has to carry a burden which (as he admitted himself, in a note found in an envelope before his death) was beyond his strength.

ROBERT LEIBER, S.J.

Pius XII

The Man

It should hardly be necessary to remind ourselves that a memorial address at the papal tomb, still unsealed, is not the

---

Father Leiber is a German Jesuit who served as secretary to Pius XII. His address was originally published in *Stimmen der Zeit*. November 1958, and reprinted in *Der Streit um Hochhuth's "Stellvertreter,"* copyright © 1963 by Basilius Presse, Basel, and was translated by Salvator Attanasio.

same as the presentation of the personality and pontificate of Pius XII which historical research will later discover, perhaps after a hundred years or even more. The historian will have sufficient perspective to appraise the Pope's accomplishment in relation to the time before and after his pontificate. He will have access to sources, and like an examining magistrate he will be able to sift and weigh all the evidence objectively and without passion. A memorial address has a different character. Nevertheless, we shall venture to get as close as we can to the core of the matter itself.

We must surely reckon Pius XII as belonging to that company of mortals to whom Providence has entrusted five talents. He came from a very good family. His father Filippo Pacelli was a papal consistorial advocate. Born on March 2, 1876, Eugenio lived under his mother's loving care up to the time in 1917 when he came to Germany as Apostolic Nuncio. His mother could barely overcome the pain of this separation from her son.

His parents had conferred a solid and many-sided education on Eugenio. He was a good horseman and swimmer and an excellent violinist. He had an unusual knowledge of musical history and a fine appreciation of music as such. From the age of ten to eighteen he attended the Visconti school, a state school where he was always the first of his class.

The classics constituted the core of his curriculum. He enjoyed and loved the ancient classic authors. They remained in his library, some of them up to the end, in the Teubner edition which he had used as a schoolboy. He loved Cicero most. On one occasion he remarked that when he had recourse to Cicero he would always lose time because he found it so difficult to break away from him. We venture to assert that this involved something more than a literary sensibility. The fact, is, rather, that there was a psychological and elective affinity between the ancient Roman statesman and Pope Pius XII. His other favorite authors were Augustine, Dante, Manzoni. On occasion he took pleasure in dipping into his copy of Goethe's *Faust*. Throughout the decades a volume of the works of Bossuet lay conveniently near his bed. Nevertheless, with the passing of the years all this claimed increasingly little, perhaps too little, of his time.

One of Eugenio's schoolmates has said that he was always somewhat unapproachable. This aloofness remained with him throughout his life. He could be captivatingly charming in company and exhibit an unconstrained cordiality and fatherliness during audiences. Nevertheless, throughout his life he belonged to the category of solitaries. It was difficult to look into the depths of his soul.

At the Sapienza, the Roman University, Eugenio Pacelli attended the lectures of Professor Karl Julius Beloch. He also went to Duchesne's Sunday lectures and it was Duchesne who brought him into contact with Franz Xavier Kraus. The latter sharply warned the young monsignor, who showed a great interest in German affairs, against the Center Party. Fortunately the warning was to bear no fruit.

Eugenio Pacelli traversed a brilliant career. Ordained as a priest in 1899, by 1902 he was already a member of the Congregation for Extraordinary Ecclesiastical Affairs. Sixteen years later he was working under the foremost canonist of the day, later Cardinal-secretary, Gasparri, secretary of the commission for the codification of canon law. From 1912 on he was also secretary of the aforementioned congregation, we would say undersecretary of state, and at the same time professor of ecclesiastical diplomacy. From 1917 on he was Apostolic Nuncio, then Cardinal-secretary, and finally Pope.

Young Eugenio Pacelli had acquired a broad knowledge of history. But he was never born to be a historian. He was almost too skeptical for that calling. When he was Apostolic Nuncio in Germany, Adolph Harnack was his table-companion at a formal dinner. In the course of the conversation the Nuncio asked him what proportion of that which has been handed down to us as history could be considered certain, indubitable fact. Without pondering the question too long, historian Harnack answered, "About half, Excellency." Our conjecture, however, is that Pius XII drew the line between the certain and the uncertain in history even below the half. In his view even the papal archives were primarily a means of administration and diplomacy. He did not, of course, reject their use in the interests of historical research but he probably took a cooler view of them than any of his predecessors.

We would say that the dominant character trait of the deceased pontiff was a sober matter-of-factness. We are aware that this appraisal will come as a surprise to not a few persons. The literary treatment accorded the Pope has enveloped him in a thick layer of obfuscation, a movie-like *mélange* which contains little that is true and much that is of a fanciful and sentimental character. The camera had followed him importunately everywhere and, perhaps, he had been somewhat too compliant toward it. But our appraisal still holds. It also holds with reference to the unspeakable article on the "Christ vision" which appeared in the questionable picture magazine *Oggi*.

A sober matter-of-factness was in keeping with the Pope's way of life. The mass media were amazingly concerned with his private life for a very long time. Of all the articles that we have had a chance to examine none reports what is truthful only. On the other hand not a few of them report only what is false. The most incredible one stems from the pen of a well-known journalist: the Pope supposedly slept on an iron bed on which every morning, at six o'clock, he was handed a small cup of coffee by four Capuchin monks. No, it was all as normal as one can imagine. Pius XII scrupulously observed ecclesiastical proscriptions, including the commandment on the Eucharistic fast as it was before the promulgation of the new regulation, even when he had to celebrate the pontifical Mass in St. Peter's which lasted three hours. The Pope's private apartment, the *Appartamento Privato,* was of an extreme simplicity, the workroom "drab" and the Pope sat at a worktable in a simple gray-white work tunic. The Pope's household was managed by three nuns from the Institute of the Teaching Sisters of the Holy Cross, Menzingen (Switzerland). He did not meet the first of them, Sister Pasqualina Lehnert from Ebersberg in Upper Bavaria, in a hermitage under romantic circumstances as was recounted over and over again. Rather, she was assigned to his domestic service after the beginning of his nunciature in Munich following his routine request for a nun who was able to run a household. During the pontificate of Pius XII, Mother Pasqualina at the same time also administered the relief and assistance program of His Holiness from which funds for the Pope's personal charities to countries, institutes, and even individuals in need were disbursed. Another of the sisters was the Pope's cook. Since cooking took up relatively little time the sister worked hours long every day with her colleague making paraments.

Pius XII had an almost physical aversion to any form of exaggeration. His utterances were always poised. He could talk in solemn tones when his high office required it. But he never indulged in exaggeration. He also pondered things for a long time before saying yes or no. Unlike his predecessor Pius XI, he did not allow himself to speak in public unless he wrote down what he had to say beforehand. Today there are still a host of inauthentic papal utterances in existence, among them a forged speech of Pius XII containing strong strictures against capitalism. It originated in the circles of so-called Left Catholics. No, the Pope was extremely cautious and proper in handling conceptions such as capitalism which are so ardently disputed nowadays and used in the most varied senses. He also avoided making any utterance that could possibly offend others. Nothing good is ever created by insults, he said. He expressed the profound philosophical opposition between Christianity and communism in the sharpest terms, but never once or in the least did he ever offend the other side. The Moscow press and radio could take a cue from Pius XII on how to remain dispassionate, truthful, and well-mannered in disputation—even in confrontations of the sharpest, most fundamental character.

Pius XII had a marked appreciation for the meaning of "power," for the very reason that he thought along realistic lines. He had little use for plans, no matter how idealistic, if there was no power behind them to effect their actualization or to assure their success. His abilities as a diplomat were also based on the fact that he approached difficulties, problems, tasks, realistically and with self-restraint, steering toward his goal without any sentimentality. The English ambassador Lord D'Abernon, in the twenties, said that Nuncio Pacelli was the most capable mind of the Berlin diplomatic corps. But matter-of-factness in connection with Pius XII in no way signified insensitivity. On the contrary, Pius XII was empathetically sensitive and perceptive to an enormous degree.

His formidable, steel-like will to work necessarily belongs to the Pope's character portrait. Pius XII did not work in haste, but along a strict, prearranged plan. Nor did he first learn systematic work habits in Germany, as can be read somewhere. Even as a schoolboy, for a whole year, every night he set aside an entire hour in order to overcome his difficulties in mastering German before beginning his assigned studies. He learned French when he was still a youngster. He spoke several languages fluently. An introductory Russian grammar had a place in his workroom in the last years of his life. In the high office which he occupied, he held to his work plan weekdays and Sundays, in Rome as well as in Castel Gandolfo. The last hour of this work plan lay beyond midnight. It is difficult to form an idea of the Pope's passion for exactness. He had a marked mistrust for footnotes and quotations and in each case he demanded to check the cited author or source work himself.

The Renaissance popes have been criticized for allegedly having spent too much time feasting and in recreation. The popes of our time do too little in this respect. The picture magazines and the film about the Pope, *Pastor Angelicus* (the expression comes from a forged papal prophecy from shortly before 1600 and it would have been better not to use it at all) give the impression that frivolous feasts are celebrated in the Vatican. But the picture magazines and the film could offer only something of a representational character, for which reason the picture they draw is necessarily incomplete and thereby falsified. No, it must be said that the Pope's life was a pitilessly hard life of constant work. The Pope took his work plan with him, at every season even during the hot months, even on his walks, which took place in the early afternoon and which were limited to the very minute.

The Pacellis were a pious family. As is known, a brother of Pius XII, the university professor and Italian water-system specialist, performed yeoman service for Pius XII as a negotiator with the Italian Government in the settlement of the Roman Question, the *Conciliazione*. Of him Pius XII remarked once in his somewhat caustic way: "Marchese Francesco Pacelli lives like the members of religious orders ought to live." As a youngster Pius XII served Mass in the Chiesa Nova, consecrated to St. Philip Neri. In his personal religious life he continued to be the pious youth of that time. The clearheaded grown man, whom life experience must have made mistrustful to some extent, had a fine appreciation for unhypocritical, humble piety and for sincere religious devotion. Eugenio Pacelli entertained a childlike love for the Mother of God from early boyhood. The visible location of his Marian devotions was the little chapel of the Madonna della Strada in the Gesu' church, iridescent with gold and precious stones. The elevation of the corporeal assumption of the Blessed Virgin into heaven to the status of an infallible dogma was a matter which Pius XII approached with a deep sense of responsibility. But it was also an affair of the heart which affected him to the very depths of his soul and at the very moment of the definition of the dogma. As regards the questions of "Mediatrix" and "Corredemptrix," however, Pius XII made known his views a few days before his death on the day immediately following the end of the Mariological Congress in Lourdes: both questions are too unclarified and unripe. He deliberately avoided taking a position toward them throughout his whole pontificate, leaving them open rather to free theological disputation. He never thought of changing this attitude.

According to Prince Constantine of Bavaria a monsignor in the Vatican declared: "No pope up to now has applied himself more to stressing what the confessions have in common and to tempering what divides them than the present one." If we rightly understand this observation it would stamp Pius XII as an accommodating Irenic. To be sure the Pope was extremely gracious in his relations with persons of other religious persuasions. Even in the denominationally mixed audiences, for example, on the occasion of international congresses before the apostolic blessing he would gladly say: "We bless those of you who are our sons and daughters as well as those of you who wish to receive our blessing." If thereupon non-Catholics genuflected, it was purely their affair. It would have grieved the Pope if they had been under the impression that it was desired to press or to force them to do so. On different occasions he also appealed to those who still believe in a personal God to join together in protection against organized atheism and in defense of the dignity and rights of man. But the blotting out or the blurring of the frontier of truth were things which aroused an almost physical aversion in Piux XII. His utterances were razor sharp and crystal clear where it was a question of the formulation and delineation of the truths of the faith. This was quite in keeping with his natural disposition. As pope he had a very lofty conception of his duty to give prominence to and to defend the Catholic faith in its full purity with lines sharply drawn against all deviations and error. Even with respect to those of other religious faiths he felt that he would be doing them an injustice by misleading them in any way on the content of the Catholic faith.

Another question revolves around the coexistence of Catholics and non-Catholics in the same community. Pius XII dealt with it fundamentally in his address to the national congress of Italian Catholic Jurists on December 6, 1953. The address, which is known as the "tolerance speech," was epoch-making. Its substance can be summarized as follows: error, of course, has no rights vis-a-vis truth. This is a generally valid proposition and applies to all who embrace an absolute truth. But the coexistence of different confessions, of Catholics and non-Catholics in the same community, cannot be regulated according to this proposition or by this proposition alone. The *bonum commune,* the common good, that of the Church, of the Church in individual countries and of the Church as a whole, as well as the common good of the State, is the ultimate and decisive norm of such regulation. The Augsburg Religious Peace of 1555 is a classical example of this. Actually the theological considerations employed in the sixteenth century regarding the moral sanction of such a coexistence (summarized by St. Peter Canisius who espoused the cause of religious peace) are in accord with the principles expounded by Pius XII in that address.

Hyper-spirituality, a withdrawal into the sphere of the "purely religious," found no favor with Pius XII. In his view faith must operate effectively in all areas of life, while showing a full respect for their relative autonomy. Also, he never accepted the notion that politics had nothing to do with religion. He felt that the exercise of the right to vote was a moral duty in any case where the cause of God, the moral order, the rights of the Church might depend on the elections. When in April, 1948 the political election in Italy would decide whether the country would remain on a Christian foundation or be delivered to communism, Pius XII imposed on all Catholics, including the last convent sister, the great responsibility of going to the polls. Pius XII gave a general audience in Castel Gandolfo on the Sunday in 1953 when the German federal elections took place. There were some Germans among those who had arrived for the audience. Before the audience the Pope, rather sharply, asked why the Germans were there in the first place. They would have done better, he said, to have fulfilled their electoral duty in their homeland. (At that time there was still no voting by mail.) Later, during the audience itself, he was markedly cool and brief in his allocution to the Germans.

Pius XII was very conscious of national sensibilities and prudently took them into consideration. He himself was above them and he probably smiled over them inwardly. He was a man of the Church, of the universal Church. In his view to work for the Church was the religious ministry which the Lord demanded from him. No national intrigues were hatched around the Pope, no nation was placed in a position of advantage vis-a-vis others.

Pius XII rarely employed the expression "Western civilization," and then only with great prudence, because it is one of the aforementioned conceptions which is wrapped in ambiguity and one which does not have the same meaning with respect to different historical epochs. He refrained from using it above all because even the appearance ought to be avoided that the Catholic Church for better or for worse identifies herself with the "Western" variety of civilization. Thus even when dealing with the relations between Europe and the emergent Asian-African world the Pope based himself on fundamentals, warning against an estrangement between them and pointing to the high values which Europe or the West could still pass on to those continents (Christmas Message,

1955). It is superfluous to recall that Pius XII greatly welcomed and promoted the economic and political cooperation which, as an example, began to be realized in Europe.

The Tasks

Not every pontificate must needs see itself placed before a task which it is called upon to fulfill. The routine administration of the whole Church by itself is already a task of sizeable dimensions. Providence, however, had set a special task before the deceased pontiff: to lead the Church through the Second World War. This was a difficult task but Pius XII discharged it brilliantly. In this era of raw violence, of hate and of murder, the Church acquired only esteem, trust, and new possibilities for widening her influence.

Space and time compel us to be content with this overall appraisal. But the following merit a more detailed discussion: the Pope's activity as mediator, the saving of Rome, his championing of the rights of peoples and of human dignity, his assistance to persons and countries in distress.

The Pope's activity as mediator: Here we shall present only some brief, sketchy remarks recalling the situation of the period. The Allies would not negotiate with Hitler under any conditions. At that time, however, it was absolutely unthinkable that Hitler would step down in order to open a path to salvation for the German people. This situation lay like a timber across any door leading to mediation and negotiation. Then the Allies, at Casablanca, proclaimed the terms of unconditional surrender. Pius XII promptly and deeply deplored this proclamation because it was perfectly tailored to drive the German people into a desperate struggle for very life.

On the other hand it was equally impossible to approach responsible parties on the German side. When the German government heard from afar, or conjectured, that the Holy See might be considering mediation, it stole a march on it by rejecting the idea outright. This happened when the suspicion arose that the Pope wanted to take steps to limit the scope of air attacks. On the first occasion Goebbels, in a markedly tactless way, publicly rejected such mediation through the international press. On the second occasion, in September, 1943, the German government through confidential channels made it known to the Pope personally that it considered air attacks to be a weapon like any other. The German government had been the first to make use of this weapon. Now the other side wanted to strike back harder with it. The German government hoped, however, that it would soon be able to deliver a still mightier counter-blow. The counter-blow never came. But the work of destruction of the bombing attacks on German cities proceeded to its shattering end. We do not contend that the Pope's mediation would have certainly put a halt to it. Nobody estimated the probability of the successful outcome of the mediation efforts with greater clearheadedness and realism than Pius XII himself. Our purpose is merely to point out how all doors were stubbornly barred even to the slightest touch.

The saving of Rome: In reply to the question: "To whom do we really owe our thanks for the saving of Rome?" Ambasador Ernst von Weizsäcker replied: "Not to me. I was only the mediator between the Vatican and Kesselring's headquarters. I would say in the first place that it was the Pope who compelled the belligerent parties to spare the city, simply through his continued presence." But there were fine, upright men on both sides, among them von Weizsäcker himself, who also helped. Pius XII was grateful to them. And he was able to help them, effectively as far as we know, when they were in trouble before war crimes tribunals after the war.

Championing the rights of peoples and human dignity: Among the many things that Pius XII said and did in this respect, we cannot fail to discuss two of his pronouncements because they are among his most valuable utterances on the question of war and peace.

In his address to the cardinals on June 2, 1940, he said: "It is not to be overlooked that the welfare of the peoples who are under occupation does not cease to be an obligatory norm in connection with the administration of public authority. Justice and equity demand that they be treated in such a way as the occupying power, in a similar case, would wish its own fellow countrymen to be treated."

An excerpt from his Easter Message of April 13, 1941, reads:

"To the powers that are holding countries in occupation during the war, without being remiss in the consideration due them, we say: may your conscience and your sense of honor direct you to treat the peoples in your areas of occupation justly and humanely and to be solicitous of them. Do not weigh them down with burdens which you, in a similar case, feel or would feel to be unjust. A prudent and helpful humaneness is the praise and pride of a sage commander, and the treatment of prisoners as well as of the population in the occupied areas is the surest foundation and measure of the culture of the heart and of nations. Beyond and above this, consider that the blessing or curse of God in regard to your own homeland can depend on the way in which you treat those whom the fortunes of war have delivered into your hands."

Assistance to persons and nations in distress: The generous assistance which the Pope ordered to be extended to the victims of political persecution, among them persecuted Jews, also belongs under this heading. Subsequently, Jews on different occasions gratefully acknowledged his help. Here also belongs the activity of the Vatican Information Office for the transmission of news from and to prisoners of war and the search service for missing persons which was set up. Under certain conditions, the only link between prisoners of war in whole theaters of operation and their homelands, this office was able to pass on news in millions of cases. There was also the pontifical emergency assistance program during the war and in the postwar period. Out of consideration for the readers of *Stimmen der Zeit* and in order to prevent any misunderstandings, we shall present only one figure in relation to Germany's postwar years of tribulation. It became possible for the Pope to have help dispatched to Germany only starting with the summer of 1946. From the summer of 1946 to the summer of 1949, the pontifical relief program or rather the personal charities of Pius XII, sent 950 freight cars, each with a capacity of 17 to 19 tons, loaded with bedding, clothes, and food provisions to Germany. All the shipments were in excellent condition, being either new or, if used, properly repaired. At that time entire female religious communities in Rome were put to work preparing papal shipments to countries in dire need.

In addition to discharging the task assigned by Providence of guiding the Catholic Church through World War II, Pius XII on his own took on another charge: to expound the Catholic world-view in its full richness and according to its manifestations in different areas of life: in the life of the individual, his human dignity, his inalienable rights, his moral duties in the sphere of conjugal and family life, in that of larger communities, and in the whole domain of public and private life.

The Pope did this in his encyclicals, messages, addresses and other speeches. Pius XII spoke a great deal. It can be said that he spoke more than any of his predecessors. Not in the least was this too much. His published pronouncements, however, give an account of how the Pope was ceaselessly invited to address words of counsel and guidance to groups of all kinds. Furthermore, Rome in our day is one of the most popular cities in which to hold national and international congresses. Almost everybody wanted to be received by the Pope and to hear him talk. In any case his messages and speeches are a rich storehouse of the first rank for relating the Catholic faith to the totality of modern existence. Pius XII, with his persuasive pronouncements, demonstrated one thing: namely, that despite all inflexibility in her supratemporal dogmas, principles, and demands which rest on divine commandments and whose meaning nothing is allowed to twist, the Church of Christ is open to the world and of relevance to our age.

We shall limit ourselves to a few brief remarks.

In questions where faith and science meet, Pius XII was very careful not to close doors hastily. He felt keenly about the case of Galileo and greatly deplored its occurrence. In his 1944 Christmas Message, Pius XII dealt with the problem of democracy. Those who understood his pronouncement in the sense of being a special praise of, and a preference for, the democratic form of government, misread its meaning. The Church remains aloof from the question of what form of government a people choose. That particular papal message had something altogether different in view. Its aim was to point out that when a nation decides for democracy, higher demands are placed on the maturity and moral reliability of its citizens. Otherwise, the danger exists that the state may sink to the level of a pseudo-democracy and fall into the dictatorship of the masses or into the clutches of ruthless tyrants. In this respect that message is even more timely today than it was fourteen years ago. It is a warning to our democratically ruled nations which they should not fail to heed.

As regards the disciplines of medicine it can be said that Pius XII dealt exhaustively with their points of contact with the injunctions of Catholic teaching in matters of faith and morals. On October 29, 1951, the Pope delivered a very detailed address to the congress of Italian Catholic midwives (Acta. Ap. Sed. Vol. 43, pp. 835-854). His words on this occasion are probably the most honorable mention and valuation that the profession of midwife has ever received in the history of mankind. The Pope took the occasion to discuss the question of conjugal morality and of moral duties toward new, or still unborn or already born life. The long address was an extension of Pius XII's encyclical "Casti Connubio." Together they form a unified whole.

Pius XII was a champion of Catholic education and

schools. His espousal of them was not merely an official duty but sprang from his heart and soul, enlisting the sympathetic response of his whole inner being. The Pope laid down his last directive in regard to the question of Catholic schools in his message to the Berlin Catholic Conference in 1958: "Our Care for Man—Your Youth!" he called out to the gathering. "We are thinking especially about fathers and mothers among the faithful who are compelled to send their children to a school in which they are systematically educated to disbelief. This school is forced upon you. Now you will be able to appreciate why the Church has always fought to the end on behalf of the right of the parent to the child, clearly circumscribed by nature and Revelation, a right which is to be reckoned among the main pillars of any social order worthy of human beings. And you will appreciate why the Church struggles to the limit for the right to entrust her children only to schools in which the life of their faith is lovingly sheltered and can unfold."

As regards liturgical reforms, the shortening of the breviary and along with it of the Roman missal stood at the center of the Pope's attentive care in this sphere. Another hurdle, which in the opinion of many was of a most formidable character, and which has been successfully negotiated for the past ten years, was the preparation of a new Latin translation of the Psalms in place of the version by Jerome. In contrast to the conjectures and assertions of others we attach great importance to stressing the fact that the inspiration to prepare new Latin texts for the Psalms came exclusively from the Pope. The directors of the Pontifical Biblical Institute were no less surprised when they received a definite directive from the Pope to prepare a new Latin version of the Psalms.

Catholics throughout the world will be thankful to Pius XII for the new regulation on the *jejunium eucharisticum,* the commandment to fast before receiving Holy Communion. A new regulation was absolutely inevitable in consequence of the communion decree issued by Pius X. Now it is in existence and it is adjusted to the tempo of modern life.

Now we should like to discuss in detail two subjects touched upon in papal pronouncements, namely Pius XII's position toward social problems as well as toward war and peace.

Pius XII and the "Social Question": In the broad field of the social question Pius XII stood fully in the tradition of the social teaching of the Church as this was begun vis-a-vis the modern world of economic man by Leo XIII in "Rerum novarum" and continued by Pius XI in "Qua dragesimo anno." Is Pius XII, therefore, to be called a "reactionary," a man who is the captive of "bourgeois" conceptions because of his social origin? Anyone who exposes himself to the influence of the rich storehouse of his addresses dealing with social problems will find an answer to this question. There is hardly a problem which modern economy, so greatly influenced by the progress of technology, has laid upon human coexistence which this Pope has not fundamentally illumined, whether it be a problem of a national, international, religious, cultural or material character, including those of automation, gold reserves and currency stabilization. He was a modern man with eyes opened wide on the world around him. Nevertheless, many found him too academic. But was not his attitude the correct one for a man of the Church who must see everything in the order of God so as to illumine the legitimate clash of opinions with the light from above which one may not overlook with impunity, but which also leaves room for possible concrete solutions?

Nevertheless, some contend that his exposition lacks the inner unity of the teachings of Pius XI. He did not bequeath a new social encyclical, a "Quinquagesimo" or a "Sexagesimo anno" to the Church and mankind. Many had expected something of this sort from him. But neither the war year of 1941, nor the year 1951, which was still under the impact of the very extensive postwar developments, permitted Pius XII to work on a message of a purely social character. This explains the external reason for his restraint. But the inner reason for this restraint is even more important: the socio-political and social-reform wishful fantasies of our time, whether from the "right" or the "left"—for instance, full employment, material security, ever increasing productivity, and currency stabilization—grappled, and grapple still, chiefly with the surface of events. What, however, was clearly pronounced in the traditional social teaching of the Church, and what Pius XII had pronounced often enough—and also could not have expressed any differently in any possible social encyclical—is the following: that the social question gives unity and coherence to those surface problems only when it is a question of the totality of being of the human person internally attuned and in all aspects, hence one concerning the opportune functioning of those three organizational structures of human society: the family, private property, and the state. Pius XII was progressive enough to alarm conservatives, and conservative enough to restrain progressives. He was neither an existentialist nor a "mystic" viewing historical being as mere process and development.

On the basis of a clear philosophy and theology, he had a keen sense for what is essential in the structure of human coexistence.

Pius XII on War and Peace

Nobody ever issued as many admonitions to preserve the peace as did Pius XII. Furthermore, he classically formulated the religious, psychological, and legal foundations of peace. It suffices to read his Christmas Messages of the first four war years. But the Pope's position toward war and peace was realistic—a position which he presupposed was shared by every Catholic, or which he demanded from Catholics, as in his 1948 Christmas Message. Pius XII was against "peace at any price." He viewed extreme pacifism not only as eccentric but as a danger to the public weal. No doubt there should be disarmament. Pius XII espoused disarmament with all his might because disarmament, honestly observed, presupposes religious, psychological, and legal foundations of peace, and is the only effective means for preventing war. But it must be universal and controlled disarmament. So long as it does not exist and any power plays with aggressive war as a means of achieving its international political aims, the peace-minded nations of the world have the right to put themselves on a defensive footing. They also have the right to build a common system of coordinated defense so strong that its mere existence deters aggressive-minded powers from unleashing an attack. Any other attitude toward the question of war and peace would surrender mankind to the morally ruthless, to criminals. This is why Pius XII did not condemn even atomic weapons out of hand and unconditionally, no matter how vigorously and pressingly he called for their universal destruction. As a necessary means of defense they can even be morally sanctioned.

Beyond and above this Pius XII saw in the tendency to achieve an organized community of nations as a surety of peace, the point of departure for a development that would make it possible to limit further the cases in which war can be morally sanctioned, along the lines of the Church's traditional teaching on war and peace. It is easy to set forth ultra-idealistic peace demands and thus stand out as a hero of the noble cause of peace. But Pius XII was far too conscientious to leave the ground of reality for the sake of popularity and to deceive the world through a misguided idea of peace.

A memorial address devoted to Pius XII and his pontificate cannot fail to mention the audiences that he gave. He gave them to the point of utter exhaustion. He was a master in the art of representation and he made brilliant use of this gift in the exercise of his high office. He considered the audiences, especially the general ones, as a special papal apostolate which he, as with all things, took very seriously. There is something about the audiences that Pius XII gave during the Second World War to the male and female members of the armed forces of both belligerent sides which is unique in the annals of papal history. These audiences were also extended to Germans. The Pope always welcomed them gladly. A prohibition to attend the audiences was never issued by the Vatican. But they certainly were from the German side, allegedly to prevent improprieties at the audiences. But no improprieties ever occurred. From June, 1944 on, the hundreds of thousands of Allied troops who marched through Rome, or who were allowed to visit the city, also paid a call on the Pope: Englishmen, Americans, Canadians, Indians, South Africans, Australians and New Zealanders and, toward the end of the war, even Brazilians. Obviously, had it not been for this circumstance it would never have occurred to most of them to see the Pope. But they were all deeply impressed by his personality, non-Catholics more so than Catholics. After all, Catholics knew who the Pope was. The others were pleasantly surprised to see a good and charming man in his august person. Ordinarily his appearance at audiences also strongly appealed to the religious sensibility of the visitors.

The general audiences which the Pope gave in the Hall of Benedictions in St. Peter's and in the inner court of the papal palace at Castel Gandolfo were world-famous. He exerted a great fascination over those who came to them, with his unconstrained, fatherly, and sincere graciousness of speech and bearing. The Vicar of Christ among his sons and daughters from the four corners of the earth—this was a powerful manifestation of the supra-national character of the Church. All felt themselves as brothers and sisters here. The many people of color who came to the audiences with increasing frequency and in ever greater numbers were probably among those most imbued with this family feeling. What was revealed here! We gladly admit that the audiences, precisely in the setting of Castel Gandolfo, created a state of suggestibility among those present. But their susceptibility was not the ultimate determining factor. The ultimate and most impressive determining factor was the powerful force of the commonly held Catholic faith which one encountered there in almost palpable form.

Pius XII and Germany

The last centuries point to no pope who had such close relations with Germany as did Pius XII. He was Apostolic Nuncio in Bavaria from 1917 to 1925, to the Reich from 1920 to 1929. German affairs had concerned him greatly, perhaps more than all other matters put together. This was the case even when he was cardinal-state secretary (1930-1939). His exchange of notes with the German ambassador, dating from those years, which has been published in part, is an eloquent testimony to this overriding interest.

His activity in Germany had a promising start with Benedict XV's mediation for peace in the summer of 1917. So far as the responsibility falls on the Germans, why did the effort at mediation fail? The German government had delayed its reply when extreme haste was imperative. Nothing can explain away this confirmed fact. Thus the yes for the restoration of complete Belgian independence was not pronounced. The English government waited for this yes as the most essential pre-condition for negotiations. If we ask why the yes was never forthcoming, newly discovered documents suggest as a decisive reason that the Germans believed they could win the game by playing the card of the Bolshevik revolution on which enormous sums had been expended since the first year of the war after the battle of the Marne had miscarried. If this is proved to be correct—what a sinister fate if we today consider things in retrospect! State-secretary von Kuhlmann is supposed to have bitterly rued his failure to take advantage of the papal efforts at mediation.

Eugenio Pacelli, as Apostolic Nuncio, had drawn up the Bavarian, Prussian, and Baden concordats from the Church side. We will add the Austrian concordat with Dollfuss to the German. The very drawing-up of a concordat for signature is an accomplishment for a papal diplomat. Pacelli could call three or four his creations. The negotiations for a concordat with Prussia turned out to be the most protracted. But once signed it was scrupulously observed. In a book on Pius XII which was translated into German—we believe it is the fanciful book by Padellaro—it is said that the Prussian concordat was the first blow which allegedly shook old Prussia. This statement is nonsense, and it is even more nonsensical that it was carried over intact in the German translation. On the part of the Church the concordat was signed in order to regulate and secure the position of Catholics in Prussia. If one wishes to inquire about its political secondary effects, it was one of the clamps that then held old Prussia together. This was how the prudent and far-seeing Minister President Otto Braun had understood it at that time.

All the fateful events that unrolled in Germany from January to March 1933—Hitler's seizure of power, the voting in the Kroll Opera House with the *Ja* of the Center Party deputies for Hitler, the proclamations of the German episcopate, or rather of Cardinal Betran, along lines that were conciliatory to the Party—all these took place without the slightest influence exerted by the Holy See or by Cardinal secretary of state Pacelli. On one of those days the Cardinal declared that he had refrained from sending even private letters to Germany in order to avoid any impression that he wanted to interfere in the course of events. He was literally astounded upon reading the March declaration of the German bishops which was favorable to the Party.

Plans and overtures between Church and State representatives had preceded the signing of the Reich concordat since 1920. But they should not be given too much weight. It is not as if the Reich concordat had been yielded on July 20 as the ripe fruit of this prior activity. The main work was carried out from Easter 1933 up to the signing of the concordat. At that time, in the early months of the Third Reich, the Holy See would have preferred a *modus vivendi* in the form of an extended validation of the individual *Länder* concordats rather than a Reich concordat. But the government exerted pressure and offered extensive concessions. The Holy See would have been wrong to refuse and thereby to have exposed Catholics in Germany to the gravest dangers. This was the considered opinion of all those who were consulted for responsible advice, even of those who had little liking for the concordat. We still remember the words that Cardinal secretary of state Pacelli pronounced in that situation: "It is easy," he remarked, "to begin a Church struggle but it is hard to stick it out. And if the Church is forced to wage this struggle, Catholics in the country must know that the highest leadership has made every attempt beforehand to spare them this struggle." How forcibly does the correctness of this observation light up the Church history of the last decades!

There was an additional factor which must not be overlooked. At the very moment that the Hitler government offered a concordat, at Easter 1933, there was a group of German Catholic political leaders in Rome, among them the former Reich Chancellor Dr. Joseph Wirth. They pointed out that the guarantees of rights and freedoms within Germany for which German Catholics had fought for the last eighty years had assumed an allegedly questionable character. Consequently the Holy See should intervene. They were told that the Holy See could do this only by way of negotiations and consultations with the German government.

This ultimately led to the signing of the concordat. It was maintained during the years of the Third Reich as a front-line position which no doubt had to be given up, piece by piece, in the face of violence and treaty violations. But it was not entirely lost because in the meanwhile it adapted the Church to the emergency situation that marked her existence during those years.

Two things, which presumably stood in the context of Cardinal secretary of state Pacelli's considerations of that time, deserve mention here: the Holy See, or rather the Cardinal, has been criticized for having been able to sign a concordat which allegedly demanded the dissolution of the Center Party. The latter was supposed to be sacrificed. We do not know exactly how its legend arose. We want merely to state that, viewed correctly, the very opposite is true. The fact is that the Center Party, as the last of the old parties, dissolved while the negotiations over the concordat were still going on. When Cardinal secretary of state Pacelli read about it in the newspapers he said, "Too bad that it should happen at this very moment. The Party, of course, would not have been able to continue much longer. If only, however, it had postponed its dissolution until the signing of the concordat. The mere fact of its existence would still have been useful to us during the negotiations."

The second thing concerns Article 32 of the concordat which prohibited the Catholic clergy to join political parties and to be active in them. On the Church side there were many misgivings over this because it placed Catholic priests under a discriminatory special provision. Naturally, with this article the government also aimed to strike a blow at "political Catholicism," i.e. the Center Party. Nevertheless, it seems to have overlooked the fact that the article was likewise directed against the NSDAP, and against it alone, following the dissolution of the Center. The article in question actually protected the Catholic clergy from forced cooperation with the NSDAP.

Cardinal secretary of state Pacelli openly acknowledged his co-responsibility in the preparation of the encyclical "Mit brennender Sorge." This was an easy and honoring acknowledgment to make later, but not so easy in 1937. Co-responsibility in another event would have grievously weighed upon

Cardinal Pacelli had it taken place: it never did. In May, 1938 Hitler made his famous state visit to Rome. Almost everywhere the situation is presented as though Pope Pius XI from the very outset had refused to receive him. This presentation is false. On the contrary the Pope had very much wished to engage in a frank conversation with the "Führer." Accordingly, he answered a confidential query as to whether he would receive Hitler in the affirmative. Thereupon intrigues were set afoot, presumably from some high echelon in the Party. No corresponding official request for an audience arrived at the Holy See through the German ambassador. The Pope waited until he was certain that Hitler would never step foot into the Vatican. Pius XI then held that it would be fitting for him not to remain in Rome at all, so at the last moment he returned to Castel Gandolfo the day before Hitler's arrival in Rome. Much comment was occasioned by Foreign Minister von Ribbentrop's visit to Pius XII in March, 1940, after the war against Poland and just before the offensive in the West. The parley between them produced no results. The Pope had most exactly prepared himself in writing beforehand, in regard to Church as well as political questions. When he began to talk about war and peace, Herr von Ribbentrop rudely interrupted him: "Holiness, any conversation on this theme must start out from the very certain presupposition that France, and not only France, England, too, will petition Germany for peace this year, in 1940."

The Pope, greatly surprised: "Excellency, how can one presuppose such a thing with certainty. The fortunes of war are fickle."

Ribbentrop: "I repeat, Holiness, France and England will petition us for peace in this very year."

The Pope: "This may be your conception, but what does the Führer think?"

Ribbentrop: "The Führer and I know that France and England will petition us for peace in this very year."

The Pope: "But what do the German people say to that?"

Ribbentrop: "The German people are also convinced of it, that France and England will petition us for peace in this very year."

Thereupon the Pope went on to another subject on the agenda. It should be recalled here that during the whole conversation in contrast to the Foreign Minister's gruff manner the Pope behaved in a way that could be described as friendly rather than sharp.

In the months that have just been discussed, i.e., from

autumn to the winter of 1939-1940, Pius XII's effort at mediation took place and was occasionally discussed in German and English publications. We shall briefly outline the main points: at that time the German politico-military resistance movement correctly grasped that Germany could be saved only at a point in time when the nation was still intact and by putting an end to Hitler, the Party, and the war itself before a further broadening of the war westward, i.e., in the relatively quiet phase of the war which existed then. Consequently, one had to be certain of the good will of the other side, of its readiness for an immediate armistice and of a mutual agreement, at least with respect to future peace negotiations. The resistance movement, therefore, through a confidant, turned to the Pope who was to forward their questions to the other side and to receive and pass on the eventual replies. Pius XII set to work if only for the reason of leaving nothing untried which perhaps might bring the war to an end. The action was carried out from November, 1939 to February, 1940. At the end of January the German confidant declared that the replies were considered so favorable that the negotiations could begin. The *coup d'état* was fixed for a day in February. It was given up at the last moment allegedly because General von Brauchitsch, on whose help the conspirators depended, had refused to participate. According to the most general agreements worked out during the negotiations, Austria was to be left fully free to determine her own fate. In regard to Poland, the situation has been presented in a way to make it appear as though the Pope had proposed the restoration of the 1914 borders to the German side. This is a complete fabrication. The Pope never, at any time, lent a hand to the dissolution or the partition of Poland. From the outset it was presupposed and proclaimed that Poland would be restored. The possibility is not to be excluded, however, that someone in the resistance movement has set this forgery before certain generals in order to make the *coup d'état* more palatable to them. Rome had to take upon itself the risk of leaving the use or misuse of the answers that arrived up to the German authorities. And not only that. In reference to this very action, in 1944 when the Allies entered Rome, a high English official told the writer: "In his efforts for peace Pius XII went to the farthest limits that it is possible for a pope to go."

The German people must surely be thankful to Providence that a man like Pius XII occupied the papal throne in the most tragic years of its history, tragic unfortunately in the first place because of the accumulated guilt in its own ranks. If the occupant of the Chair of Peter had been another who did not have a personal knowledge of Germany it would have been difficult, if not impossible, to administer objective measures properly at all times. Pius XII could do so because he had formed an independent judgment about us and our conditions as the result of his twelve-year activity in Germany. As Apostolic Nuncio he learned to know the German people, primarily, of course, in its better and best representatives. For this reason in the bitterest hours his judgment could strike a greater note of understanding than was possible even for us Germans.

Pius XII never again touched on the thorny question of Germany's eastern borders after 1945. It is a political question in which the Pope did not consider himself competent. What Pius XII did discuss, in his famous letter to the German bishops on March 4, 1948, was the forced expulsion of millions of Germans from their homelands, from East Germany and from the eastern and southwestern regions, no matter how these territories were governmentally divided. We should not blame the Pope for publicly sympathizing with their plight and for openly discussing these shocking events. Here, however, we do not wish to recall, much less point to, the shocking events which took place in those areas during the war years through German guilt.

Every personality, every capacity has its limits. But the evidence can show that Pope Pius XII unreservedly and uninterruptedly placed his ability and his energies in the service of the Church of Christ, a service during which he was increasingly assigned higher tasks and which found its fulfillment in a pontificate which lasted almost twenty years. A future time, which will have acquired the necessary perspective, will ultimately judge the significance of this pontificate whose richness for the Church and mankind meantime leaves no doubt. Pius XII masterfully steered the Church through the war and the postwar period, a time for which it is difficult to find historical parallels in upheavals, in the tragic fate of individuals as well as of whole peoples, in acts of atrocity, as well as in acts that were imbued with the spirit of God. The deceased Pope fulfilled the task of being the Vicar of Christ, the teacher of nations to so great a measure that, in this respect, one may be tempted to place him alongside the greatest of his predecessors. In the end, through personal contact with statesmen, diplomats, and high-ranking military officers, especially in the first postwar years, he contributed infinitely much to the quelling of passions, to the reduction of hate and estrangement, and to the *rapprochement* of peoples and nations.

The world-wide sympathy in response to the death of the Pope was of an unprecedented character. Veneration and love for the memory of Pius XII were expressed throughout the world from the highest leaders in public life down to simple employees and workers. What was most deeply impressive about this universal sympathy was its authenticity and sincerity. From Moscow too came a friendly word of farewell from the Patriarch resident there. For a moment it seemed as if our sundered world were one. It was a quiet triumph for the Church and her greatness, for whom Pius XII had staked his all.

GUENTER LEWY

Pius XII, the Jews, and the German Catholic Church

Rolf Hochhuth's controversial "Christian tragedy," dealing with the failure of Pope Pius XII to protest publicly against the incredible horrors that Nazi Germany was inflicting upon the Jews of Europe, has dramatized a problem that is as old as Christianity itself. Hochhuth, to be sure, relates this failure to the personality of Pius XII himself, who is portrayed in *The Deputy* as a cold, unfeeling politician worried only about the interests of the Church. But the truth is that the Pope's stand cannot adequately be understood in terms of personalities. For one thing, we must remember that the Nazi assault upon the Jews of Europe took place in a climate of opinion

---

Born in Germany in 1923, the author came to the U.S. in 1947 and received a Ph.D. in political theory from Columbia. He has taught at Columbia and Smith Colleges. With permission of the McGraw-Hill Book Company, division of McGraw-Hill, Inc., this article is adapted from *The Catholic Church and Nazi Germany* by Guenter Lewy.

conditioned by centuries of Christian hostility to Jews and Judaism. And for another, we must realize that in acting—or failing to act—as he did, Pius XII was to a considerable extent influenced by the behavior of his "constituency" within Germany itself. Consequently, it is with German Catholicism that any effort to explain the Pope's silence must begin.

1. The Weimar Period

From the time the National Socialist movement appeared in the 20's, organized German Catholicism came into repeated conflict with it, but anti-Semitism was not one of the primary bones of contention. On the contrary, many Catholic publicists—like the Franciscan Father, Erhard Schlund—agreed with the Nazis on the importance of fighting "the destructive influence of the Jews in religion, morality, literature and art, and political and social life," and objected only to the extremist tone of the movement. Thus, for example, the Jesuit Gustav Gundlach, writing in a reference work edited by Bishop Buchberger of Regensburg, argued that a political anti-Semitism, directed against the "exaggerated and harmful influence" of the Jews, was permitted so long as it utilized morally admissible means. And Bishop Buchberger himself, while deploring racialism, concluded that it was "justified self-defense" to ward off the rule of "an overly powerful Jewish capital."

Concentrating her fire upon liberals and free thinkers, many of whom were of Jewish descent, the Church did practically nothing to stem the inroads anti-Semitism was making on German life throughout the period of the Weimar Republic. Though the German bishops during these years spoke up against Hitler's glorification of race and blood, they rarely found anything specific to say about the virulent anti-Semitic propaganda the Nazis were spreading or about the acts of violence against Jews that were becoming more and more common. So far as individual Catholic clerics in the pre-Hitler years were concerned, the *Verein für die Abwehr des Antisemitismus,* an organization of Christians and Jews struggling against the rising anti-Semitic agitation, counted two Catholic priests as members of its board of sponsors, while only a few Catholic laymen—like the journalist Franz Steffen and the editor Felix Langer—ever raised their voices against the anti-Semitic tirades of the Nazis and their allies.

2. The Pre-War Hitler Years

On April, 26, 1933, shortly after coming to power, Hitler had a talk with two dignitaries of the German church, Bishop

Berning and Prelate Steinmann. In the course of this talk he reminded his visitors that the Church for 1500 years had regarded the Jews as parasites, had banished them into ghettos, and had forbidden Christians to work for them; he, Hitler said, merely intended to do more effectively what the Church had attempted to accomplish for so long.

The reaction of the two Church dignitaries to Hitler's attempt to identify his brand of anti-Semitism with the age-old anti-Judaism of the Church is not known. What we do know, however, is that from the time Hitler came to power all the German bishops began declaring their appreciation of the important natural values of race and racial purity, and they limited their dissent to insisting that this goal be achieved without resort to immoral means. The article on "Race" in an authoritative handbook on topical religious problems, edited by Archbishop Gröber, expressed this position in the following words:

> Every people bears itself the responsibility for its successful existence, and the intake of entirely foreign blood will always represent a risk for a nationality that has proven its historical worth. Hence, no people may be denied the right to maintain undisturbed their previous racial stock and to enact safeguards for this purpose. The Christian religion merely demands that the means used do not offend against the moral law and natural justice.

Similarly, in his celebrated Advent sermons of 1933, Cardinal Faulhaber observed that the Church did not have "any objection to the endeavor to keep the national characteristics of a people as far as possible pure and unadulterated, and to foster their national spirit by emphasis upon the common ties of blood which unite them." To what, then, did the Church object? To hatred of other nations, said Faulhaber, and to setting loyalty to race above the obligations one owed to the Church.

Faulhaber was severely criticized by the Nazis for these qualifications, and his palace was fired on—a fact which has been taken as proof that German Catholicism actually did condemn the Nazi persecution of the Jews. Yet in the same series of sermons, in his eloquent vindication of the sacred character of the Old Testament (which Rosenberg had attacked as the "Jewish Bible"), Faulhaber went out of his way to make clear that he was not concerned with defending the Jews of his time. We must distinguish, he told the faithful, between the people of Israel before the death of Christ, who were vehicles of divine revelation, and the Jews after the death of Christ, who have become restless wanderers over the earth. But even the Jewish people of ancient times could not justly claim credit for the wisdom of the Old Testament: "People of Israel, this did not grow in your own garden of your own planting. This condemnation of usurious land-grabbing, this war against the oppression of the farmer by debt, this prohibition of usury, is not the product of your spirit."

Whatever ambiguity may still have attached to his position after these pronouncements, Faulhaber soon acted to dispel. In the summer of 1934 a Social Democratic paper in Prague published a sermon against race hatred which Faulhaber had allegedly preached. The Basel *National-Zeitung* in Switzerland reprinted excerpts from this sermon, and the World Jewish Congress at a meeting in Geneva praised the Cardinal's courageous stand. But the sermon turned out to be a fabrication, and Faulhaber had his secretary write a widely publicized letter to the Jewish organization protesting against "the use of his name by a conference that demands the commercial boycott of Germany, that is, economic war." The Cardinal, the letter continued, "in his Advent sermons of the previous year has defended the Old Testament of the Children of Israel but not taken a position with regard to the Jewish question of today."

Lesser Church dignitaries quite naturally took the cue from their Archbishop. An article written by a canon of the cathedral chapter of Regensburg, and published in *Klerusblatt*, the organ of the Bavarian priests' association, advised Catholic teachers to point out to pupils that the sacred books of the Old Testament were not only beyond the Jewish mentality but in direct conflict with it. "The greatest miracle of the Bible is that the true religion could hold its own and maintain itself against the voice of the Semitic blood."

The embarrassing fact that Jesus had been a Jew was handled in a similar manner. In a pastoral letter of 1939 Archbishop Gröber conceded that Jesus Christ could not be made into an Aryan, but the Son of God had been fundamentally different from the Jews of his time — so much so that they had hated him and demanded his crucifixion; and "their murderous hatred has continued in later centuries." Jesus had been a Jew, admitted Bishop Hilfrich of Limburg in his pastoral letter for Lent 1939, but "the Christian religion has not grown out of the nature of this people, that is, is not influenced by their racial characteristics. Rather it has had to make its way against this people." The Jewish people, the Bishop added, were guilty of the murder of God and had been under a curse since the day of the crucifixion.

The attempt to swim with the anti-Semitic tide was even

more pronounced in the previously cited *Handbook* of Archbishop Gröber. Marxism here was defined as "the materialistic socialism founded primarily by the Jew Karl Marx," and Bolshevism was characterized as "an Asiatic state despotism, in point of fact in the service of a group of terrorists led by Jews." The Führer had correctly described the struggle against this evil force as a defense of European civilization against Asiatic barbarism. "No people can avoid this clash between its natural tradition and Marxism which is opposed to national ties and led mostly by Jewish agitators and revolutionaries." And in yet another article, the *Handbook* asserted that most of the unhealthy and un-German developments in art since the 19th century had been the work of "the uprooted and atheistically perverted Jew," or those under Jewish influence.

If such language could be endorsed by an archbishop, it is no wonder that lower ranking figures in the Church felt free to express their anti-Semitic sentiments still more openly. Thus the theologian Karl Adam spoke of the need to purge the press, literature, science, and art of the "Jewish mentality," adding the usual caveat that "the Christian conscience must insist that these legal ordinances be implemented in a spirit of justice and love." Thus also an article on the revolution of 1918 in the paper of the Bavarian priests accused the Jew [sic] Karl Liebknecht of treason, and told how "the Jew Emil Barth equipped his *Untermenschen* [inferior humans] with hand grenades and automatic pistols in order to attack the national defense from the rear."

And so it went. The Jews had had a "demoralizing influence on religiosity and national character." The Jews, as a spiritual community, had brought the German people "more damage than benefit." The Jews had been "the first and most cruel persecutors of the young Church." The Jews had killed Jesus and in their boundless hatred of Christianity were still in the forefront of those seeking to destroy the Church.

If we take into account this climate of opinion within the Church—all the sentiments just cited were published between 1933 and 1939 in journals edited by priests or in books bearing the *Imprimatur* — we will find it easier to understand how it happened that the Church retreated in the face of the Nazis' anti-Semitic legislation, even where these ordinances touched upon vital domains of ecclesiastical jurisdiction such as matrimony.

According to canon law, the Church had exclusive jurisdiction over the marriage of Catholics. In practice, however, the Church in many countries had recognized the right of the state to impose certain conditions on marriage, so long as these did not conflict with natural law. Thus in Germany, the Church had long agreed to the provision that a civil marriage ceremony normally had to precede the ceremony conducted by the priest, and this agreement was ratified by the Concordat of 1933 between the Nazi government and the Vatican.

As early as 1934 the Church had made clear to the Nazi government that the enactment of a law forbidding racially mixed marriages would create a very difficult situation. In the eyes of the Church, the German bishops pointed out in a memorandum, every Catholic, whether born to a pure German or to a racially mixed marriage, whether baptized as a child or as an adult, was equally entitled to the sacraments. Hence if two baptized persons of racially mixed stock insisted on being married by a priest, the latter would have to comply, even if the state were to have prohibited such a union.

This, however, is precisely what the state soon did, for one of the practical results of the so-called Nuremberg laws of September 15, 1935, was to make it illegal for two Catholics to marry when one was considered racially "non-Aryan" under the standards set up by the law. (Since the persecution of the Jews had led to many new conversions to the Catholic religion, the number of such marriages was undoubtedly rising at the time.) The central office of information of the German episcopate in Berlin reported in September 1935 that earlier Catholic couples of racially mixed descent had been traveling to England to get married there, but now even those marriages had become illegal, and the Church had a very serious problem on its hands. What did she do? In some instances priests circumvented the law by using a provision of the Concordat of 1933 which, in cases of "great moral emergency," permitted a church marriage without a preceding civil ceremony, but by and large the Church conformed to the law, bowing to what earlier she had termed an inadmissible infringement of her spiritual jurisdiction.

For some elements in the Church, to be sure, bowing was unnecessary, for they actually welcomed the Nuremberg laws. While a distinguished German Catholic in exile, Waldemar Gurian, was denouncing the Nuremberg ordinances as violations of natural law and of the moral teachings of the Church, and declaring that they were "only a stage on the way toward the complete physical destruction of the Jews," an article in the *Klerusblatt* of January 1936 was justifying the new anti-Jewish statutes as indispensable safeguards for the qualitative makeup of the German people. So, too, Bishop Hudal, the head of the German Church in Rome, said that the Nuremberg laws were a necessary measure of self-defense against the influx of foreign elements. The Church in her own legislation, the Bishop contended, had held a radical position on the Jewish question "until the walls of the Ghetto had been torn down in the 19th century by the liberal state first and not by the Church." Consequently, from the point of view of the Church, there could be no objection to laws containing discriminatory provisions for Jews. "The principles of the modern state [based on the rule of equal treatment before the law] have been created by the French Revolution and are not the best from the standpoint of Christianity and nationality."

The Church surrendered in a similar fashion when the so-called Aryan clause was applied to clerical teachers of religion. This ordinance, enacted in 1938, meant that priests teaching religion in the public schools had to submit proof of their Aryan descent before they could continue in their posts. However, the policy in question affected very few clerics and had no further ramifications. Such was not the case when the Church agreed to supply data from her own records on the religious origin of those under her care. A decree of April 7, 1933 which resulted in the discharge of numerous Catholic civil servants, had also provided for the dismissal of all Jews, except veterans of the first World War, from the civil service. Henceforth, anyone applying for government employment—and soon for various other positions as well—had to submit proof that he was not a Jew. Since prior to 1874-76 births had been registered only by the churches, the latter were asked to help in determining who was or was not fully Aryan, for under Nazi law this depended on the racial (i.e., religious) status of parents and grandparents. The Church cooperated as a matter of course, complaining only that priests already overburdened with work were not receiving compensation for this special service to the state. The very question of whether the Church should lend its help to the Nazi state in sorting out people of Jewish descent was never debated. On the contrary. "We have always unselfishly worked for the people without regard to gratitude or ingratitude," a priest wrote in the *Klerusblatt* in September of 1934. "We shall also do our best to help in this service to the people." And the cooperation of the Church in this matter continued right through the war years when the price of being Jewish was no longer dismissal from a government job and loss of livelihood, but deportation and outright physical destruction.

The bishops sometimes showed concern for these non-Aryan Catholics, for whom the Church felt a special responsibility. Already in September 1933, Archbishop Bertram inquired from the Papal Secretary of State whether the Holy See could not put in a good word with the German government for the Jewish converts to the Catholic religion who were being made destitute on account of their non-Aryan descent. Soon the *St. Raphaelsverein,* a Catholic organization founded in 1871 for the protection of German émigrés, and presided over by Bishop Berning, began to take care of these Catholics. In the years 1936-37 the *St. Raphaelsverein* helped 516 Catholic non-Aryans to emigrate; in 1938 it facilitated the emigration of 1,850 such persons.

But what of non-Aryans who were not members of the Catholic faith? During these years prior to the adoption of the Final Solution, a few instances are on record where individual churchmen did speak up in defense of the Jews. In March, 1933, a priest in the Rhineland in a sermon characterized the vilification of the Jews as unjust and was fined 500 marks for abuse of the pulpit. In 1934 another priest, who for reasons of safety chose to remain anonymous, took his Church to task for not helping the Jews. And yet another priest, in Bavaria in 1936, declared that the stories being told in Germany about the Jews were a pack of lies. In Berlin on the morning after the *Kristallnacht* pogrom of November 1938, Provost Bernhard Lichtenberg prayed for the persecuted non-Aryan Christians and Jews and added: "What took place yesterday, we know; what will be tomorrow, we do not know; but what happens today, that we have witnessed; outside [this church] the synagogue is burning, and that also is a house of God."

There probably were other such statements, and here and there acts of Samaritanism may have taken place that have remained unrecorded. But the Church as such, speaking through the voice of her bishops, extended neither aid nor sympathy to other than Catholic non-Aryans, and remained silent in the face of anti-Jewish legislation, burning temples, and the first round-ups of Jews.

3. The Final Solution

In a speech delivered on January 30, 1939, the Führer served public notice of his intentions: "If international Jewry should succeed, in Europe or elsewhere, in precipitating nations into a world war, the result will not be the bolshevization of Europe and a victory for Judaism, but the extermination of the Jewish race." A few months later Hitler attacked Poland and World War II began. On July 31, 1941 Heydrich was charged "with making all necessary preparations . . . for bringing about a complete solution of the Jewish question in the German sphere of influence in Europe." The machinery of destruction went into action.

It began with a decree dated September 1, 1941 which provided that no Jew was to leave his place of domicile without special permission, and could appear in public only when marked with a yellow star. The idea of marking the Jews had first been applied in Poland, and now the system of identification was extended to the entire Reich. The decree covered so-called Mosaic Jews as well as baptized Jews; only those who had converted before September 15, 1935 (the date of the Nuremberg laws) and non-Aryans married to Aryan partners were exempt.

The wearing of the yellow star had a paralyzing effect upon those who were forced to do so. Many were afraid to leave their houses, and this fear created a special problem for the Catholics affected. In a number of towns these non-Aryan Catholics applied to the police for permission to remove the yellow star while going to and attending church services, and they asked their bishops to support the request. Accordingly, Bishops Wienken and Berning in Berlin tried to obtain permission from the Gestapo for the "Jewish" Catholics not to wear the Star of David while in church. But their efforts failed—the Gestapo was adamant.

Meanwhile, on September 17, Cardinal Bertram addressed a letter to the episcopate in which he counseled the avoidance of such "rash measures that could hurt the feelings of the Jewish Catholics as the introduction of special Jewish benches, separation when administering the sacraments, introduction of special services in specific churches or private houses." The segregation of the Catholic non-Aryans would violate Christian principles and therefore should be avoided as long as possible. (Priests might, however, advise Jewish Catholics to attend early mass whenever possible.) Admonitions to the faithful to exercise brotherly love toward the non-Aryans similarly should be postponed until disturbances resulted; and "Only when substantial difficulties result from attendance at church by the non-Aryan Catholics (like staying away of officials, party members and others . . .), should the Catholic non-Aryans be consulted about the holding of special services."

Mass deportations of German Jews to the East began on October 15, 1941. Bishop Berning, in a letter of October 27, informed Cardinal Bertram that while discussing the question of the Jewish star with the Gestapo he had also pointed to the harshness accompanying "the evacuation of the non-Aryans" and had requested some amelioration. He had been told that Christian non-Aryans would be evacuated only in exceptional cases (such as where earlier conflicts with the

Gestapo had occurred). For the time being non-Aryans in mixed marriages would not be affected by these measures.

The promises made by the Gestapo to Bishop Berning were of course not honored. On October 27, Bishop Hilfrich of Limburg informed Bishop Wienken, the episcopate's troubleshooter in Berlin, that the transport of Jews from Frankfurt earlier in the month had included Catholic non-Aryans to whom no preferred treatment had been granted. Their fate was especially sad since they were being regarded by their "*Rassengenossen*" (fellow Jews) as apostates. Hilfrich inquired whether for this reason it might not be possible to secure their exemption; if that could not be done, they should at least be put into special settlements where they could be given religious care more easily. Wienken replied a few days later that negotiations in the matter of the deportation of Catholic non-Aryans had been started at the highest level. The bishops of the Cologne and Paderborn church provinces, meeting in November 1941, also suggested that the government be petitioned in the matter of the deportations. They furthermore recommended that non-Aryan or half-Aryan priests and nuns volunteer to accompany the deportees in order to hold services for them and provide religious instruction for the children.

Meanwhile, rumors were spreading about the fate of the Jews in the East. These rumors had been making the rounds ever since the attack upon Russia on June 22, 1941, which had brought in its wake the employment of special detachments (*Einsatzgruppen*) assigned to the job of machine-gunning Jews. By the end of 1941 the first news had also trickled back about the fate of the deported German Jews who had been shot by mobile killing detachments near Riga and Minsk. And in the spring of 1942 the "White Rose," an organization made up of a group of students and a professor of philosophy at the University of Munich, distributed leaflets telling of the murder of 300,000 Jews in Poland and asking why the German people were being so apathetic in the face of these revolting crimes.

In December, 1941, the first death camp began operations near Lodz. Sobibor, Treblinka, and Auschwitz went into operation in the course of the year 1942. By the end of 1942 more than 100,000 German Jews had been sent to their death in the East, and the vague rumors about their fate had been replaced now by hard and persistent reports that included details of the mass gassings. In August, 1942, Colonel Kurt Gerstein, who had joined the S.S. to investigate the stories of extermination for himself, tried to tell the Papal Nuncio in

Berlin about a gassing he had witnessed near Lublin. When Monsignor Orsenigo refused to receive him, he told his story to Dr. Winter, the legal advisor of Bishop Preysing of Berlin, and to numbers of other persons. He also requested that the report be forwarded to the Holy See. During the same period, other reports about the extermination of the Jews reached the bishops through Catholic officers serving in Poland and Russia. For a long time Dr. Joseph Müller, an officer in Canaris's Military Intelligence Service and also a confidant of Cardinal Faulhaber, had kept the episcopate well informed about the systematic atrocities committed in Poland. Another source of information was Dr. Hans Globke, a Catholic and a high official in the Ministry of the Interior entrusted with handling racial matters. It is, then, clear that by the end of the year 1942 at the latest, the German episcopate was possessed of quite accurate knowledge of the horrible events unfolding in the East.

Until 1942 half-Jews and quarter-Jews, the so-called *Mischlinge,* as well as non-Aryans married to Aryans, had been exempt both from wearing the yellow star and from deportation. (The number of such persons in the Reich-Protektorat area was estimated at above 150,000.) Though the Nuremberg laws had forbidden marriages between Jews and Aryans, they had not annulled existing mixed marriages. With the progress of the Final Solution, however, this loophole was now to be closed. A conference of experts in March, 1942 decided upon the compulsory dissolution of racially mixed marriages, to be followed by the deportation of the Jewish partner. If the Aryan partner failed to apply for a divorce within a certain period of time, the public prosecutor was to file a petition for divorce which the courts would have to grant.

The bishops heard of the contemplated measure through Dr. Globke in the Ministry of the Interior, and they reacted promptly. On November 11, 1942, Archbishop Bertram in the name of the episcopate addressed a letter of protest against the planned compulsory divorce legislation to the Ministers of Justice, Interior, and Ecclesiastical Affairs. The intervention of the bishops, he insisted, was not due "to lack of love for the German nationality, lack of a feeling of national dignity, and also not to underestimation of the harmful Jewish influences upon German culture and national interests." The bishops merely felt called upon to emphasize that the duty of humane treatment also existed toward the members of other races. Among the persons affected by the contemplated measure, Bertram went on, were many thousands of Catholics whose marriages, according to Catholic doctrine, were indissoluble. Respect for the religious rights of the Catholic Christians was an indispensable condition for the peaceful cooperation of Church and State, which had never been as necessary as in the present situation. The bishops therefore hoped, the letter ended, that the government would withdraw the planned divorce ordinance.

Despite the fact that the ordinance was still tied up in bureaucratic difficulties, the Gestapo in February 1943, in the course of deporting the last German Jews, seized several thousand Christian non-Aryans, partners of mixed marriages. In Berlin alone about 6,000 such men were arrested on February 27. But then something unexpected and unparalleled happened: their Aryan wives followed them to the place of temporary detention and there they stood for several hours screaming and howling for their men. With the secrecy of the whole machinery of destruction threatened, the Gestapo yielded, and the non-Aryan husbands were released.

A few days after this unique event Bertram composed another letter. This time he also sent copies to the chief of the Reich Chancellery and to the *Reichssicherheitshauptamt* (RSHA), Himmler's headquarters. About 8,000 non-Aryan Catholics, Bertram complained, had been seized and deported. The episcopate could not silently accept these measures. He then repeated what he had said in November 1942 about the illegitimacy of compulsory divorce. On April 16, Bishop Preysing informed his fellow bishops that the contemplated divorce decree was soon to be made public. He urged that for the time being the matter be treated as strictly confidential; but in the event that the order should be issued, a statement drawn up by Bertram was to be read from the pulpits. The statement reaffirmed the indissolubility of Christian marriage and the validity of this principle even in the case of racially mixed marriages, and it asked for prayer for the unfortunates affected by the decree.

About two months later Preysing sent word to his colleagues through a messenger that the threatened decree had been postponed. The bishops were asked to write letters to all the ministries; they should inquire in strong language as to the whereabouts of the deportees, demanding pastoral care for the Christians and threatening a public protest. The point of departure should be concern for the Christian Jews, "but beyond this one should speak clearly about the outrages inflicted upon the Jews generally." We do not know how many bishops acted upon Preysing's request.

In November 1943, Bertram sent out another appeal in

the name of the entire episcopate to the Minister of the Interior and the RSHA. The episcopate, he wrote, had received information according to which the non-Aryans evacuated from Germany were living in camps under conditions that would have to be called inhuman. A large number of the sufferers had already succumbed. "In view of the reputation of the German name at home and abroad," and in view of the commands of the Christian moral law concerning the duties owed fellow men even of foreign races, the bishops considered it necessary to plead for an amelioration of conditions in these camps. In particular, Bertram continued, the bishops wished to demand the benefit of pastoral care for the imprisoned Catholics. The episcopate would gladly designate priests for divine services and the administration of the sacraments in the camps.

Bertram's letter neither employed strong language nor said anything very definite about the outrages against the Jews, as Bishop Preysing had suggested. Such vagueness was typical of the few public pronouncements the bishops made on this matter in the years following the adoption of the Final Solution. They spoke of the right to life and liberty, not to be denied even those "who are not of our blood," to "men of foreign races and descent," and to "the resettled," but the word "Jew" never once appeared in any of these documents.

In his next and last letter to the government, dispatched in January 1944, Bertram wrote that reports had been received to the effect that measures which had previously been applied only to Jews were now to be applied also to the *Mischlinge*. These Christians had already been barred from military service and institutions of higher learning, but now, it seemed, they were to be conscripted into special formations for labor service. "All these measures," Bertram continued, "aim clearly at segregation, at the end of which extermination threatens." In the name of the episcopate he felt obligated to point out that any change in the meaning of the term "Jew" — when the Nuremberg statutes had been accepted as the final word on this question for almost ten years—would seriously undermine confidence in the law. The *Mischlinge* were Germans and Christians and had always been rejected by the Jews. "The German Catholics, indeed numerous Christians in Germany," Bertram warned, "would be deeply hurt if these fellow Christians now had to meet a fate similar to that of the Jews." The bishops would not be able to reconcile it with their conscience to remain silent in the face of such measures.

As against the case of the euthanasia program of the early

war years, then—when the episcopate did not mince words and succeeded in putting a stop to the killings—the bishops continually played it safe where the Jews were concerned. Such public protests as they did register could, indeed, have been seen as referring to the Jews, but any Catholic who chose to interpret them otherwise (as referring, say, only to Slavs) was left free to do so. Close to half the population of the Greater German Reich (43.1 per cent in 1939) was Catholic, and even among the S.S., despite all pressures to leave the Church, almost a fourth (22.7 per cent on December 31, 1938) belonged to the Catholic faith. Yet while the episcopate had in the past issued orders to deny the sacraments to Catholics who engaged in dueling or agreed to have their bodies cremated, the word that would have forbidden the faithful, on pain of excommunication, to go on participating in the massacre of the Jews was never spoken. And so Catholics went on participating conscientiously, along with other Germans.

There was, however, at least one Catholic churchman in Germany for whom the Christian duty to love one's neighbor amounted to more than a pious formula—the sixty-six-year-old Provost Lichtenberg of Berlin, who, right through the stepped-up anti-Semitic agitation, continued to say a daily prayer for the Jews. He was finally arrested on October 23, 1941, a week after the first of the mass deportations of Jews had begun. During questioning by Himmler's henchmen, the Provost asserted that the deportation of the Jews was irreconcilable with the Christian moral law, and asked to be allowed to accompany the deportees as their spiritual adviser. Sentenced to two years imprisonment for abuse of the pulpit, Lichtenberg was seized by the Gestapo upon his release in October, 1943, and shipped off to the concentration camp at Dachau. He died during the transport on November 5, 1943.

The passivity of the German episcopate in the face of the Jewish tragedy stands in marked contrast to the conduct of the French, Belgian, and Dutch bishops. In Holland, where the Church as early as 1934 had prohibited the participation of Catholics in the Dutch Nazi movement, the bishops in 1942 immediately and publicly protested the first deportations of Dutch Jews, and in May 1943, they forbade the collaboration of Catholic policemen in the hunting down of Jews even at the cost of losing their jobs. In Belgium members of the episcopate actively supported the rescue efforts of their clergy, who hid many hundreds of Jewish children. And in France, the highest dignitaries of the Church repeatedly used their pulpits to denounce the deportations and to condemn the barbarous treatment of the Jews.

Throughout Western Europe untold numbers of priests and members of the monastic clergy organized the rescue of Jews, hid them in monasteries, parish houses, and private homes. Many lay Catholics in France, Holland, and Belgium acted in a similar fashion, thus saving thousands of Jewish lives. The concern of the Gentile populations of these countries for their Jewish fellow-citizens was undoubtedly one of the key factors behind the bold public protests of the French, Dutch, and Belgian bishops—just as the absence of such solicitude in Germany goes a long way toward explaining the apathy of their German counterparts. In France, Belgium, and Holland, declarations of solidarity and help for the Jews were almost universally regarded as signs of patriotism; in Germany, on the other hand, the bishops in so acting would have incurred new charges of being un-German and of being in league with Germany's mortal enemies. Their own parishioners, moreover, would probably have failed to understand or support any signs of sympathy for the Jews—whom the Church, after all, had herself long been branding as a harmful factor in German life. Consequently, at the very moment when the bishops might perhaps have wanted to protest the inhuman treatment of the Jews, they found themselves the prisoners of their own anti-Semitic teachings.

Indeed, in Germany only a handful of Jews was hidden by the clergy or otherwise helped by them in their hour of distress. In Freiburg there was Dr. Gertrud Luckner, an official of the *Caritas* (the large Catholic philanthropic organization) who helped Jews get across the Swiss border, sent packages to deportees, and distributed money from a special fund established by the episcopate for non-Aryans. She was arrested in November 1943, while trying to bring a sum of money to the few remaining Jews in Berlin and spent the rest of the war in a concentration camp. A few cases are also recorded of individual Catholics hiding and saving Jews, but only in Berlin did a significant number of Jews find refuge with friends and neighbors; according to Provost Grüber, most of these courageous people were workers, many of them were unconnected with any church.

There were, then, exceptions, but the overall picture was one of indifference and apathy. "Among the Christians," a group of German Protestant and Catholic theologians concluded in 1950, "a few courageously helped the persecuted, but the large majority failed disgracefully in the face of this unheard-of provocation of the merciful God."

4. The Role of the Papacy

In April 1933 a communication reached Pope Pius XI from Germany expressing grave concern over the Nazis' anti-Semitic aims and requesting the Supreme Pontiff to issue an encyclical on the Jewish question. The letter was written by the philosopher Dr. Edith Stein, a Jewish convert to Catholicism and later known as Sister Teresia Benedicta a Cruce of the Order of the Carmelites. Edith Stein's request was not granted and nine years later, in August 1942, she was seized by the Gestapo from a Dutch monastery in which she had sought refuge, and sent to Auschwitz to be gassed. The debate over whether the Papacy could have prevented or should at least have vigorously protested the massacre of the Jews of Europe, of which Edith Stein was one of the victims, has been going on ever since and has acquired new vigor as a result of the Hochhuth play.

In response to Hitler's anti-Semitic drive, Pius XII's predecessor, Pius XI, like the German episcopate, seems to have limited his concern to Catholic non-Aryans. At the request of Cardinal Bertram, the Papal Secretary of State in September 1933 put in "a word on behalf of those German Catholics" who were of Jewish descent and for this reason suffering "social and economic difficulties." In the years that followed the Holy See often took issue with the Nazis' glorification of race, but the Jewish question specifically was never discussed. In 1934 the influential Jesuit magazine *Civiltà Cattolica,* published in Rome and traditionally close to Vatican thinking, noted with regret that the anti-Semitism of the Nazis "did not stem from the religious convictions nor the Christian conscience . . . , but from . . . their desire to upset the order of religion and society." The *Civiltà Cattolica* added that "we could understand them, or even praise them, if their policy were restricted within acceptable bounds of defense against the Jewish organizations and institutions . . ." In 1936 the same journal published another article on the subject, emphasizing that opposition to Nazi racialism should not be interpreted as a rejection of anti-Semitism, and arguing—as the magazine had done since 1890—that the Christian world (though without un-Christian hatred) must defend itself against the Jewish threat by suspending the civic rights of Jews and returning them to the ghettos.

Pius XI's encyclical *"Mit brennender Sorge"* of March 1937 rejected the myths of race and blood as contrary to revealed Christian truth, but it neither mentioned nor criticized anti-Semitism *per se.* Nor was anti-Semitism mentioned in the statement of the Roman Congregation of Seminaries and

Universities, issued on April 13, 1938 and attacking as erroneous eight theses taken from the arsenal of Nazi doctrine. On September 7, 1938, during a reception for Catholic pilgrims from Belgium, Pius XI is said to have condemned the participation of Catholics in anti-Semitic movements and to have added that Christians, the spiritual descendants of the patriarch Abraham, were "spiritually Semites." But this statement was omitted by all the Italian papers, including *L'Osservatore Romano,* from their account of the Pope's address.

The elevation of Cardinal Pacelli to the Papacy in the spring of 1939 brought to the chair of St. Peter a man who, in contrast to his predecessor, was unemotional and dispassionate, as well as a master of the language of diplomatic ambiguity. "Pius XII," recalls Cardinal Tardini, "was by nature meek and almost timid. He was not born with the temperament of a fighter. In this he was different from his great predecessor." But whether, as Hochhuth has speculated, Pius XI would have reacted to the massacre of the Jews during World War II differently from Pacelli, is a question to which no definite answer is possible.

That the Holy See had no intrinsic objection to a policy of subjecting the Jews to discriminatory legislation again became clear when in June 1941 Marshal Pétain's Vichy government introduced a series of "Jewish statutes." The Cardinals and Archbishops of France made known their strong disapproval of these measures, but Léon Bérard, the Vichy ambassador at the Holy See, was able to report to Pétain after lengthy consultations with high Church officials that the Vatican did not consider such laws in conflict with Catholic teaching. The Holy See merely counseled that no provisions on marriage be added to the statutes and "that the precepts of justice and charity be considered in the application of the law." In August 1941 the consequences of this discriminatory policy could not yet be clearly seen, but when mass deportations from France got under way in 1942, the Papal Nuncio, without invoking the authority of the Holy See, requested Laval to mitigate the severity of the measures taken against the Jews of Vichy France. By that time, however, such pleas could no longer halt the machinery of destruction.

Meanwhile, there was growing criticism of the Pope's failure to protest publicly against Nazi atrocities, and especially against the murder of the Jews in the Polish death factories. In July 1942, Harold H. Tittmann, the assistant to Roosevelt's personal representative at the Holy See, Myron C. Taylor, pointed out to the Vatican that its silence was "endangering its moral prestige and is undermining faith both in the Church and in the Holy Father himself." In September 1942, after authorization by Secretary of State Hull, Tittmann and several other diplomatic representatives at the Vatican formally requested that the Pope condemn the "incredible horrors" perpetrated by the Nazis. A few days later Taylor forwarded to the Papal Secretary of State, Luigi Maglione, a memorandum from the Jewish Agency for Palestine reporting mass executions of Jews in Poland and occupied Russia, and telling of deportations to death camps from Germany, Belgium, Holland, France, Slovakia, etc. Taylor inquired whether the Vatican could confirm these reports, and if so, "whether the Holy Father has any suggestions as to any practical manner in which the forces of civilized opinion could be utilized in order to prevent a continuation of these barbarities." On October 10 the Holy See, in reply to Taylor's note, said that up to the present time it had not been possible to verify the accuracy of reports concerning the severe measures that were being taken against the Jews. "It is well known," the statement added, "that the Holy See is taking advantage of every opportunity offered in order to mitigate the suffering of non-Aryans."

After the Western Allies in December 1942 had vigorously denounced the cold-blooded extermination of the Jews, Tittmann again asked the Papal Secretary of State whether the Holy See could not issue a similar pronouncement. Maglione answered that the Holy See, in line with its policy of neutrality, could not protest particular atrocities and had to limit itself to condemning immoral actions in general. He assured Tittmann that everything possible was being done behind the scenes to help the Jews.

Two days later, in the course of a lengthy Christmas message broadcast by the Vatican radio, Pope Pius made another of his many calls for a more humane conduct of hostilities. Humanity, the Pope declared, owed the resolution to build a better world to "the hundreds of thousands who without personal guilt, sometimes for no other reason but on account of their nationality or descent, were doomed to death or exposed to a progressive deterioration of their condition." Again, addressing the Sacred College of Cardinals in June 1943, the Pontiff spoke of his twofold duty to be impartial and to point up moral errors. He had given special attention, he recalled, to the plight of those who were still being harassed because of their nationality or descent and who without personal guilt were subjected to measures that spelled destruction. Much had been done for the unfortunates that could not be described yet. Every public statement had had to be carefully weighed "in the interest of those suffering so that their situation would not inadvertently be made still more difficult and unbearable." Unfortunately, Pius XII added, the Church's pleas for compassion and for the observance of the elementary norms of humanity had encountered doors "which no key was able to open."

The precise nature of these interventions has not been revealed to this day. We do know, however, that Nuncio Orsenigo in Berlin made inquiries several times about mass shootings and the fate of deported Jews. (Ernst Woermann, the director of the Political Department of the German Foreign Ministry, recorded on October 15, 1942 that the Nuncio had made his representation with "some embarrassment and without emphasis." State Secretary Weizsäcker told Monsignor Orsenigo on another such occasion that the Vatican had so far conducted itself "very cleverly" in these matters, and that he would hope for a continuation of this policy. The Nuncio took the hint and "pointed out that he had not really touched this topic and that he had no desire to touch it."

The Pope's policy of neutrality encountered its most crucial test when the Nazis began rounding up the 8,000 Jews of Rome in the fall of 1943. Prior to the start of the arrests, the Jewish community was told by the Nazis that unless it raised 50 kilograms of gold (the equivalent of $56,000) within 36 hours, 300 hostages would be taken. When it turned out that the Jews themselves could only raise 35 kgs., the Chief Rabbi, Israel Zolli, asked for and received a loan from the Vatican treasury to cover the balance. The Pope approved this transaction. But the big question in everyone's mind was how the Supreme Pontiff would react when the deportation of the Jews from the Eternal City began.

The test came on the night of October 15/16. While the round-up was still going on, a letter was delivered to General Stahel, the German military commander of Rome. Bearing the signature of Bishop Hudal, the head of the German Church in Rome, it said:

I have just been informed by a high Vatican office in the immediate circle of the Holy Father that the arrests of Jews of Italian nationality have begun this morning. In the interest of the good relations which have existed until now between the Vatican and the high German military command . . . I would be very grateful if you would give an order to stop these arrests in Rome and its vicinity right away; I fear that otherwise the Pope will have to make an open stand which will serve the anti-German propaganda as a weapon against us.

A day later, Ernst von Weizsäcker, the new German Ambassador at the Holy See, reported to Berlin that the Vatican was upset, especially since the deportations had taken place, as it were, right under the Pope's window:

The people hostile to us in Rome are taking advantage of this affair to force the Vatican from its reserve. People say that the bishops of French cities, where similar incidents occurred, have taken a firm stand. The Pope, as supreme head of the Church and Bishop of Rome, cannot be more reticent than they. They are also drawing a parallel between the stronger character of Pius XI and that of the present Pope.

Contrary to Hudal's and Weizsäcker's apprehensions, however, the man in the Vatican palace remained silent. On October 18, over one thousand Roman Jews—more than two-thirds of them women and children—were shipped off to the killing center of Auschwitz. Fourteen men and one woman returned alive. About 7,000 Roman Jews—that is, seven out of eight—were able to elude their hunters by going into hiding. More than 4,000, with the knowledge and approval of the Pope, found refuge in the numerous monasteries and houses of religious orders in Rome, and a few dozen were sheltered in the Vatican itself. The rest were hidden by their Italian neighbors, among whom the anti-Jewish policy of the Fascists had never been popular. But for the Germans, overwhelmingly relieved at having averted a public protest by the Pope, the fact that a few thousand Jews had escaped the net was of minor significance. On October 28 Ambassador Weizsäcker was able to report:

Although under pressure from all sides, the Pope has not let himself be drawn into any demonstrative censure of the deportation of Jews from Rome. Although he must expect that his attitude will be criticized by our enemies and exploited by the Protestant and Anglo-Saxon countries in their propaganda against Catholicism, he has done everything he could in this delicate matter not to strain relations with the German government, and German circles in Rome. As there is probably no reason to expect other German actions against the Jews of Rome, we can consider that a question so disturbing to German-Vatican relations has been liquidated.

In any case, an indication for this state of affairs can be seen in the Vatican's attitude. *L'Osservatore Romano* has in fact prominently published in its issue of October 25-26, an official communiqué on the Pope's charitable activities. The communiqué, in the Vatican's distinctive style, that is, very vague and complicated, declares that all men, without distinction of nationality, race, or religion, benefit from the Pope's paternal solicitude. The continual and varied activities of Pius XII have probably increased lately because of the greater sufferings of so many unfortunates.

There is less reason to object to the terms of this message . . . as only a very small number of people will recognize in it a special allusion to the Jewish question.

Since the end of World War II, Pius XII has often been criticized for his silence. It has been argued—and most recently by Hochhuth—that the Pope could have saved numerous lives, if indeed he could not have halted the machinery of destruction altogether, had he chosen to take a public stand, and had he confronted the Germans with the threat of an interdict or with the excommunication of Hitler, Goebbels, and other leading Nazis belonging to the Catholic faith. As examples of the effectiveness of public protests, it is possible to cite the resolute reaction of the German episcopate to the euthanasia program. Also, in Slovakia, Hungary, and Rumania, the forceful intervention of Papal nuncios, who threatened the Quisling governments with public condemnation by the Pope, was able, albeit temporarily, to stop the deportations. At the very least, it has been suggested, a public denunciation of the mass murders by Pius XII, broadcast widely over the Vatican radio, would have revealed to Jews and Christians alike what deportation to the East actually meant. The Pope would have been believed, whereas the broadcasts of the Allies were often shrugged off as war propaganda. Many of the deportees who accepted the assurances of the Germans that they were merely being resettled, might thus have been warned and given an impetus to escape; many more Christians might have helped and sheltered Jews, and many more lives might have been saved.

There exists, of course, no way of definitively proving or disproving these arguments. Whether a papal decree of excommunication against Hitler would have dissuaded the Führer from carrying out his plan to destroy the Jews is very doubtful, and revocation of the Concordat by the Holy See would have bothered Hitler still less. However, a flaming protest against the massacre of the Jews coupled with an imposition of the interdict upon all of Germany or the excommunication of all Catholics in any way involved with the apparatus of the "Final Solution" would have been a more formidable and effective weapon. Yet this was precisely the kind of action which the Pope could not take without risking the allegiance of the German Catholics. Given the indifference of the German population toward the fate of the Jews and the highly ambivalent attitude of the German hierarchy toward Nazi anti-Semitism, a forceful stand by the Supreme Pontiff on the Jewish question might well have led to a large-scale desertion from the Church. When Dr. Edoardo Senatro, the correspondent of *L'Osservatore Romano* in Berlin, asked Pius XII whether he would not protest the extermination of the Jews, the Pope is reported to have answered, "Dear friend, do not forget that millions of Catholics serve in the German armies. Shall I bring them into conflicts of conscience?" The Pope knew that the German Catholics were not prepared to suffer martyrdom for their Church; still less were they willing to incur the wrath of their Nazi rulers for the sake of the Jews, whom their own bishops for years had castigated as a harmful influence in German life. In the final analysis, then, "the Vatican's silence only reflected the deep feeling of the Catholic masses of Europe."

Some Catholic writers have suggested that a public protest by the Pope would not only have been unsuccessful in helping the Jews but might have caused additional damage—to the Jews, to the *Mischlinge,* to the Church, to the territorial integrity of the Vatican, and to Catholics in all of Nazi-occupied Europe. So far as the Jews are concerned, it is tempting to dismiss this argument by asking what worse fate could possibly have befallen them than the one that actually did. But in any case, the Catholic bishops of Holland tried the gamble and failed. In July 1942, together with the Protestant Churches, they sent a telegram of protest against the deportation of the Dutch Jews to the German *Reichskommissar* (commissioner) and threatened to make their protest public unless the deportations were halted. The Germans responded by offering to exempt from deportation non-Aryans converted to Christianity before 1941 if the churches agreed to remain silent. The Dutch Reformed Church accepted the bargain, but the Catholic Archbishop of Utrecht refused and issued a pastoral letter in which he denounced the wrong done to the Jews. The Germans retaliated by seizing and deporting all the Catholic non-Aryans they could find, among them Edith Stein. There was thus some basis for the fear that a public protest, along with any good that could come of it, might make some things worse, if not for the Jews, at least for the *Mischlinge* and the Catholics themselves.

The Pope had other, perhaps still weightier, reasons for remaining silent. As Mr. Tittmann was told by highly placed officials of the Curia, the Holy See did not want to jeopardize its neutrality by condemning German atrocities, and the Pope was unwilling to risk later charges of having been partial and contributing to a German defeat. Moreover, the Vatican did not wish to undermine and weaken Germany's struggle against Russia. In the late summer of 1943, the Papal Secretary of State declared that the fate of Europe depended upon a German victory on the Eastern front; and Father Robert Leiber, one of Pius XII's secretaries, recalls that the late Pope had always looked upon Russian Bolshevism as more dangerous than German National Socialism.

Finally, one is inclined to conclude that the Pope and his advisors—influenced by the long tradition of moderate anti-Semitism so widely accepted in Vatican circles—did not view the plight of the Jews with a real sense of urgency and moral outrage. For this assertion no documentation is possible, but it is a conclusion difficult to avoid. Pius XII broke his policy of strict neutrality during World War II to express concern over the German violation of the neutrality of Holland, Belgium, and Luxemburg in May 1940. When some German Catholics criticized him for this action, the Pope wrote the German bishops that neutrality was not synonymous "with indifference and apathy where moral and humane considerations demanded a candid word." All things told, did not the murder of several million Jews demand a similarly "candid word"?

GOLO MANN

The Real Accomplishment

If I remember correctly, the opinion explaining the verdict which concluded the Eichmann trial had this to say: we are

---

Noted German historian, son of Thomas Mann, the author has written extensively on contemporary history including his study *Deutsche Geschichte des 19. und 20. Jahrhunderts.* This article was originally published in *Basler Nachrichten,* September 17, 1963 and was translated by William Duell, Jr.

incapable of depicting the human dimensions of the crime or the suffering of the victims; that is the task of great writers. I do not want to state definitely that Rolf Hochhuth is a great writer—the future will prove that. But a writer he is; I admire his accomplishment in *The Deputy*. It is really a miracle that in the stagnant atmosphere of the Federal Republic of Germany—where there is a well-trained, self-justified officialdom, by now again very secure, opposed by an equally self-justified and mostly uncreative radicalism—this courageous work of art could be created by a young man who knew the outrages of the Hitler period only from documents. If Hochhuth's play does not accomplish everything the Jerusalem judges expect from writers in the future, it does accomplish much of it; it gives form to the human reality of the murder of the Jews, of the murderers themselves, of the victims and the few who helped them. The typifying and idealizing artistic means which he risks include versified prose. The discussion prompted by the play was centered almost completely on the question of the complicity or non-complicity of the Pope and the Catholic hierarchy. The defenders of Pope and Church offered, in effect, an admonition to the Germans or "Nazis" to clean up their own mess first and questioned whether an open protest by the Pope could have improved the situation. This was countered by the question whether an open papal protest could have worsened the situation, quite aside from the unforeseeable effect and usefulness of a step never taken, and if there was not an absolute obligation to speak the truth about such horrors. Everything that could be said about this has been said; in the meantime new historical studies and document collections have proven the Catholic hierarchy's guilty involvement in the beginnings, and more than the beginnings, of the Third Reich. If there is a weakness in the liberal criticism it is the argument that a person who absolutely does not believe in the holiness of an institution in the first place is in no position to accuse it of unholiness or ineffectiveness in a time of great peril.

It seems to me that in this dispute Hochhuth's accomplishment has not been fully appreciated. His accomplishment is not, at least not chiefly, his portrait of the Pope, the dignitaries, and financial administrators, be it accurate or distorted—and I think it is by no means wholly distorted. Hochhuth is too good a psychologist, too careful a historian, and too much of a writer not to have sought out the precise nuance here as he has elsewhere. Had he left out the Vatican completely, or constructed his play on a different moral theme, it would have lost none of its value. The tension between the hierarchy and the idealists who demand more from the hierarchy than it is willing to give is basically nothing more than the really dramatic, necessary, but exchangeable opportunity to do something else: to give form to this terrible history, something which no historian or novelist before Hochhuth had been able to do. Up to now the power of the word has always failed when confronted with this subject; here it does not fail. How viably the criminals are pictured: the Germans and their non-German accomplices, from the wretches on top—who, with one exception, are not "monsters"—all the way down to the vulgar, sly, infinitely common sergeant who rounded up the Roman Jews. How tangible the destiny of a single family, the Luccanis, makes things which no statistics, no comprehensive report, not even a documentary, could convey! How much perception for things human, how much empathy, fantasy and pity, sorrow, deep revulsion and anger are forced under the yoke of art. This is the true accomplishment. It explains why the German public has been affected by this drama as no trial in Nuremberg or Jerusalem, no study by the Institute for Contemporary History, no matter how exhaustive, has affected it. It is for this that we must thank the writer.

JAMES O'GARA

The Real Issue

It is hard to realize that the Berlin premiere of Hochhuth's *The Deputy* took place only a year ago. Since then the play has been translated into many languages and has been staged in several countries. I cannot remember another play that has

---

Mr. O'Gara is managing editor of *Commonweal,* from which this piece of February 28, 1964 is reprinted.

been so widely discussed, and an American production is scheduled to open here late this month.

I saw the Hochhuth play in London last fall—or at least I saw the two and a half hours which have been culled from a play that would take seven or eight hours to put on in its entirety. It is, I think, quite a bad play; when Pius XII washes his hands like Pilate on stage—literally—one realizes there is no limit to which Hochhuth will not go. *The Deputy* has power, but not because of any worth as a play; it can move us only because it is a historico-legal statement about the most monstrous crime of our time, and perhaps of any time—the systematic murder of six million Jews in the heart of civilized Europe. It is this crime that gives *The Deputy* its importance, and it is on this level rather than as a play that I would like to discuss it.

The Hochhuth thesis is a simple one. Pope Pius XII, he maintains, could have stopped Hitler from exterminating the Jews by a forthright denunciation before the whole world. That condemnation Pope Pius never delivered, at least in the explicit terms Hochhuth wanted. The motives for the Pope's silence, as Hochhuth sees them, were these: first of all, and most incredibly, that the Vatican was profiteering from the war; secondly, that Nazism was fighting the great enemy in the East, atheistic Communism; thirdly, the hope that a silent, "neutral" Pope would eventually be called on to mediate between the warring parties. In *The Deputy* Pius is a far cry from the saintly portrait of the Catholic press; Hochhuth's Pope was sly, he was greedy, he was morally insensitive, he was a politician without principle. In short, for Hochhuth the Deputy of Christ on earth was a villain.

How is a Catholic to respond to all this? In Germany and England some made plain their conviction that any discussion of the Pope's conduct is completely out of order. In France, a few Catholics even became violent when the play was produced. Both reactions seem to me inappropriate. Catholics claim for the Pope infallibility under certain circumstances; we don't say he can do no wrong. The only valid question about *The Deputy* as a historico-legal document is its truth. On this score, and on this score alone, then, I would throw Hochhuth's indictment out.

This is not to say that on the Jewish question Pope Pius did all some of us would have wanted. It is true that he condemned racism, but he did so in such general terms that for many the effect was muted. It is true that he personally was responsible for the sheltering of many Jews, in the Vatican and elsewhere, but these amounted only to thousands while millions were dying in the concentration camps and gas chambers.

Part of this may have been temperament. Pope Pius was a shy and rather retiring man; it is possible that another Pope, a John XXIII, for example, might have succeeded in rousing the conscience of the world against Hitler and forced him to stop his planned extermination of the Jews. Or, on the other hand, the effort might have backfired, as it did in Holland, where the condemnation of a Nazi deportation program by the Catholic bishops only led to more extensive measures.

In any case, it can certainly be argued that Pius erred. But this is not what Hochhuth charges. The playwright does not say Pius made a mistake in judgment; he says he followed the wrong course because he was a vain, greedy and unprincipled man. Hochhuth does what no man can do; he inserts himself into the mind of Pius and draws only the worst conclusions. He is guilty of the worst kind of McCarthyism, and only the staggering immensity of his charge has kept people from seeing this fact.

All this, I think, is true. And yet something more needs to be said, for if one is content simply to defend Pius, one risks collaborating with a lie, or at least with a half-truth. For if Hochhuth is wrong in his indictment, he is wrong only in the man he singles out; correct that, and Hochhuth has given us a true bill.

Nineteen hundred years after the birth of Our Lord, a monstrous form of pagan barbarism arose in the heart of Christian Europe. By the thousands and by the hundreds of thousands, men who called themselves Christian abandoned the one true God in order to worship in the Nazis' cult of blood and race. By the thousands and the hundreds of thousands, they were at best silent and at worst cooperative with Hitler's "final solution" to the Jewish problem. And while this went on in Germany, Christians in other countries watched, most of them in silence, some even approving what Hitler was doing. What are we to say about that? As far as that goes, what are we to say about the conspiracy of silence that greeted Gordon Zahn's attempt to weigh Catholic responsibility for Hitler in *German Catholics and Hitler's Wars* (Sheed & Ward), and this only two years ago, not in Germany but in the United States?

Hochhuth is wrong, then, and people should know this. They should know it because it is altogether too easy to lay the blame on Pius XII, and this can easily be just one more act of evasion where there has been too much evasion already.

LEON POLIAKOV

Pope Pius XII and the Nazis

Why did Pope Pius XII never protest against Hitler's extermination of the Jews?

Der Stellvertreter or *The Deputy,* a play by a young, previously unknown German Protestant author, Rolf Hochhuth, has triggered renewed international controversy around this twenty-year-old question. The Catholic diocese in Berlin circulated tracts attacking the play the day it opened there last February. In Basle, Switzerland, this September, protesters marched by torchlight the night of the premiere, and police cordons guarding the theater intervened to halt an incipient riot. In London, where *The Deputy* opened the same month, the Royal Shakespeare Company's program included at the request of the Lord Chamberlain, a letter written by Pope Paul VI while he was still Cardinal Montini denouncing the play. In Israel, according to reports, the Government has brought pressure to bear upon the Habimah troupe not to produce *The Deputy*. In newspapers and magazine articles, on radio and television, discussion — and acrimony — has been raging, centering on two distinct issues:

Politically, would protest by Pius XII have been of help to the Jews or not? And, for the Catholic Church, without danger or fraught with consequences?

Morally, and regardless of any political evaluation, was the Pope justified in keeping silent?

The question is not new. I myself raised it in an article in *Commentary* in 1950. Catholics, too, and of no mean standing, have expressed regret at Pius XII's silence. In 1951, for example, François Mauriac spoke of "we French Catholics whose honor, certainly, was saved by the heroism

---

Member of the French Resistance and research director of the Paris Centre de Documentation Juive Contemporaine, the author is an historian whose book, *Harvest of Hate,* documents the Nazi extermination program. This article is reprinted from *Jewish Frontier* of April 1964 by permission of the author and *Jewish Frontier*. It originally appeared in the French magazine *L'Arche.* The translation from the French is by Abe Karlikoff.

and charity shown hunted Jews by so many bishops, priests, nuns and monks; but who never had the consolation of hearing Galilean Simon Peter's successor clearly condemn the crucifixion of these innumerable 'brethren of the Lord' in plain terms, not diplomatic allusion . . ." Mauriac characterized the Pope's silence as a "horrible duty."

In *The Deputy,* however, Hochhuth has given these questions a dramatic turn of such boldness and intensity that the Holy See itself has taken a stand on historical and moral points about which it previously kept silent. Real and imaginary events and characters are welded together in a long, complex and impassioned drama: uncut, it is estimated, the play would run seven hours. The central figure is a young Italian Jesuit, a member of the Vatican's foreign service, Father Riccardo Fontana. Shocked on learning of the Nazi mass murder of Jews he seeks public condemnation by the Pope, pleading the case for action before the Pontiff himself in the play's key — and certainly most controversial — scene. When Pius refuses, citing political considerations, Fontana is appalled. He pins the Star of David to his cassock and goes to join Jews being deported to Auschwitz, perishing with them. (Hochhuth's play is dedicated to two priests who sacrificed themselves in such a manner — Bernard Lichtenberg and Maximilian Kolbe.)

The scene is set in the Rome of October, 1943. The Germans, it will be remembered, had just entered the City. Jews were being seized at the gates of the Vatican. This was the time when the German Ambassador to the Holy See, Ernst von Weizsäcker, warned his government (probably with the accord of the Curia[1]) that the Pope might protest. He pointed out the stand that French bishops had taken under similar circumstances and affirmed that the Pope, as supreme head of the Church and bishop of Rome, could be expected to act in a similar fashion. Some ten days later, however, von Weizsäcker informed his government that "although pressed on all sides" the Pope had abstained from protesting "so as not to put to the test relations with the German government and German circles in Rome." It is on the reading of these lines that the play closes.

For Hochhuth's Father Riccardo a Pope who knows of the

[1] According to the testimony at Nuremberg of von Weizsäcker and his aide Albrecht von Kessel, they did their best in the autumn of 1943, in concert with the Curia, to forestall and lessen the sufferings of the Rome population. Public protest by the Pope against the deportation of Jews may have been one of the steps envisaged at the time. We have no direct evidence from the Curia on this point.

deportation of Jews, "a Vicar of Christ who has *that* under his eyes and who still keeps silent for reasons of state, who reflects a single day, who hesitates for a single hour to raise his voice in grief to pronounce a solemn malediction — such a Pope is a criminal," he cries.

The quotation gives some idea of the play's violence. Together with this goes a portrayal of the Pope as a cold, calculating politician, primarily concerned to avoid an open conflict with Hitler lest the vast and multiple interests of the Roman Church suffer, and lest Communism make any advance.

Hochhuth argues, moreover, (both through his character and in a lengthy historical supplement to the play), that a protest by the Pope would have been effective: that the Pope not only would have saved Roman Jews but also would have stopped the extermination at Auschwitz and elsewhere. He advances as evidence for this the fact that in August, 1941, Hitler, faced by the protests of Catholic and Protestant German clergy, halted the mass murder of German mentally sick undertaken when the war began.

Little wonder then that, from the outset, *The Deputy* has aroused emotion and argument, discussion and denunciation. The tracts put out by the Berlin diocese attacking the play cited past praise by Jewish personalities — Rome's Chief Rabbi Elio Toaff, the Jewish Agency's Kurt R. Grossman, the Nuremberg prosecutor Robert M. Kempner, and Dr. Nahum Goldmann — for Pius XII and his help to Jews. Hochhuth's critics charge that by imputing responsibility for the holocaust of the Jews to the Pope, Hochhuth is, in effect, trying to lift the guilt from Nazism. "Should the rest of us Germans tolerate such theater, should we not refute it mercilessly, we should again compromise ourselves in the eyes of the entire world," declared one spokesman of German Catholicism, Fürst zu Löwenstein. Bonn Foreign Minister Gerhard Schroeder advanced the same idea without naming Hochhuth or the play, deploring the attacks on Pius and lauding his actions on behalf of Jews. Generally, although gingerly, Protestant voices were more favorable to *The Deputy* than Catholic ones, but the *pros* and *cons* were by no means divided along religious lines.

Two critics of Hochhuth merit special attention. Both had been close to, and had even played roles in, the events of October, 1943.

One is the German Jesuit Father Robert Leiber, a former secretary of Pius XII. Father Leiber calls Hochhuth's accusations blasphemous. One should praise Providence, Father

Leiber writes, for having placed at the head of the Church in this tragic period a Pope of absolute impartiality, one who raised only general protests against injustice, violence and cruelty so as not to give an advantage to either side, since virtually all belligerents were guilty of such conduct. Father Leiber recalls Pius's tireless efforts on behalf of peace, and the risk he took in serving as an intermediary between the Allies and the Germans who sought to overthrow Hitler in the plot of July 20, 1944. He acknowledges that Pius, looking towards the future, held the Communist system more dangerous than the Nazi — a view the Pope did not hide. He makes particular mention of the numerous actions of the Pope in bringing aid to Jews, discreetly and in silence, and thus helping save thousands of lives. (I wrote about this in my 1950 *Commentary* article.) Public protest, writes Father Leiber, would have been of no help. It would have been very dangerous in view of the insane grudges of which Hitler was capable. He makes it clear, finally, that Pius XII by no means failed to ask himself whether or not he should protest against the extermination of the Jews; but he had to choose silence. "Let him who dares judge him," Father Leiber concludes.

A second, more eminent critic is the present Pope, Paul VI, Under-Secretary for Ordinary Affairs of the Secretariat of State at the Vatican during the war years. On June 29th of last year, then Cardinal Montini, he wrote a letter about *The Deputy* to the British Catholic publication, *The Tablet,* a letter reprinted in the *Osservatore Romano* a week after Montini's accession to the papacy. He described his predecessor as "a man of exquisite sensibility and the most delicate human sympathies. True, he did love solitude; his richly cultivated mind, his unusual capacity for thought and study, led him to avoid all useless distractions, every unnecessary relaxation; but he was quite the reverse of a man shut away from life and indifferent to people and events around him . . ."

Public protest, Cardinal Montini insisted, would have been ineffectual and perilous: "Let us suppose that Pius XII had done what Hochhuth blames him for not doing. His action would have led to such reprisals and devastations that Hochhuth himself, the war over and now possessed of a better historical, political and moral judgment, would have been able to write another play, more realistic and far more interesting than the one he has cleverly but in fact also ineptly put together: a play, that is, about 'The Deputy' who, through political exhibitionism or psychological myopia, had been guilty of unleashing on the already tormented world still greater calamities involving innumerable innocent victims, let alone himself . . . In the present case the real drama — and tragedy — is not what the playright imagines it to be: it is the tragedy of one who tries to impute to a Pope who was acutely aware both of his own moral obligations and of historical reality — and was moreover a loyal as well as impartial friend of the people of Germany — the horrible crimes of German Nazism." [1a]

What were the "reprisals and devastations" open to Hitler referred to by the present Pope? Denunciation of the Concordat, increased persecution of Catholic clergy throughout Europe — these were always possible. The fall of Rome brought new dangers, as we know thanks to the Nuremberg Trial testimony and various historical memoirs: violation of the Holy See's extraterritoriality; destruction of its only means of communication with the outside world, Radio Vatican; blind, vengeful destruction visited upon the Roman population; the kidnapping, or even assassination, of the Pope.

Were I a Catholic, perhaps I should end my article here, joining in agreement with the present Pope. But I am not a Catholic. And it is impossible to say how I should judge as a Catholic — with the Church permitting me my freedom of judgment. Moreover, in judging a hypothetical situation, who can say with any certainty what would have occurred had Pius XII hazarded a public protest and proclaimed his indignation to the world? The issue, too, must be placed in the perspective of the period. In any event, the Holy See feared some calamity, some savage blow by Hitler at the time; in particular, that he might kidnap the Pope, an act for which there were two famous historic precedents[2] And our best

1a During Pope Paul VI's visit to Israel this January, according to *The New York Times* (Jan. 6, 1964), he defended Pope Pius XII against "unjust accusations," apparently referring to Hochhuth's play. The Pontiff said just before he left Israel, "in a voice heavy with emotion:" "Pope Pius XII did all he could during World War II for all those who were in need without distinction." —*Ed.*

2 These precedents were the kidnapping of Boniface VIII by King Philippe le Bel of France, beginning the Church's "Exile in Babylon" in the 14th century, and that of Pius VII by Napoleon, following his excommunication of the Emperor.

On Sept. 19, 1963 (after this article was written) the Italian magazine *Oggi* published an article about plans to kidnap Pius XII. This seems reliable, though inaccurate in certain details.

source (for the time being, at least) for forming some idea of the then current Vatican worries and fears — the Nuremberg testimony of von Weizäcker and his aide von Kessel — leaves the impression that the Jews of Rome did not constitute so much a major problem for the Curia as for the Germans.

If so, it is not unreasonable to put forward hypotheses other than those advanced by Cardinal Montini: to think that the Führer, given what was to him a secondary question, would not wish to add the Vatican to his list of adversaries and so strain the loyalty of thirty-five million German Catholics; would abstain from reprisals, as in the case of the protest of the French bishops; or might limit them to victims condemned in any case.

The extermination of the Jews was halted in October, 1944, seven months before the war's end, when Himmler judged the conflict lost. Perhaps it would have stopped sooner had the Pope thrown the weight of his authority into the scales. Perhaps such a protest would have encouraged internal German resistance. And, whatever the incalculable calamity risked in October, 1943, assuming Cardinal Montini's view, public protest presented no such danger before the entry of the Germans into Rome, that is, before the autumn of 1943. Why did the Pope not lift his voice from the summer of 1942 onwards, with the annihilation of Polish Jewry? Since he knew, why did he not seek to inform the world about the assassination of a people? And what prestige, what honor for the Catholic Church had it ended, or even opposed, genocide! What gratitude, what hope, in the breasts of Jews!

Historians of the future will make better-informed judgments once the archives of the Vatican have been opened.[3] Rather, let us ask why the Pope, who manifested such solicitude for the Jews of Rome, in October, 1943, felt that his hands were tied. May not the answer lie — as is usual in cases of blackmail — in what went on before?

The concordat governing relations between the Catholic Church and the Third Reich was signed in 1933 by Pius XII's predecessor, Pius XI. It was Pius XI who, in 1937, issued the celebrated encyclical, "With Burning Concern" that denounced the "road of suffering" and the persecution of the German Church and the havoc of racial dogma to religious

[3] In his work *The War and the Vatican,* C. Cianfarra, Rome correspondent of *The New York Times* during the war, advances an astonishing argument to justify the silence of the Vatican: it was to spare German Catholics the conflict of conscience between duty to Church and State!

life. This was the Pope who, to underline the incompatibility between Christianity and racism, exclaimed: "Spiritually, we are all Semites." When Hitler came to Rome in 1938 Pius XI demonstratively left the Eternal City. "This air makes us sick," he said.

Such doctrinal and moral intransigence exposed him to all kinds of attacks in Germany. The government of the Third Reich officially reproached him with "mobilizing the entire world against the new Germany." A whispering campaign spread the rumor that he had Jewish blood in his veins. It is interesting to note the way in which the head of the German Catholic hierarchy, Cardinal Faulhaber, gave the lie to this rumor in 1936. In the course of a sermon he declared that "a hateful untruth has been bruited about concerning the Holy Father, according to which the Pope is half-Jewish, his mother having been a Dutch Jewess. I see my listeners tremble with horror. This lie is especially likely to expose the Pope's reputation to derision in Germany."

Such phrases show the inroads of racism among Germans, including faithful Catholics. With such a spirit prevailing one can better understand why, in 1933, the same Cardinal Faulhaber had affirmed that "from the point of view of the Church there was nothing to object to against honest pursuit of — and devotion to — race." The German Catholic Church never went as far as certain Protestant sects that proclaimed the "Aryanism" of Jesus, but it did take timid steps in this direction. Probably, as the German historian Carl Amery writes, had the German episcopate adopted an intransigent attitude the faithful would have deserted the Church *en masse*. Obliged to compromise with, if not infected by, the Hitler virus, the German Catholic hierarchy never adopted the firm, courageous position of Pius XI. It faced with determination Nazi anti-religious campaigns and attacks on its works and institutions. On the racial question, however — that is to say the Jewish question — it failed almost completely. Neither the anti-Semitic persecutions that marked the beginning of the Hitler regime nor the Crystal Night of 1938 nor the horrors of the "Final Solution" were ever denounced publicly by the German Catholic Church.

Incidentally, there is a weak point in Hochhuth's thesis, I feel, when he compares the extermination of the mentally ill in Germany and that of the Jews, inasmuch as it was not a protest by the Pope that caused Hitler to beat a retreat but, rather, that by German pastors and prelates. Noteworthy was the resounding sermon of August 3, 1941, by the Bishop of Münster, Monsignor von Galen: ". . . Why must they suffer, these poor defenseless sick? . . . Woe to mankind! Woe to our German people if the sacred commandment, 'Thou Shalt Not Kill' . . . should be transgressed, and if this transgression is tolerated and goes unpunished . . ." Nothing of the sort was said in Germany from the pulpit to condemn the murder of Jews, as if the fate of these victims, supposedly of "another race," was completely outside the competence of German priests. Who, then, was competent to say "Woe to mankind!" on behalf of the Jews?

To return to the head of the Roman Church: is it necessary to point out that his authority has limits, that he, too, in turn, must compromise, must take into account the state of mind of national churches, the passions, errors, and weaknesses of the times? In so doing, however, the manner in which he conceives his high mission and his personal temperament both play a role. Contemporaries and historians alike have contrasted the fighting character of Pius XI and that of Pius XII who, it is generally agreed, was a "political Pope."

On the eve of Pius XI's death, relations between the Holy See and the Third Reich were approaching the breaking-point. Pius XII set about bettering them. In keeping with the noble and natural ambition of so many pontiffs, he hoped to be a peace-maker — in an epoch when such were legion. His ascension to the pontifical throne coincided with the zenith of the appeasement era, those months between Munich and the dismemberment of Czechoslovakia when universal fear of war and of Communism permitted Hitler to practice blackmail on a European scale, and to march from triumph to triumph. Among responsible statesmen and leaders of the time only rare, prophetic souls saw that with concession after concession the West was moving towards catastrophe. Pius XII cannot be included in their company. On the eve of war, tirelessly, he multiplied appeals for negotiation and attempts at mediation. Even after the invasion of the Catholic nation of Poland he refrained from condemning aggression. "With peace, nothing is lost; with war, everything can be," he said, expressing all Europe's views.

The Jewish question cannot be separated from this historic context. Hitler's paranoic dialectic — "You are a Jew; I make war upon you; now you are a warmonger, responsible for Europe's affliction" — nourished by centuries-old, endemic anti-Semitism, made Jews suspect in lands threatened by war even before the fighting began. Afterwards, they were generally held responsible for defeat. And the special treatment to which they were subjected was tacitly accepted, if not openly applauded, by public opinion in subjugated

Europe. (A report by a Nazi planner, Dr. Wetzel, relating to the Poles, illustrates this: ". . . it goes without saying," he wrote, "that one cannot resolve the Polish problem by liquidating Poles as the Jews were liquidated. Such a solution would brand the German people into the far future and would cost us sympathy on all sides, especially since other peoples might envisage that they would be similarly treated at a future time . . .")

In the last analysis, it was because Jews needed the most help that they got the least. Responsible men and organizations believed that by yielding with regard to "these plague-bearers" they might the better alleviate other griefs. This was the case of the International Red Cross, which refrained from denouncing massacres in the death-camps for fear that to do so would deny it access to civil internment and prisoner-of-war camps and which justified its silence on the ground that it had no legal or traditional basis, no international convention, permitting it to intervene.[4] Thus, official consciences salved their silence. The German resistant Kurt Gerstein, that "spy of God" in S.S. uniform, provides us with a tragic example. He succeeded in penetrating into the death-camps; but he could not get himself received at the Berlin nunciature to bear witness to the hell he had seen with his own eyes.

Still, Christians did raise their voices in many a place, saying what had to be said when and how it had to be said. With the first deportation of foreign Jews from France Archbishop Saliège of Toulouse drew up a memorable declaration for the priests of his diocese to read from their pulpits: "Why does the right of asylum no longer exist in our churches? Lord, take pity upon us! Our Lady of God, pray for France! In our diocese, horrible scenes are taking place in the camps of Noé and Récébédou. Jews are men, Jews are women. Not everything is permitted against them, against these men, these women, these fathers and mothers of families. They are part of mankind. They are our brothers like so many others. A Christian cannot forget it . . ." (August 22, 1942).

Other French prelates followed the example of the Toulouse archbishop. Priests, members of religious orders, and

[4] Cf. *Rapport du Comité International de la Croix-Rouge pendant la Seconde Guerre Mondiale,* Geneva, 1947, vol. III. p. 559: "[The Commission] had to exercise a certain prudence, therefore, and forbid itself all intervention without chance of success which, without profiting anyone, would have compromised those of its activities founded on traditions and Conventions."

laymen were rivals in giving asylum, saving, as Mauriac wrote, the honor of French Catholics. The saving of their honor saved tens of thousands of Jewish lives. Deportations from France, though not stopped altogether, were widely spaced after August, 1942. Under the pressure of public opinion the Vichy authorities stopped giving assistance to Eichmann's administration. As a result, about three-quarters of the Jews in France lived through the years of trial.

One can discuss indefinitely whether or not protest by the Pope in October, 1943, or at any other time would have saved Jewish lives or, on the contrary, compromised the humanitarian work he carried on in silence. One can argue forever whether such a protest, whatever the effect for Jews, would have brought down calamity on the Church, on men and works closer to the Holy Father's heart. A host of precedents and analogies have been invoked by both sides in the debate about *The Deputy,* but none are wholly convincing. One example is that of Holland, often mentioned by defenders of the Pope. In the summer of 1942 deportation of "Jews by Religion" began in Holland. The Dutch Catholic episcopate raised a solemn protest. German reprisal consisted in the immediate deportation of Jews converted to Catholicism, among them the well-known Carmelite nun Edith Stein. Yet though Protestant religious authorities refrained from protest, this did not prevent deportation of converts to Protestantism, too, even if at a later date.

On one aspect of the subject, however, there can be no discussion. At the most tragic moment of modern history Christianity's highest spiritual authority, one who did not fail to condemn injustice, cruelty, aggression and massacre throughout the war years regardless of source, confined himself to diplomatic allusion — that is to say virtually kept silent — about the most odious crime of all.

Agreed: the very immensity of the crime befuddled judgment. This can account for the explanations that the Holy See (like the Red Cross) kept from protesting so as not to aggravate the plight of the Jews. But, as matters stood, what worse could happen to the Jews? Nothing more, certainly, than what they were already suffering. Not to understand this was to cover one's eyes to the horror of their fate (a weakness not unlike that of those ghetto Jews who opposed a hopeless rebellion undertaken to save Jewish honor).

Fallacious, too, is another argument of apologists for Pius, drawn from the fact that Jews were not the only victims of Hitler.[5] One can understand that Catholic victims (whose fate could be aggravated by untimely protest)[6] should be dearer to the heart of the Pope. Yet was not Christian honor peculiarly bound up with the very sign, the very criterion, used to designate the victims of the Final Solution — the absence of baptism? I pose the problem for the theologians. Let them bear in mind, however, the holocaust of nearly two million innocent Jewish children whose executioners, to be sure, had received Christian baptism. Let them judge if this was one of those "minor cases" in which the Holy See could or should resolve to say nothing.

If Pius XII was not of a kind to meet such a situation, his silence, we have seen, had its story. For how can one separate it from the compromises of the German Catholic hierarchy with the Third Reich? Hitler, receiving the official representatives of the German episcopate in April, 1934, told them that his anti-Semitic policies but followed the example given by the Catholic Church which "for 1,500 years considered Jews as pernicious beings"; and in binding himself with this past, he said, he rendered "perhaps the greatest service to Christianity." The bishops found nothing to object to in this.[7]

[5] Mgr. Giovanetti in *L'Osservatore Romano* of April 5, 1963: "Certainly, the Jews were the first and most numerous to suffer the application of the absurd Nazi *Weltanschauung;* but neither in time of peace nor war were they the only ones to be offered up to the National Socialist Moloch . . . but he who thinks that their contribution to civilization lessens that of others only casts a shadow over the nobility of this sacrifice."

Pushing such reasoning much further, certain German critics of Hochhuth have ironically asked why the playwright did not hold the Pope responsible for all the 55 million victims of the last war (although this number included executioners as well as victims).

[6] In the autumn of 1939 the Vatican Radio halted its broadcasts about the persecution of the Polish clergy at the request of the Polish episcopate, having been informed that every such program brought cruel reprisals.

[7] I cite from Hans Muller's *Katholische Kirche und National-Sozialismus,* Munich, 1963, p. 118. According to the resumé made by Church representatives, Hitler, after having spoken with respect of the Catholic Church, went on to the Jewish question: "I have been attacked because of the way I treat the Jews. For 1500 years the Catholic Church has considered Jews as pernicious, has relegated them to ghettos, understand what Jews were. With [the coming of] liberalism the danger was not seen any more. I join myself to [literally,

Hence, behind the tragic dilemma of Pius XII stands silhouetted the failure of the German Church (permitting us the better to understand the fury of certain of the attacks on Hochhuth). And, behind this, centuries of Christian history, with its train of prejudice, persecution, and theological doctrine about the deserved bondage of the Children of Israel: *"culpae suae perpetuae servituti addicti,"* in the phrase of St. Thomas Aquinas. What has Hochhuth done with his play but to distill the historic responsibilities of Christianity into a drama centering in a few protagonists and a few months?

A point where I tend to agree with Hochhuth's critics, however, is in his portrayal of the Pope's personality. As discussion goes on, new witnesses draw new pictures of Pius XII. Here is von Kessel's: ". . . a great figure who, such remains my conviction, almost succumbed to the weight on his conscience. He struggled, I know, day after day, week after week, month after month, to find an answer. . . ." I do not know if this portrait is the just one; let us remember, too, the priest of intensely religious life, lost in his fervors and visions. At any rate, it seems more plausible to me than the one pictured by Hochhuth: a person who is not even *in*human so much as *a*-human, a fleshless abstraction, the symbol, perhaps, of historic Christianity, to which a young Christian in anger has come to seek an accounting.

I do not know if this interpretation is correct. Others are possible when dealing with this complex work reflecting the shame, indignation and fury of young Germany. One of the most subtle of Hochhuth's Catholic critics, Father Willhard Eckert, reproaches the playwright (whose drama bears the subtitle "A Christian Tragedy") with the absence of true faith. He sees the proof of this in the doubts that assail the young Jesuit priest, Riccardo Fontana, once he arrives at Auschwitz. For Fontana's mission ends in failure. Far from consoling other deportees, he himself succumbs to despair before being killed. In debate with "the Doctor" of Auschwitz (based, partially, on the infamous Nazi Dr. Mengele but meant, in the play, to represent the Devil) Fontana is bested.

"The Doctor" defies him: "In truth, the Creator, creation and the created are refuted by Auschwitz. Life as an idea is

---

tie a band with] what was done for 1500 years. I do not place race above religion; I consider the representatives of the race in question as pernicious for both State and Church and, in so doing, I am perhaps rendering the greatest service to Christianity; that's why I expel Jews from the intellectual professions and State service . . ."

dead. This may be the beginning of a great return, of a liberation from all suffering. You must understand: henceforth there will be but one sin: the accursed sin of creating life. I destroy life. This is humanity's sole hope of being saved from its destiny."

Thus, through the Sovereign Pontiff, it is God who is defied and accused in Hochhuth's drama: God who allows the Devil to run rampant at Auschwitz, and who keeps silent; God, of whom the Pope is the incarnation on earth for Protestant Hochhuth. Does not the young and impassioned iconoclast in this fashion indirectly render homage to the Catholic Church?

I. F. STONE

What Some People Have Forgotten About God's "Deputy"

One of the elements missing in Rolf Hochhuth's play *The Deputy* and in comment upon it is recognition of the crucial role played by the Vatican in the rise of Fascism. The Vatican opposed modern liberalism from its very inception. It denounced Marxism, whether democratic or totalitarian. But everywhere it welcomed Fascism — in Italy, in Germany, in Spain, in Austria, in Slovakia and in Hungary. Many commentators have contrasted Pius XII, the central figure in Hochhuth's play, with his predecessor, Pius XI. But Pius XII, in being friendly to Hitler, was only following in the footsteps of Pius XI. Mussolini's seizure of power in Italy could have been blocked if the powerful Catholic Popular Party, and its priestly leader, Don Luigi Sturzo, had been allowed to follow the policy now being applied by Italy's Christian Democrats. An "opening to the left" which united the Popular

---

This article is reprinted from *I. F. Stone's Weekly*, issue of March 9, 1964, published by Mr. Stone, an independent journalist, in Washington, D. C.

Party with the Socialists and the Liberals against *Fascismo,* would have choked off this pestilence at the start.

But Pius XI decided otherwise. He disliked Don Luigi and his party, which had won a following among the peasantry by its advocacy of land reform. He joined the industrialists and the army officers who, like their counterparts a decade later in Germany, saw Fascism as a protection for property rights against the clamor for social reform. The Popular Party was dissolved and Don Luigi driven into exile. In Italy, as in Germany, Catholic anti-Fascists were sacrificed for a concordant with the dictatorships. These pacts with the devil lent first Il Duce and then Der Fuehrer a cloak of Catholic approval when they most needed it. The March on Rome which Pius XI facilitated was the first step toward Auschwitz which Pius XII never condemned. The louts and paranoids Mussolini marshalled for his coup were the same type who later stoked the human furnaces for Hitler with Jews, gypsies and Slavs too weak to work for Krupp and I. G. Farben. More than the sin of silence lies on the consciences of God's "deputies." They were accessories in the creation of these criminal regimes.

A second element has to do with Allied policy. While the Allies were pressing Pius XII to condemn Nazi atrocities against the Jews for its propaganda value, they were far from whole-hearted about saving the victims. I remember as a young newspaperman the coldness one encountered in the State Department on the subject of refugees and the inhumanity with which the British turned away from Palestine boatloads of Jews fleeing from Hitler's ovens; two, the Struma and the Patria, sank with their human cargoes. Last October 12, the State Department released a volume of diplomatic papers from the year 1943 (Vol. I: General) in which two painful stories are disclosed. One (at p. 134) is a British Embassy memorandum expressing fear lest the Germans "change over from the policy of extermination to one of extrusion, and aim as they did before the war at embarrassing other countries by flooding them with alien immigrants." Milton Friedman of *Jewish Telegraphic Agency,* the only Washington correspondent who paid attention to these documents, commented: "It would appear the concern existed 20 years ago in some high places that too many Jews might escape from Hitler and burden the democracies with their presence."

His Majesty's Government in the same memorandum said it was ready to take 4500 Jewish children and 300 women from Bulgaria but could not accept adult males from enemy occupied countries in Palestine owing to "the acute security problem" and the White Paper of 1939, which severely restricted Jewish immigration to the Holy Land lest this antagonize the Arabs. The British were not alone in this kind of thinking. The same volume at p. 296 contains a memorandum from the U.S. Chiefs of Staff objecting to a plan to move 4500 refugees from Spain to camps in North Africa lest this "cause resentment on the part of the Arab population." From a Jewish point of view, it was not the Pope alone who failed the test of conscience. Neither the Gospel of Jesus nor the Gospel of Marx prevented their highest respective spokesmen from making pacts with Hitler. In all the great capitals, political expediency came before humanity. The whole bitter story still feeds Jewish nationalism. When our people were thrown to the furnaces, few really cared.

It helps to heal our hearts that a young German should have written *The Deputy*. It is also a good sign that the play should have aroused such animosity — like a painful memory dragged unwillingly from the subconscious of a whole generation. The protest and the shame indicate that under the hypocrisy and the cant there lives on a concern for human and moral values. The crematoriums should not be forgotten. That one set of human beings could do this to another set condemns our whole species. There are savages within us against whom we must be on guard. The excuses of race and statecraft that are used to justify murder, and silence about it, now threaten the entire human race with a "final solution."

For the play as presented in New York, Herman Shumlin deserves a high mark for courage, a lesser one for artistry. His version is an oversimplified and sometimes vulgarized shadow of the original. Gerstein, Jacobson and Fontana are all debased from Hochhuth's original conception. In the original, the SS man, Gerstein, who tried to help the Jews, was not a hysteric. Jacobson, the Jew hiding out in his apartment, was not the vulgar creature in Jerome Rothenberg's adaptation. Fontana, the young Jesuit who goes to Auschwitz in protest, is also diminished in the New York version. But Emlyn Williams is magnificent as the Pope. Severely shortened, the play as produced also focuses too narrowly on the moral responsibility of the Pope while Hochhuth's original brings the German people into the full orbit of guilt. But to see the play is still an experience we recommend as a moral and political duty, though the play in book form (excellently translated by Richard and Clara Winston for Grove Press) is essential to grasp the author's full design and memorable intention. It is Hochhuth's achievement so painfully to have twisted the conscience of the Church and the world.

8 | Bibliography

DAVID BEAMS

Bibliography

Advocate, The (Newark): Editorial, February 27, 1964.
———Column (Joseph Thomas), March 12, 1964.
America: Article (Philip Land, S. J.), May 25, 1963.
———Editorial, July 20, 1963.
———Editorial, August 24, 1963.
———Article (Edgar Alexander), October 12, 1963.
———Discussion, November 2, 1963.
———Article (Msgr. John Osterreicher), November 9, 1963.
———Discussion, November 23, 1963.
———Discussion, November 30, 1963.
———Editorial, January 4, 1964.
———Editorial, January 11, 1964.
———Editorial, January 18, 1964.
———Theater Review (Mary Zavada), January 25, 1964.
———Editorial, February 15, 1964.
———Article (Rabbi Arthur Gilbert), March 14, 1964.
———Editorial, March 21, 1964.
———Editorial and Discussion, March 28, 1964.
———Theater Review (C. J. McNaspy), April 4, 1964.
———Discussion, April 11, 1964.
———Editorial and Article (G. A. Gripenberg), April 18, 1964.
———Discussion, May 2, 1964.
———Editorial, May 16, 1964.
———Article (Robert Graham), June 27, 1964.
American Dialog: Article (M. S. Arnoni), July-August, 1964.
American Examiner (New York): Column (Boris Smolar), August 29, 1963.

———Editorial, October 24, 1963.
———Editorial, January 16, 1964.
———Article (Julio Dressner), January 30, 1964.
———Statement (Maximilian Moss) and Column (Barry Hyams), February 6, 1964.
———Column (Rabbi Philip Alstat) and Discussion, March 12, 1964.
———Column (Albert Friedman), April 2, 1964.
American-German Review, The: Article (Alfred Gong), February-March, 1964.
American Israelite, The (Cincinnati): Column (Robert Segal), October 31, 1963.
American Opinion: Column (Jack Moffitt), March, 1964.
American Post, The (Paterson): Editorial, February 14, 1964.
Anchor, The (Fall River, Mass.): Editorial, March 5, 1964.
Asbury Park Evening Press: (N. J.) Article (E. Burke Maloney), October 19, 1963.
———Theater Reviews (James T. Norris and Rabbi Morris A. Schmidman), March 8, 1964.
Ave Maria (Notre Dame): Editorial and Article (Harry W. Flannery), August 24, 1963.
Awake!: Article, May 8, 1964.
Back Stage (New York): Article (Ernest Oppenheimer), June 7, 1963.
———News Report, October 11, 1963.
———Editorial (Allen Zwerdling), March 6, 1964.
Banner, The (Grand Rapids): Article (Richard J. Frens), January 10, 1964.
Beacon, The (Oceanside, N.Y.): Column (Lynne Ianniello), February 27, 1964.
Best Sellers (Scranton): Book Review (Dominic Maruca, S.J.), March 15, 1964.
B'nai B'rith Messenger, The (Los Angeles): Column (Samuel Schreig), December 27, 1963.
———Editorial, February 28, 1964.
———Article (Levi Zvi), March 27, 1964.
Book-of-the-Month Club News: Book Review (G. C. Hedge), May, 1964.
Boston Globe, The: Theater Review (Kevin Kelly), February 27, 1964.
———Discussion, March 19, 1964.
Boston Herald, The: Book Review (Harry Moore), March 1, 1964.
———Article (Elinor Hughes), March 8, 1964.
Brooklyn Bay News, The: Discussion, November 9, 1963.
Catholic Accent (Greensburg, Pa.): Editorial, March 5, 1964.

Catholic Courier Journal, The (Rochester, NY): Editorial, July 26, 1963.
———Theater Review (Euphemia Wyatt), March 6, 1964.
Catholic Exponent, The (Youngstown): Article, March 6, 1964.
———Column (Joseph Breig), March 13, 1964.
Catholic Free Press, The (Worcester, Mass.): Book Review (H. Channing Bowles), March 6, 1964.
Catholic Herald, The (Sacramento): Column (Msgr. Mark Hurley), March 12, 1964.
Catholic Herald Citizen, The (Milwaukee): News Report, January 18, 1964.
Catholic Messenger, The (Davenport, Ia.): Discussion, January 16, 1964.
———Editorial and Article (Msgr. John Osterreicher), March 12, 1964.
———News Report (James C. O'Neill), March 19, 1964.
———Article (Joseph Lichten), April 2, 1964.
Catholic News, The (New York): Article (Floyd Stuart), August 15, 1963.
———News Report, September 19, 1963.
———Article (Bill Mooring), September 26, 1963.
———News Report, October 3, 1963.
———News Report, December 19, 1963.
———Editorial, January 23, 1964.
———News Report and Theater Review (Joan T. Nourse), March 5, 1964.
———Article (Dr. William F. Rosenblum), March 12, 1964.
———Discussion, March 26, 1964.
———Discussion, April 2, 1964.
———Article (Msgr. Thomas Reginek), April 9, 1964.
Catholic Northwest Progress (Seattle): Editorial, January 24, 1964.
Catholic Reporter, The (Kansas City, Mo.): News Report, July 19, 1963.
———News Report, January 24, 1964.
———News Report (John Leo) and Editorial, March 6, 1964.
Catholic Review, The (Baltimore): Editorial, January 3, 1964.
———Editorial, February 28, 1964.
———Theater Review (Thomas X. Murn), March 6, 1964.
Catholic Standard, The (Washington, D.C.): Article (Kathleen Carmody), October 4, 1963.
———Column (Father John B. Sheerin), October 11, 1963.
———Theater Review (George Gent), March 6, 1964.

———Editorial, March 13, 1964.
Catholic Standard and Times (Philadelphia): News Report and Editorial, February 7, 1964.
———News Report, February 21, 1964.
———Column (Father John B. Sheerin) and Book Review (D. Bernard Theall), March 13, 1964.
Catholic Star Herald, The (Camden): Articles (Arthur Jones), December 13, 1963.
———Editorial and News Report (Arthur Jones), February 28, 1964.
———News Report, Column (Msgr. S. J. Adamo), and Discussion, March 6, 1964.
Catholic Sun, The (Syracuse): Book Review (Rev. John W. Lynch), March 5, 1964.
Catholic Telegraph, The (Cincinnati): News Report, November 15, 1963.
———Editorial, March 6, 1964.
Catholic Transcript, The (Hartford): Editorial, March 5, 1964.
Catholic Union and Echo (Buffalo): Editorial, March 13, 1964.
Catholic Universe Bulletin (Cleveland): Editorial, May 31, 1963.
Catholic World, The: Article (Hilda Graef), September, 1963.
———Theater Review (Norman J. O'Connor, C.S.P.), May 1964.
Charlotte News, The: Editorial, March 3, 1964.
Chicago Daily Defender: Column (Chuck Stone), March 3, 1964.
Chicago Daily News: Article (Richard Christianson), February 22, 1964.
———Theater Review (Jack Gaver), February 27, 1964.
———Discussion, February 29, 1964.
Chicago Sun-Times: Book Review (Gordon C. Zahn), March 8, 1964.
Chicago Tribune: Column (Claudia Cassidy), October 31, 1963.
———Column (Claudia Cassidy), February 26, 1964.
———Theater Review (Claudia Cassidy), June 1, 1964
Christian Century, The: Article (Bert Stoop), August 7, 1963.
———Editorial, September 18, 1963.
———Article (Ewart E. Turner), October 16, 1963.
———Editorial, March 4, 1964.
———Editorial, April 22, 1964.
———Discussion, July 1, 1964.

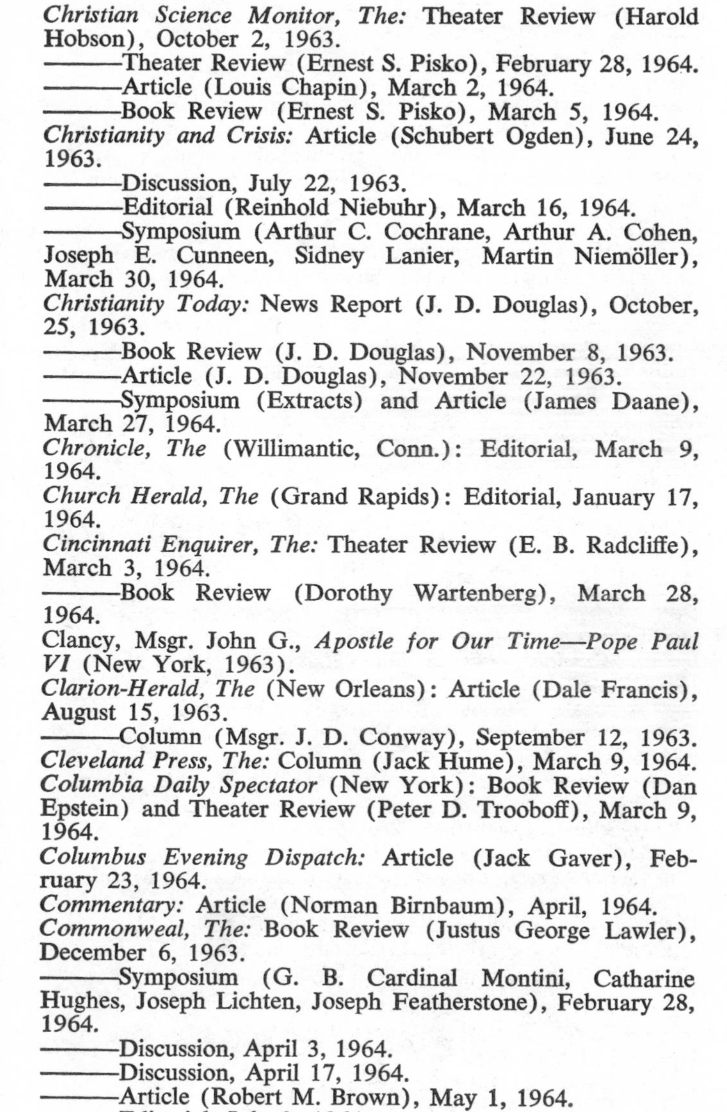

Christian Science Monitor, The: Theater Review (Harold Hobson), October 2, 1963.
———Theater Review (Ernest S. Pisko), February 28, 1964.
———Article (Louis Chapin), March 2, 1964.
———Book Review (Ernest S. Pisko), March 5, 1964.
Christianity and Crisis: Article (Schubert Ogden), June 24, 1963.
———Discussion, July 22, 1963.
———Editorial (Reinhold Niebuhr), March 16, 1964.
———Symposium (Arthur C. Cochrane, Arthur A. Cohen, Joseph E. Cunneen, Sidney Lanier, Martin Niemöller), March 30, 1964.
Christianity Today: News Report (J. D. Douglas), October, 25, 1963.
———Book Review (J. D. Douglas), November 8, 1963.
———Article (J. D. Douglas), November 22, 1963.
———Symposium (Extracts) and Article (James Daane), March 27, 1964.
Chronicle, The (Willimantic, Conn.): Editorial, March 9, 1964.
Church Herald, The (Grand Rapids): Editorial, January 17, 1964.
Cincinnati Enquirer, The: Theater Review (E. B. Radcliffe), March 3, 1964.
———Book Review (Dorothy Wartenberg), March 28, 1964.
Clancy, Msgr. John G., *Apostle for Our Time—Pope Paul VI* (New York, 1963).
Clarion-Herald, The (New Orleans): Article (Dale Francis), August 15, 1963.
———Column (Msgr. J. D. Conway), September 12, 1963.
Cleveland Press, The: Column (Jack Hume), March 9, 1964.
Columbia Daily Spectator (New York): Book Review (Dan Epstein) and Theater Review (Peter D. Trooboff), March 9, 1964.
Columbus Evening Dispatch: Article (Jack Gaver), February 23, 1964.
Commentary: Article (Norman Birnbaum), April, 1964.
Commonweal, The: Book Review (Justus George Lawler), December 6, 1963.
———Symposium (G. B. Cardinal Montini, Catharine Hughes, Joseph Lichten, Joseph Featherstone), February 28, 1964.
———Discussion, April 3, 1964.
———Discussion, April 17, 1964.
———Article (Robert M. Brown), May 1, 1964.
———Editorial, July 3, 1964.

Community News (Merchantville, N.J.): Editorial, March 12, 1964.
Congress Bi-Weekly: Article (S. L. Shneiderman), June 24, 1963.
———Editorial, February 10, 1964.
———Article (S. L. Shneiderman), February 24, 1964.
Courier, The (Winona, Minn.): Editorial, January 16, 1964.
Critic, The: Article (Gordon C. Zahn), October-November, 1963.
———Discussion, December, 1963.
———Discussion, February, 1964.
Cue (New York): Theater Review (Emory Lewis), March 7, 1964.
Daily Express, The (London): Theater Review (Herbert Kretzmer) September 26, 1963.
Daily Herald, The (London): Theater Review (David Nathan) September 26, 1963.
Daily Mail, The (London): Theater Review (Bernard Levin), September 26, 1963.
Daily Mirror, The (London): Theater Review (Arthur Thirkell), September 26, 1963.
Daily News (New York): News Report, February 2, 1964.
———Theater Review (John Chapman), February 27, 1964.
Daily Sketch, The (London): Theater Review (Fergus Cashin), September 26, 1963.
Daily Telegraph, The (London): Theater Review (W. A. Darlington), September 26, 1963.
Dallas Morning News: Article (Harry Bowman), March 8, 1964.
———Theater Review (Rual Askew), March 21, 1964.
Dallas Times Herald: Book Review (A. C. Greene), March 8, 1964.
Dayton Daily News: News Report (Kay Black), February 27, 1964.
———Editorial, February 28, 1964.
Des Moines Register, The: Editorial, March 1, 1964.
Detroit Free Press: Theater Review (Louis Cook), March 29, 1964.
Dispatch, The (Moline, Ill.): Editorial, February 26, 1964.
Dispatch, The (York, Pa.): Discussion, March 17, 1964.
Drama: Theater Review (J. W. Lambert), Winter, 1963.
Educational Theatre Journal: Theater Review (John Gassner), May, 1964.
Encore: Theater Review (Ian Dallas), November-December, 1963.
Encounter: Article (François Bondy), October, 1963.

Evangelist, The (Albany): News Report, August 8, 1963.
———Editorial, January 30, 1964.
———Column (Leon Paul), February 27, 1964.
———Article (Rev. Aiden Carr), March 5, 1964.
Evening Journal, The (Wilmington): Theater Review (Philip F. Crosland), April 4, 1964.
Evening News, The (London): Theater Review (Felix Barker), September 26, 1963.
Evening Press, The (Binghamton, NY): Editorial, February 25, 1964.
Evening Standard, The (London): Theater Review (Milton Shulman), September 26, 1963.
Evening Star, The (Washington, D.C.): Book Review, March 1, 1964.
Financial Times, The (London): Theater Review (T. C. Worsley), September 26, 1963.
Fisher, Desmond, *Pope Pius XII and the Jews* (Glen Rock, N.J., 1963).
For Your Information: 'The Deputy' (New York playbill).
Free Press, The (Burlington, Vt.): News Report, March 20, 1964.
Gazette-Mail, The (Charleston, W. Va.): Book Review (Peter H. Olden), March 1, 1964.
Greensboro Daily News: Editorial, March 14, 1964.
Guardian, The (London): Theater Review (Philip Hope-Wallace), September 26, 1963.
Hadassah Magazine: Article (Marlin Levin), February, 1964.
Hampshire Gazette, The (Northampton, Mass.): Column (B. Decker), March 3, 1964.
Harper's Bazaar: Article (Martin Esslin), May, 1964.
Hartford Courant, The: Article (William J. Clew), February 16, 1964.
Hartford Times, The: Article (Thomas E. Willey), March 20, 1964.
Herald The (New Britain, Conn.): Editorial, February 29, 1964.
———Editorial, March 5, 1964.
Herald Banner, The (Greenville, Tex.): Book Review (George Near) March 19, 1964.
Hollywood Reporter: Theater Review (Leonard Hoffman), February 27, 1964.
Home Reporter and Sunset News (Brooklyn): Column (Robert P. Whelan), March 6, 1964.
Houston Chronicle, The: Theater Review (Ann Holmes), March 10, 1964.

Hudson Review, The: Theater Review (John Simon), Summer, 1964.
Hyde Park Herald, The (Chicago): Theater Review (Robert Pollak), March 11, 1964.
Illustrated London News: Theater Review (J. C. Trewin), October 19, 1963.
Independent Star-News (Pasadena): Book Review (Leonard Brown), March 22, 1964.
Interfaith Observer: Book Review (Thelma Lewisohn), March, 1964.
Intermountain Jewish News (Denver): News Report, October 25, 1963.
Israel Horizons: Editorial, February, 1964.
Jewish Advocate, The (Boston): Column (Joseph G. Weisberg), February 20, 1964.
Jewish Chronicle, The (Pittsburgh): Editorial, February 21, 1964.
———Column (Albert Bloom), March 6, 1964.
———Column (Milton K. Susman), March 13, 1964.
Jewish Civic Leader, The (Worcester, Mass.): Discussion, November 7, 1963.
Jewish Currents: Article (Harry Zohn), February, 1964.
———Editorial, April, 1964.
———Theater Review (Arthur Vogel), May, 1964.
———Editorial, June, 1964.
Jewish Exponent (Philadelphia): Article (Boris Smolar), July 26, 1963.
———Article (Eleazar Lipsky) and Book Review (Charles Angoff), March 6, 1964.
Jewish Floridian, The (Miami): Column (Leo Mindlin), March 20, 1964.
Jewish Frontier: Article (Moshe Bar-Natan), March, 1964.
Jewish Independent, The (Cleveland): News Report, February 14, 1964.
Jewish Ledger, The (Rochester, NY): News Report, October 11, 1963.
———Editorial, February 28, 1964.
———Article (Joachim Prinz) and Column (Boris Smolar), March 6, 1964.
———Article (Rabbi Philip S. Bernstein), March 20 and March 27, 1964.
Jewish News, The (Detroit): News Report, March 6, 1964.
———Book Review (Philip Slomovitz), March 27, 1964.
Jewish News, The (Newark): News Report, May 24, 1963.
———News Report, February 21, 1964.
———Theater Review, March 6, 1964.

Jewish News, The (Phoenix): Article (Paula Sobol), December 27, 1963.
Jewish Press, The (Brooklyn): Discussion, December 27, 1963.
———Article (Avraham Tov), February 28 and March 6, 1964.
Jewish Review, The (Buffalo): Column (Boris Smolar), February 21, 1964.
Jewish Spectator, The Article (Joseph Litvin), December, 1963.
———Editorial (Trude Weiss-Rosmarin), February, 1964.
———Editorial (Trude Weiss-Rosmarin), March, 1964.
Jewish Times, The (Brookline, Mass.): News Report, February 13, 1964.
Jewish Times, The (Youngstown): Editorial, February 28, 1964.
Jewish World, The: Article (Herman Shumlin), Letter (Albert Schweitzer), and News Report, February, 1964.
Journal of Commerce, The (New York): Theater Review, February 28, 1964.
Journal of Existential Psychiatry: Article (Robert Meister), Winter, 1964.
Jubilee: Article (Peter White), June, 1963.
———Article (Wilfrid Sheed), April, 1964.
Lamp, The: Editorial, April, 1964.
Lewy, Guenter, *The Catholic Church and Nazi Germany* (New York, 1964).
Lichten, Joseph, *A Question of Judgment* (Washington, D.C., 1963).
Life: News Report (Tom Prideaux), March 13, 1964.
———Editorial, March 27, 1964.
———Article (Carl Mydans), May 1, 1964.
Life International: Article, March 11, 1963.
Long Island Catholic (Rockville Centre, NY): Column (Leon Paul), November 7, 1963.
———Editorial, March 5, 1964.
Long Island Press, The (Jamaica, NY): Theater Review (Ward Morehouse), February 27, 1964.
Look: Article (Howard and Arlene Eisenberg), June 2, 1964
Los Angeles Times: Theater Review (William Glover), February 28, 1964.
———Book Review (Dan L. Thrapp), March 22, 1964.
Lutheran, The: Theater Review (Edgar S. Brown), March 11, 1964.
———Editorial (Elson Ruff), March 25, 1964.

Mainliner and Dispatch (Cresson, Pa.): Article (William Wallace), March 12, 1964.
Manchester Guardian Weekly: Theater Review, September 26, 1963.
Massachusetts Review, The: Article (Clara Winston), Spring, 1964.
Messenger, The (East St. Louis, Ill.): Article (J. J. Gilbert), March 13, 1964.
———Editorial, March 27, 1964.
Miami Herald, The: News Report, August 28, 1963.
Michigan Catholic, The (Detroit): Editorial, March 12, 1964.
Michigan Times, The (Grand Rapids): Column (Marilyn Gibson), March 21, 1964.
Midstream: Article (Michael Harrington), December, 1963.
———Book Review (*of Summa iniuria*) (Theodore Frankel), June, 1964.
Milwaukee Journal, The: Article (Alicia Armstrong), April 4, 1964.
Minnesota Review, The: Book Review (John B. Freund), Spring, 1964.
Minority of One, The: Editorial, April, 1964.
Mississippi Register, The (Jackson): Editorial, March 27, 1964.
Monitor, The (San Francisco): News Report, May 24, 1963.
———Editorial, March 6, 1964.
Monitor, The (Trenton): Editorial, February 28, 1964.
Montreal Star, The: Articles (Hal Winter and Walter Poronovich), March 2, 1964.
Morning Telegraph, The (New York): Theater Review (Whitney Bolton), February 28, 1964.
———Article (Whitney Bolton), March 3, 1964.
Nation, The: Article (Clive Barnes), November 2, 1963.
———Discussion, March 30, 1964.
National Chronicle, The (Clifton, N.J.): Editorial (Marianna Rossi), April 3, 1964.
National Jewish Ledger, The (Washington, D.C.): Article S. J. Goldsmith) and Column (Dorothy Steinberg), July 5, 1963.
National Jewish Post and Opinion (Indianapolis): Editorial, October 11, 1963.
———Article (Jean R. Herschaft), March 20, 1964.
———News Report and Book Review (Meyer Levin), March 27, 1964.
National Observer, The (Washington, D.C.): Article (Jack Bolter), August 19, 1963.

———Theater Review (David Boroff), March 2, 1964.
New Haven Register, The: Book Review (E. Nelson Hayes), March 22, 1964.
New Leader, The: Article (Jacob Baal-Teshuva), February 17, 1964.
———Article (Reinhold Niebuhr), March 16, 1964.
New Republic, The: Discussion, April 4, 1964.
New Statesman, The: Theater Review (Ronald Bryden), October 4, 1963.
New Theatre Magazine: Book Review (Nicholas Hern), January-March, 1964.
New York Amsterdam News: Column (Gertrude Wilson), March 14, 1964.
New York Herald Tribune: News Report (Stuart Little), August 6, 1963.
———News Report (Alvin Rosenfeld), September 27, 1963.
———Article (Stuart Little), October 18, 1963.
———Article (John Molleson), October 21, 1963.
———Article (Stuart Little), January 30, 1964.
———Article (Sam Rubenstein), February 2, 1964.
———News Report (John Molleson), February 25, 1964.
———News Report (John Molleson) and Theater Review (Walter Kerr), February 27, 1964.
———Articles (Stuart Little and Jimmy Breslin), February 28, 1964.
———Discussion, March 1, 1964.
———News Report (Albin Krebs) and Discussion, March 3, 1964.
———Discussion, March 7, 1964.
———Article (Walter Kerr), March 15, 1964.
———News Report, March 25, 1964.
New York Journal American: Column (Frank Coniff), December 2, 1963.
———Column (Frank Coniff), December 9, 1963.
———Discussion, December 16, 1963.
———Synopsis of Broadway script, Symposium (Extracts), and Article (John Mitchell), February 26, 1964.
———Theater Review (John McClain), February 27, 1964.
———Column (Leon Monsky), February 29, 1964.
———Article (Harry Demarsky), March 1, 1964.
———Column (Frank Coniff), March 4, 1964.
New York Post: News Report, September 25, 1963.
———Column (Joseph Barry), October 11, 1963.
———Column (Max Lerner), October 18, 1963.
———Column (Joseph Barry), December 19, 1963.
———News Report, January 21, 1964.

———Theater Review (Richard Watts, Jr.), February 27, 1964.
———Article (Judy Michaelson), March 1, 1964.
———Column (Max Lerner), March 2, 1964.
———Column (Harry Golden), March 4, 1964.
———News Report (Judy Michaelson), March 10, 1964.
———Article (Richard Watts, Jr.), March 15, 1964.
———News Report, June 19, 1964.
New York Times, The: Theater Review, February 21, 1963.
———News Report, April 28, 1963.
———Article (Arthur Olsen), May 5, 1963.
———News Report (Sam Zolotow), May 20, 1963.
———News Report, September 10, 1963.
———News Report (Sam Zolotow), November 6, 1963.
———News Report, November 18, 1963.
———News Report, January 6, 1964.
———News Report, January 11, 1964.
———News Report, January 25, 1964.
———News Report (Lewis Funke), February 9, 1964.
———News Report, February 11, 1964.
———News Report, February 17, 1964.
———Article (Robert C. Doty), February 23, 1964.
———News Report, February 24, 1964.
———News Report (Richard F. Shepard), February 25, 1964.
———News Report, February 26, 1964.
———Theater Review (Howard Taubman), February 27, 1964.
———News Report (Richard F. Shepard), February 28, 1964.
———News Report, March 1, 1964.
———Discussion, March 6, 1964.
———Article (Howard Taubman), News Report (Paul Hofmann), Symposium (Extracts), and Discussion, March 8, 1964.
———News Report, March 9, 1964.
———News Report (Sam Zolotow), March 16, 1964.
———News Report, March 21, 1964.
———News Report (Paul Hofmann), March 26, 1964.
———News Report, June 27, 1964.
———News Report, Book Review (George N. Shuster), March 1, 1964.
New York Times Book Review, The: Article (Arthur Olsen), March 1, 1964.
———Discussion, March 22, 1964.

New York Times Magazine, The: Article (Constantine Fitzgibbon), August 18, 1963.
———Article (Gertrude Samuels), January 5, 1964.
New York World-Telegram: Article (John Ferris), May 28, 1963.
———Discussion, December 5, 1963.
———Article (Norman Nadel), January 30, 1964.
———Discussion, February 4, 1964.
———Theater Review (Norman Nadel), February 27, 1964.
New Yorker, The: Article (Genet), December 28, 1963.
———Article (Genet), January 25, 1964.
———Theater Review (John McCarten), March 7, 1964.
Newark Evening News, The: Theater Review [of *The Burning*] (Gene Palatsky), December 4, 1963.
———Theater Review (Edward S. Hipp), February 27, 1964.
Newark Sunday News, The: Article (Edward S. Hipp), March 8, 1964.
Newsday (Garden City, NY): Theater Review (George Oppenheimer), February 27, 1964.
———News Report (Arnold Abrams), March 5, 1964.
———Discussion, March 10, 1964.
News-Herald, The (Marshfield, Wis.): Editorial, February 28, 1964.
News Times, The (Danbury, Conn.): Book Review (Larry Vershel), March 7, 1964.
Newsweek: News Report, March 11, 1963.
———News Report, October 7, 1963.
———Article, March 2, 1964.
———Theater Review, March 9, 1964.
———Discussion, March 16, 1964.
———Discussion, March 23, 1964.
North Carolina Catholic (Raleigh): Column (Dale Francis), February 16, 1964.
Oakland Tribune, The: Book Review (Dennis Powers), March 4, 1964.
Observer, The (London): Column (Pendennis) and Text of Papal scene, September 22, 1963.
———Theater Review (Bamber Gascoigne) and Discussion, September 29, 1963.
Observer, The (Rockford, Ill.): Column (Frank Morriss), February 28, 1964.
Ohio Jewish Chronicle (Columbus): Column (David Horowitz), March 20, 1964.
Old Colony Memorial (Plymouth, Mass.): Editorial, March 5, 1964.

Oregonian, The (Portland): Editorial, March 1, 1964.
Our Sunday Visitor (Gary): News Report, March 8, 1964.
Partisan Review: Theater Review (Susan Sontag), Spring, 1964.
Pilot, The (Boston): News Report, June 15, 1963.
———News Report, August 24, 1963.
———News Report, September 14, 1963.
———News Report, October 5, 1963.
———News Report, November 2, 1963.
———Editorial and Article (John J. Grant), November 9, 1963.
———News Report, November 23, 1963.
———Article (Wladimir d'Ormesson), January 4, 1964.
———Article (George Ryan), February 22, 1964.
———Editorial, February 29, 1964.
———Column (Joseph McLellan), March 7, 1964.
———News Report, March 21, 1964.
Pittsburgh Catholic, The: News Report, February 27, 1964.
———Book Review (Msgr. Charles Owen Rice), March 19, 1964.
Plain Dealer, The (Cleveland): Article (Norman Melnick) and Book Review (Peter Bellamy), March 22, 1964.
Plays and Players: Editorial, November, 1963.
———Theater Reviews (Hugh Leonard and Charles Marowitz), December, 1963.
Portland Evening Express (Maine): Column (Franklin Wright), March 18, 1964.
Post-Crescent, The (Appleton, Wis.): Editorial, March 6, 1964.
Presbyterian Life: Editorial, March 1, 1964.
———Theater Review (John R. Fry), April 1, 1964.
Progressive, The: Article (George L. Mosse), June, 1964.
Providence Journal, The: Theater Review (Henry Popkin), December 8, 1963.
———Article (Wolfe Kaufman), January 5, 1964.
———Theater Review (Henry Popkin) and Book Review (George Troy), March 8, 1964.
Ramparts: Book Reviews (Edward M. Keating and Trude Weiss-Rosmarin), Summer, 1964.
Reconstructionist, The: Article (Eliahu Ben-Horin), December 27, 1963.
———Article (Barry Hyams), February 21, 1964.
———Editorial, March 6, 1964.
———Editorial and Theater Review (Barry Hyams), March 20, 1964.
———Articles (Arthur Gilbert and Charles E. Shulman), April 17, 1964.

Record, The (Hackensack, N.J.): Article (William A. Caldwell), February 26, 1964.
———News Report, February 28, 1964.
———Book Review (John Barkham) and Discussion, February 29, 1964.
———Editorial, March 7, 1964.
Record, The (Passaic, N.J.): Editorial (Jerry Fuchs), March 4, 1964.
Record American, The (Boston): Theater Review (Elliot Norton), February 28, 1964.
———Column (Austen Lake), March 4, 1964.
Register, The (Denver): Column (Frank Scully), November 17, 1963.
———Column (Joseph P. Kiefer), March 15, 1964.
———Editorial, March 29, 1964.
Register, The (Green Bay, Wis.): Editorial, March 13, 1964.
Register, The (Steubenville, Ohio): Editorial, March 5, 1964.
Report: Article, December, 1963.
———Article, March, 1964.
Reporter, The: Article (Frederic Grunfeld), January 30, 1964.
———Editorial (Max Ascoli) April 9, 1964.
Republican, The (Columbus): Article (Tom Cullen), October 12, 1963.
Review, The (St. Louis): News Report, October 11, 1963.
———Editorial, February 28, 1964.
Rocky Mountain News (Denver): Column (Wes French), November 16, 1963.
———Theater Review (Janet Cohn), March 22, 1964.
Sacramento Union, The: Editorial, March 8, 1964.
St. Anthony Messenger: Article (J. J. Hanlin), March, 1964.
St. Louis Post-Dispatch: Book Review (Thomas B. Sherman), March 1, 1964.
———Editorial, March 8, 1964.
San Francisco Chronicle: Book Review (Edward M. Keating), March 1, 1964.
San Francisco Examiner: Article (William Glover), February 16, 1964.
———Article (Stanley Eichelbaum), April 2, 1964.
Saturday Evening Post, The: Article (Alfred G. Aronowitz), February 29, 1964.
Saturday Review: Theater Review (Henry Hewes), March 14, 1964.
———Book Review (Emile Capouya), March 21, 1964.
Sentinel, The (Chicago): Editorial (J. Fishbein), February 20, 1964.

———Article and Column (Rabbi Irving J. Rosenbaum), March 5, 1964.

Show: Articles (Franz Spelman and William Rospigliosi), July, 1963.

———Theater Review (Otis Guernsey), May, 1964.

Show Business (New York): Theater Review (Tom Dash), March 7, 1964.

Sign, The: Editorial, February, 1964.

———Theater Review (Jerry Cotter), April, 1964.

Spectator, The: Theater Review (Malcolm Rutherford), October 4, 1963.

Spectator, The (Roselle, N.J.): Discussion, March 5, 1964.

Stage, The (London): Theater Review (R. B. Marriott), September 26, 1963.

Standard-Times, The (New Bedford, Mass.): Discussion, March 1, 1964.

Star, The (Oneonta, NY): Editorial, February 26, 1964.

Sudbury Enterprise, The (Marlboro, Mass.): Article (Ed Bridges), March 19, 1964.

Sun, The (Baltimore): Article (Francis Ofner), January 8, 1964.

———Article (Tania Bothezat), January 10, 1964.

———Book Review (William H. McClain), March 8, 1964.

Sunday Times, The (London): Article (George Steiner), May 5, 1963.

Tablet, The (Brooklyn): Column (Jim Greene) October 24, 1963.

———News Report, January 9, 1964.

———Editorial, February 27, 1964.

———Article (Jim Greene), March 5, 1964.

———News Report, March 26, 1964.

Tablet, The (London): Theater Review (Douglas Woodruff), September 28, 1963.

Theatre Arts: Article (Schwab-Felisch), June, 1963.

Theatre World: Article, November, 1963.

Tidings, The (Los Angeles): Editorial, March 6, 1964.

Time: Article, November 1, 1963.

———Theater Review, March 6, 1964.

Times, The (London): Article, May 10, 1963.

———Discussion, May 13, 1963.

———Discussion, May 15, 1963.

———Discussion, May 17, 1963.

———Discussion, May 20, 1963.

———Discussion, May 22, 1963.

———Discussion, May 25, 1963.

———Theater Review, September 26, 1963.

Times Literary Supplement, The (London): Book Review, September 27, 1963.
———Discussion, October 11, 1963.
Times, The (Reading, Pa.): Editorial, February 25, 1964.
Times-Dispatch, The (Richmond, Va.): Column (Ross Valentine), March 1, 1964.
Times Union, The (Albany): Column (Rabbi Alvin S. Roth), April 4, 1964.
Toronto Daily Star: Article (Nathan Cohen), March 11, 1964.
Travel Trade: Theater Review (Joel M. Abels), March, 1964.
True Voice (Omaha): Editorial, February 28, 1964.
Union Leader, The (Manchester, N.H.): Discussion, March 18, 1964.
———Editorial, March 25, 1964.
U.S. News and World Report: News Report, March 16, 1964.
Variety: News Report and Theater Review, March 6, 1963.
———News Report, May 29, 1963.
———News Report, July 17, 1963.
———News Report and Theater Review, October 2, 1963.
———Article, October 16, 1963.
———Discussion, October 23, 1963.
———News Report, November 20, 1963.
———News Report, December 18, 1963.
———Article (Gene Moskowitz), December 25, 1963.
———News Report, January 8, 1964.
———News Report, January 15, 1963.
———News Report and Theater Review, March 4, 1964.
Village Voice, The (New York): Theater Review (Daniel Wolf), March 12, 1964.
Virginia Pilot, The (Norfolk): Theater Review (Creighton Peet), March 8, 1964.
Visitor, The (Providence): Discussion, November 1, 1963.
———Editorial, February 28, 1964.
Vogue: Theater Review (Henry Popkin), April 15, 1964.
Wall Street Journal, The: Theater Review (Richard P. Cooke), February 28, 1964.
Washington Post, The: Article (Richard L. Coe), September 26, 1963.
———Article (Flora Lewis), November 3, 1963.
Watertown Daily Press: Editorial, February 26, 1964.
Weekly People (New York): Article, March 28, 1964.
Wisconsin Jewish Chronicle (Milwaukee): Article (S. J. Goldsmith), November 22, 1963.
———News Report, January 17, 1964.

Wiseman Review, The: Article (Sir Alec Randall), Summer, 1963.
Women's Wear Daily (New York): Theater Review (Martin Gottfried), February 28, 1964.
———Article (Martin Gottfried), March 19, 1964.
World Theatre: Theater Review (Ingvelde Geleng), Summer, 1963.